# ROB RA

# THE INVISIBLE WAR

## WAR

### LIVING IN VICTORY OVER THE ENEMY

21ST CENTURY
PRESS
PUBLISHING WITH PURPOSE
WWW.21STCENTURYPRESS.COM

CHRISTIAN PUBLISHING WITH A PURPOSE
WWW.21STCENTURYPRESS.COM

# The Invisible War
## Living in Victory Over the Enemy

Copyright © 2008  by *Rob Randall*

Published by 21st Century Press

Springfield, MO 65807

21st Century Press
2131 W. Republic Rd.
PMB 41
Springfield, MO 65807

ISBN 978-0-9725719-0-6

Cover: Keith Locke
Book Design: Lee Fredrickson and Terry White

First Ediiton  2003
Second Edition 2008

21ST CENTURY
PRESS
PUBLISHING WITH PURPOSE
WWW.21STCENTURYPRESS.COM

CHRISTIAN PUBLISHING WITH A PURPOSE
WWW.21STCENTURYPRESS.COM

# Dedications

To my precious help-meet and soul-mate, Pattie: Thank you for your love of our Lord and faithfulness to Him. You are my gift from our Lord. I love you more with each passing day.

To Tina, Jason, and precious Callum: Praise God for new beginnings. You are my "sweet baby girl."

To my first born Son, Bobby: Through your faith, I have seen God's great work and power. You are a wonderful blessing from our Lord.

To Michael: Your encouragement has been heaven-sent when I needed it the most. You have God's blessing upon you.

# Acknowledgments

To Dr. Eaves: Thank you for standing in as my encourager and counselor.

To Jack and Gwen Shaw: Thank you for loving our Lord and allowing Him to use you in our lives.

To Norm and Beverly Coad: Thank you for the countless hours of your petitions and prayers on the Randall's behalf.

To my late Pastor and wonderful encourager, Dr. W.A. Criswell: You sir, taught me to love the Word of God and the people of God.

To my Father and Mother: I'm so sorry I didn't know how to help you find the freedom of our Lord you so longed for. I love you both.

To Oliver and Peggy: Thank you for believing in me and entrusting me with your precious Pattie.

To Mama Quillin: What a privilege it is to remember your godly love to all who knew you. Thank you for loving and praying for me.

To LeeRoy and Hannah Till: Through the darkest of the night, the light of Christ's love and grace has shown the brightest through you.

To Joe and Judy Atkinson: Thank you for being there. You have carried the torch well.

To Dr. Bill Nix: You have allowed me to cry, scream, and argue with you. You have remained a friend through it all. You are a great blessing.

To Johnny and Carlene Jackson: Your love and prayers mean more to the Kingdom of God than you could ever know this side of our heavenly home.

To our many partners in ministry: Because you have sown your good seed into the souls of men, tens of thousands have heard and will hear the good news of Christ. Through your faithfulness to our Lord, Heaven is now richer.

To the Conference of Texas Baptist Evangelists: Thank you for allowing me to be your President. May our Lord grant you His great freedom and power in His harvest.

To the hundreds of pastors who have been willing to share their pulpits in evangelism: May God grant you His freedom and power as you minister His truth that will set the captives free.

My Dear Heavenly Father,

As I come into your presence, I thank You that in my union with You in the Lord Jesus Christ, my petitions are heard and answered according to Thy will. I thank You that You have entrusted me with the writing of this book. I ask You Sir that the Holy Spirit will place this book in the lives of those who need it the most. I ask You to protect this work through the power of the blood of Christ. Bring forth in your time great victory and freedom in the lives of the many who are in spiritual bondage. As they come to study and apply the truth of the Word of God to their lives, may the truth of God set them free from the lies and schemes of the Enemy. May the Lord Jesus Christ be exalted above all *(John 3:31)*.

*Rob Randall*
*Eph. 3:20-21*

# The Invisible War
# Living in Victory over the Enemy
## Table of Contents

# Foreword

There is a noticeable shortage of books about the Devil. I might suggest that this is something the Devil very much appreciates since the one thing he desperately fears is exposure. That is the precise purpose of the book *The Invisible War,* and it is a well-done and thorough exposure of the Enemy and his tactics.

The book is written out of the context of the author's own first hand experience. Rob Randall is far more than a theoretician when it comes to knowledge of the Enemy. But in spite of this, the author never looks to experience as the final authority in demonology. There is the prevailing insistence that the criterion by which one's experience is judged is by the plumb line of Scripture.

All of us know of preachers and even books which, in spiritual warfare, find a "demon behind every bush." *The Invisible War* doesn't fall into this error. The message of the book is extremely balanced at this point. In fact one of the great strengths of *The Invisible War* is its balanced approach. The deceptive activity of the Devil is a major thrust of the author, but this is skillfully balanced by the positive aspect of the power and authority given to the believer in our union with Christ. A wholesome emphasis on the Christian's armor is seen as obviously superior to the wiles of the Devil.

This book does not deal in generalities. It provides a number of specific prayers of deliverance which parry various attacks of the Enemy. The last chapter deals with specific ways in which the Devil hinders revival and how to respond to his efforts.

The real strength of this book is that it is soundly biblical and intensely practical. If you are looking for something that challenges your heart and stretches your mind, you will be greatly helped by this book. *The Invisible War* is the biblical and practical study on spiritual warfare we as Baptists have long needed.

**Dr. Roy J. Fish,**
**Distinguished Professor of Evangelism**
**Southwestern Baptist Theological Seminary**
**Ft. Worth, Texas**

# PREFACE TO THE FIRST EDITION

To many people, spiritual warfare is not something they want to think about or to deal with. Yet the reality is we, as believers, are involved in spiritual conflict. Many choose not to think about it, others have put it out of their mind, but the Word of God is clear that we are involved in this battle. Rob Randall, in his latest book *The Invisible War*, details his own personal experience and that of his family. More importantly, he turns to the Word of God to give the reader direction and instruction on how we are to face the Enemy.

You will find this practical tool a tremendous help in understanding what God's Word has to say about this invisible war. As you are guided by these chapters it is my prayer that your spiritual eyes will be opened, that you will put on the full armor of God and that the strength and wisdom of our Lord will carry you through the battle.

**Dr. Mac Brunson, Pastor**
**First Baptist Church, Dallas, TX**
**President, Southern Baptist Convention-**
**Pastor's Conference 2002**

Writing on spiritual warfare has fallen on disfavor in recent days. Perhaps it is because we have been lulled to sleep by the adversary, and he has us exactly where he wants us.

*The Invisible War* is not only an important work; it is an essential one. Well researched and thoughtful, it comes from the heart of Rob Randall, a preacher, evangelist and scholar. Read it carefully and read it thoroughly.

**Dr. Ergun Caner,**
**Professor of Theology and Church History, Criswell College,**
**Dallas, TX**

Evangelist Rob Randall has been at the forefront of the spiritual battle for the past thirty years. He has drawn on his personal encounters in the crucible of experience to delineate specific issues confronting multitudes of individuals, families, and churches today.

His investigation has taken him into difficult areas where his reliance on the authority of God's Word in speaking to the needs of humankind has given him boldness to go where few have dared to travel. It has also provided him a sound basis for the practical procedures he offers to apply God's Word in their personal arena of spiritual warfare.

May His endeavor, *The Invisible War,* be an encouragement to all who seek guidance, support, and encouragement along the way.

**Dr. William E. Nix,**
**Professor of Theology,**
**Southern Evangelical Seminary, Charlotte, NC**
**President, Electronic Bible Society, Dallas, TX**

Evangelist Rob Randall has a genuine concern for people who too often become victims of the spiritual battles of life. He really cares! He has spent many long hours in searching the Scriptures, in praying, and ministering to hurting people. Out of this kind of ministry he has been led to write this book.

*The Invisible War* will be of great help to those who are seeking spiritual freedom and victory. Dr. Randall leads them step by step, saturated with the Word of God, in open communication with other Christians, and permeated with earnest prayer to true victory.

Read it slowly and thoughtfully while lingering in the many Scripture references. Pray for the Holy Spirit to be your Teacher. You will find the journey as I did eternally rewarding. You will be blessed!

**Dr. James F. Eaves, Professor of Evangelism**
**Southwestern Baptist Theological Seminary**
**Ft. Worth, Texas**

I have known Rob Randall since he was a two year old toddler son of my dear friend, Evangelist Bob Randall. I have watched him grow through the years to his now exciting evangelistic ministry. In recent years God has given him tremendous insight into spiritual warfare. *The Invisible War* is must reading for every serious soldier of the Cross.

**Evangelist Johnny Jackson, Little Rock, Arkansas**
**President Arkansas Baptist Convention 1978-79**
**Chairman of Southern Baptist Convention**
**North American Mission Board 1991-92**

11

I received a phone call from Brother Randall. He poured out his soul relating how the Enemy established a hold of his son's life and was seeking to destroy him *(John 10:10)*. He asked if I would council them.

The *Invisible War* was not written from a purely academic point of view. It was written by a man who experienced first hand the struggle to free his son from Satan's grip. As Rob entered the battle, he began a pilgrimage of learning the strategies of the Enemy that caused something like this to happen to his own family. A wise man once said, "If Satan cannot get the parents, he will go after the children."

This book is must reading for every Bible believing Christian. It will equip you to understand Satan's tactics today and how you can experience the victory of the Cross of Christ not only for yourself, but also for those you love.

**Dr. Jim Logan, Counselor**
**International Center for Biblical Counseling**
**Sioux City, Iowa**

# PREFACE TO THE SECOND EDITION

## BOB'S STORY

First of all, I would like to say how proud I am of my father for writing *The Invisible War*. Although unglamorous and often neglected, the ministry of seeing people set free from addictions and bondages is incredibly vital to the church today. I believe this book is a most helpful tool for believers who are involved in the process of getting free from demonic oppression not only for themselves but also in praying for others in spiritual bondage. This book gives biblical answers to those who are tormented with questions and thoughts such as:

"This is just the way I am."

"Why am I this way?"

"Something is just not right. What is it?"

"Is there any way out for me from this terrible darkness?"

*The Invisible War* directs those who need help to the One who can help—JESUS CHRIST and HIS BLOOD.

Today, we still overcome the enemy by the blood of the Lamb (what Jesus has done on the cross) and the word of our testimony (telling the truth of how we have found freedom in Christ and how the work of the devil has been defeated in our lives). Here, then, is a brief look into my own journey from bondage to freedom in Christ.

Being a preacher's kid, I was in church every time the doors were open. Although my parents loved Jesus, the enemy was able to get my attention on the religion of the church and how it was focused on man. As I grew older, I witnessed leaders in the church fall into immorality. (I want to make it clear that I do not judge, and I have no stone to throw.) I saw the local church struggle spiritually. The faith that people professed with their mouths was different from the faith they practiced. Much of what I saw reinforced the enemy's lie that I was beginning to believe—the power of Jesus just did not work in the real world. The lines between Jesus, The true Son of God and religion were being blurred. Well, I wanted and needed something that worked, so I went on my own journey to find the truth. This quest took me through a six-year journey of drug addiction that was so hellish that I couldn't go for four hours without taking more "stuff." Without it, I felt such terrible

13

physical, emotional, and spiritual pain I didn't think I could live another day.

One night, as I lay sober on my parents' couch, I was in such torment that I cried aloud, "I don't want anything to do with God. I choose darkness. I will control my own life. I want God to leave me alone." At that moment, I literally began to die. I couldn't breathe or move. I began to panic. I remember thinking, "This is it. I am leaving this earth."

At an instant, light filled the room. Jesus was standing before me. I felt peace. I could see the room I was in again. I gasped for air. Then, I began to move. Suddenly, to my astonishment, I heard the audible voice of God say, "I am in control, and if you don't start living for Me, you will not be here on this earth any longer."

This encounter with the living Lord Jesus was the turning point in my battle for freedom from addiction. Through the unrelenting intercession of my precious brother, Michael, my sister, Tina, and the willingness of my Mom and Dad, Dr. Norman and his sweet wife, Beverly, and Jack Shaw to stand in the gap while battling for me against the powers of darkness, I can honestly say I would not be here today. God used every prayer.

There is no greater one to follow than Jesus Christ. I have seen His face, and I love Him with all my heart. I will forever follow Him and His Light and His Truth. True Christianity is not a dead religion like the enemy has persuaded me to believe. It's a dynamic, intimate relationship with a very much alive Jesus who wants us to be free more than we could possible imagine.

My prayer is that we will all take the journey into freedom, and I believe *The Invisible War* can help. This book is not simply a Bible study that will hit the best seller list and then fade away as a "new fangled" ministry idea. It will endure as a vital tool that should be referred to through the years to come by those who need to gain more and more freedom in their walk with the Living Lord Jesus and by those who are interceding for those who are still yet in bondage. May our Lord Jesus use this book to help you in your journey into true freedom.

**Bob Randall**
**Missionary Staff**
**Antioch Community Church, Waco, Texas**

Taboo—"A social or religious custom prohibiting or restricting a particular practice or forbidding association with a particular person, place or thing."

There could be no better word selected, in my opinion, for the theology of and practice of "deliverance" in American Evangelical churches. Those who practice this type of ministry are immediately hedged into the corner of "radical Pentecostalism." Churches who profess in the ministry of deliverance are rarely if ever given any credence, whether from a denomination or local governing body, but Jesus proclaimed that He came *"to set captives free... [and] ye shall know the truth and the truth shall set you free" (Luke 4:18; John 8:32).*

So, who is in error? Often both. Why? Because the biblical concept of deliverance that Jesus, the apostles, and the early church believed in and practiced has been too often hi-jacked, slandered, and masticated at the hands of far too many pseudo-religious charlatans and "TV evangelists" who manipulate, take advantage of, and prey upon the well intended ignorance of their audience.

In my religious tradition I was led to believe Jesus saves but deliverance came in the after-life. However after several mission trips overseas and studying the concepts found within these pages, I have come to believe that the ministry of deliverance is essential for today's church in America. I've seen the fruit of deliverance in both personal and corporate environments.

Although I've never been able to see into the invisible spirit world, I have seen the effects of deliverance. I've witnessed those who were in bondage to addictions, fears, others, etc. literally set free. The ministry of deliverance, when done biblically, is not a "Dog and Pony show." It is a reverent and humble act of allowing God to operate through the lives of those whom He came to set free–you.

Why, or should I say how, did my perspective change?—desperation. Often people do not take the words of Scripture literally until they are placed in a desperate situation or scenario. Rob experienced this with his family and so have I. The question is—Are you desperate enough for God's miraculous intervention in your life that you do not care anymore what a denomination, or group of people think, but rather what God thinks *(Gal. 1:10)*?

This book, or should I say Bible study, is about change–our willingness to allow God to change us. This is not a self-help book because only Jesus Christ can deliver someone out of misery, bondage, bitterness, fear, addiction, abandonment, etc. This is a study that will, if received, lead you to the life in Christ you have heard so much about.

As a pastor, I have witness the life and ministry of my friend and fellow servant of Christ, Dr. Rob Randall. I believe in what God is doing through Rob. I have gladly trusted my people to Rob's God given ministry of true revival and cleansing. I have literally handed out dozens of copies of this study. Why? Because it is just that—a study. You hold in your hands a guide to biblical principles of deliverance. Not a man's opinion or a certain scheme of theology, but rather "what the Bible says."

If you want to be free, truly free in Christ then begin the study found in these pages and allow the Lord Jesus to do His cleansing work in your life.

**Dr. Jeff Meyers, Pastor**
**East Booneville Baptist Church**
**Booneville, Mississippi**

# Introduction to the First Edition of
# THE INVISIBLE WAR

*...while we look not at the things which are seen, but at the things which are not seen; for the things which are seen are temporal, but the things which are not seen are eternal (2 Cor. 4:18). Now faith is the assurance of things hoped for, the conviction of things not seen (Heb. 11:1).*

We are surrounded by the invisible war. We see casualties of the war on every side. It is becoming more and more impossible to ignore the supernatural battle in which we find ourselves. As the return of our Lord approaches ever closer, Hell is unleashing its fury on this generation of our children. Those who should be living in great victory and power more often fall into great sorrow and defeat. This is the "pill" generation. If a child has the behavior problem we give him a pill to manipulate his behavior. We look to the doctor and pharmacist for the peace of mind we do not possess.

There's never been a generation like this one. A time filled with education but without truth. It is a time of great promise but without hope. Everywhere we look, people are seeking answers from psychiatrists and self help books and psychics. Husbands and wives having lost all hope run to lawyers to solve marital problems. The struggle to find some peace at home so often leads to divorce which brings more guilt and more hopelessness. Mothers are killing their own children for the sake of selfish convenience. Men and women are confused as to their own sex. Out of control are they even in the face of AIDS and certain death. We are witnessing a generation out of control with all kinds of addictions, seeking to medicate the pain of grief, sorrow, and endless loneliness.

From Columbine High School to Pearle Mississippi, across our land we watch in horror the epidemic of kids killing kids as a result of a hopeless rage. Children walking into our schools dazed in a trance, loaded for war with an appetite for the shedding of Christian blood. Our prisons are filled with children who could not find any reason to live straight. Our graveyards are filled with the bodies of children that lived in such defeat they could not find a reason to live. Beautiful young girls, their hearts filled with anorexic confusion, believing a lie that they are fat commit slow suicide as their bodies waste away headed for the graveyard. Children filled with such guilt and heartache that they cut themselves to relieve their spiritual pain. Truly our generation is the generation that will be remembered as the hopeless generation.

Even the pulpit is too often a place for psychoanalyzing rather than the preaching of the Word of God. Preachers filled with prescription drugs find no peace within themselves. A deluge of dark desperation and depression has baptized those who should be living in great joy and victory. The more society looks for answers the more confused and lost it becomes. Education has not solved our search for truth. More people carry degrees today than ever and yet people live in hopelessness. When we have a problem we throw money at it, and it doesn't solve a thing. Our politicians pontificate declaring they have the answers so we will re-elect them to their own selfish carnal realities. The tragedy is we don't seem to know how to appropriate the victory that is ours in Christ.

We find ourselves in the midst of a revival of interest of the supernatural. From physic hotlines to government studies of the paranormal, people everywhere are searching for spiritual answers. From religions of witchcraft to blasphemous rituals in the church, we see a strange marriage between the holy and the unholy. We read with shock when our First Lady, Nancy Reagan sought answers from the world of the psychics and spiritual mediums.[1] Well publicized was the spiritual encounter Hillary Clinton had with Eleanor Roosevelt through the medium of a spiritist. And just think the "Harry Potter Generation" is just ahead. Billy Graham has said, "Certainly, the activity of Satan is evident on every side. We can see it in the wars and other crises that affect all men daily. We can also see it in the attacks of Satan against individual members of the body of Christ. Demonic activity and Satan worship are on the increase in all parts of the world. The Devil is alive and more at work than at any other time. The Bible says that he realizes his time is short, his activity will increase."[2]

If we are to know the truth, we must go to the Word of God. *Forever Oh, Lord thy word is settled in heaven (Psalm 119:89). Heaven and earth shall pass away, but my Word will never pass away (Luke 21:33).* All we can know for certain concerning spiritual things is what we read in the Bible. There must be a non-hysterical biblically balanced approach to spiritual warfare. We have nothing to fear but our ignorance of God's

18

truth. For *you shall know the truth and the truth shall make you free (John 8:32)*.

It was a normal day, most like any other day. In my heart, I knew I needed to spend some time with the Lord. As I went before Him, an acute longing came over my soul for real revival. I began to cry out to the Lord concerning our spiritual needs as the people of God. Serving as the President of the Conference of Texas Baptist Evangelists, as well as serving on the Evangelism Committee of a strong conservative evangelical denomination, I was aware of most of what the Lord was doing in our churches. Although we were regularly seeing people come to Christ, the work of evangelism was not seeing near the harvest I was convinced God had for us. Having served now in evangelism for a quarter of a century as well as growing up in an evangelist's home, my heart became very heavy for a genuine move of God in our time. As a student of the history of revival and spiritual awakenings, it was obvious what I read in the history books, we had never experienced.

As I prayed, I told the Lord I was not ungrateful. "Lord, You have blessed me far beyond my greatest expectations. You have given me a precious wife and three wonderful and gifted children. My ministry as an evangelist has your hand upon it. I see more people come to Christ in a year than many churches with their multi-million dollar budgets, and I'm just one guy. I am so grateful for all you have done for me. Lord, You know my heart, I am not whining and ungrateful." My heart became heavy as soul began to cry. "Oh God, Would you do a new work in my life for a new work in our churches?" I long to see real revival in my lifetime. Even now I remember confessing to our Lord that I didn't even know what I was asking of Him. I just knew I needed for the Lord to do a new work in my life for a new work in the churches where I would serve as an evangelist.

Had I known what I was praying, had I known what my family and I was going to go through in the next three years, I would have never prayed that prayer. My dear friend, I've seen things I didn't want to see. I've heard things I didn't want to hear. I've learned things I didn't really want to know. There were times I didn't believe we would survive the battle with the powers of darkness. There were days I was convinced I would be buying a casket for one or more of my family members or they would be buying one for me.

As soon as I became aware of the Enemy's evil intent and the work of demons and their unholy assignments against my family, I told the Lord two things. Number one: I would distance myself from the highly emotionally charged charismatic world to learn of these matters. Although, I have great love and respect for our charismatic brothers for their zeal in evangelism, I believe way too much deception has characterized the most recent charismatic movements. I didn't need any more confusion in my life concerning these spiritual truths. Number two: If I was to learn anything, I would learn it from God himself. I claimed that He alone would be my guide into all truth. I told Him that He would have to teach me the truth that would set men free. I took a red highlighter and marked every passage in the Bible that related to our spiritual battle. I began to pray and study over each of them to allow the Lord to teach me about the "invisible war."

### God's Answer to my prayer,
### "Do a new work in my life for a new work in Your Church."

After months and months of battling for my son's spiritual cleansing, The Lord came to me and said, "It's your turn. There is a work I need to do in your life." I had learned enough concerning the invisible war to know that no one is exempt from the deceptions and lies of the Enemy. So I willingly said, "Yes, Sir. What do You want me to do?" The Lord instructed me to go before Him and He would show me the areas of deception in my life. He would show me the times I had believed Satan's lies. He would show me the times I had been unwilling to believe God's truth.

With pen and pad in my hand, I humbled myself before Holy God. I went into His presence with fear and trembling in obedience. He told me that I did not have to come up with the list. That He would show me every time I refused to believe God. The list began to fill with all matters of unbelief. As soon as the Lord would bring them to my attention, I confessed them to Him. I asked Him to cleanse me of these matters that had separated me from Him and His will in my life. When the list was finished, I looked up and more than two hours had gone by. I was exhausted. This was extremely difficult especially to my flesh. The flesh doesn't like any of this. I was so tired I went to bed to take a nap.

In my sleep, the Lord woke me up and said, "We're not done yet." I told the Lord I didn't believe I could take any more. He assured me I could and that this work of cleansing was not finished. He said, "I want you to come before me again and I will show you every time you let the *sun go down on your anger.* There you will find the work of the Enemy in your life." *Eph. 4:26-27* says, *Be angry, and yet do not sin, do not let the sun go down on your anger, and do not give the Devil an opportunity.* I had learned in my study of the invisible war that the Devil exploited the times of anger when that anger was not turned over to our Lord through confession.

So obediently, I went before the Throne of God and into His Holy presence. With the same pen and pad in my hand, The Lord began to show me the times I had joined Satan's rebellion by not trusting the Lord to take care of matters that had hurt me and those I loved. He showed me the time as a teenager when I became so angry at my Mother I wanted to hit her. I couldn't hit her, so I rammed my fist through a door in our house. He reminded me that I never asked Him to forgive me of that sin. I told Him I was so sorry, and confessed these areas of disobedience to Him. It was a precious time, but also a painful time before Holy God. Once again the flesh, our pride wants nothing of holiness. When this time was done before the Lord, several more hours had passed. I was completely emptied of all my strength. I crawled into bed for a nights rest.

Early the next morning, the Lord woke me again and said, "We're not done yet. I want you to come before me again." I began to cry out to Him and say, "I can't take it any more, Lord. I don't believe I can survive any more of this." He assured me once again that I could and that His work of cleansing was not finished. He told me to go before Him and write down the armor of God. And under each piece of His armor, He would show me the times when I did not have on my spiritual armor. He said, "There you will find the work of the Enemy in your life."

So I went before Holy God again. I did as He had instructed me to do. I wrote down each piece of the armor in *Eph. 6*: Belt of Truth, Breastplate of Righteousness, Shoes of the Preparation of the Gospel of Peace, Shield of Faith, Helmet of Salvation, and Sword of the Spirit – Word of God. Under each piece I began to write what the Lord was showing me. He showed me every time I refused to believe what He said was true. He showed me the times in my life when I relied on my righteousness instead of His. He showed me those times in my life

21

I was unwilling to be at peace with Him and with others. He showed me each time in my life when I walked in the flesh instead of faith. Everything He told me, I wrote it down on the pad. Each time I asked Him to forgive me for my disobedience. I thanked Him that through Calvary I had His full forgiveness. I quoted *I John 1:9, If we confess our sins, He is faithful and righteous to forgive us our sins and to cleanse us from all unrighteousness.* He showed me the times when I chose to walk in selfishness instead of the Spirit of Christ. He showed me the times in my life when I did not trust His salvation and all that He had done for me on Calvary. He showed me the times when although I proclaimed to believe the Bible, I didn't walk in its truth.

My time of spiritual cleansing was now in its second day. When we were through, I literally couldn't walk. My strength was gone. I truly thought that I might die. It was like major surgery. My wife, Pattie walked into the room. She asked, "Honey, what's hurting you?" There it was. When my sin and disobedience had been cleansed by the Lord, underneath was the "Big Lie" that the Devil had been able to use in my life. I saw a young boy who believed he had been abandoned by everyone. Oh, I hadn't been. But I believed I was. Remember, all of Satan's work is based upon lies. It doesn't have to be true; you just have to believe it.

Tears began to roll off my face in ways I have never known. These tears were almost like molasses. I began to see clearly how I had set up my life and ministry so as not to be abandoned. I had smothered my friends so I wouldn't loose them. All the while, I had lost most of them. The Enemy had used this lie to manipulate my life all these years. All kinds of fears and the desire to fix my family's name because of my parent's divorce came up. Only the Lord justifies and forgives. Forgiveness is only found in the work of Christ on Calvary. To believe or practice otherwise is to join Satan's rebellion.

After two days of cleansing in my life. I told my wife that she didn't need to miss the movement of God in her life. Since we were "one flesh" before Him, no doubt there was a work of cleaning He wanted to do in her. That began three more days of spiritual cleansing in the Randall home. Our lives will never be the same. The Lord has taught us how to pray. Our prayer time is not just a few minutes as it used to be. Now our time before our precious Lord can be hours. The Lord has taught us how to trust Him. The Lord has taught us to believe in His

Holy and living Word. Our Lord has taught us about Himself. There is no one like Him. There is no one who is more faithful than Christ. There is no one who is worthy of all praise but Jesus Christ.

Through it all, our Lord has taught us how to walk in the victory that is ours in Christ. He has revealed Himself to me in ways I had never known. Our Lord is faithful! Our Lord is great and mighty to save! Our Lord is able to do exceeding abundantly above all that we ask or think, according to the power that works within us! I have always been a praying Christian. However, now the Lord has taught me how to listen to Him when He speaks. In the Randall Home we have learned you can trust the Lord! We can trust Him to do what He said He would do! In the churches we are seeing real revival cleansing from our Lord. Heaven is pouring out revival rain in most all the churches now where we serve. Praise the Lord! There is nobody like our Lord Jesus Christ! He is Lord of all! His Word is alive and more powerful than we can imagine. No matter what wicked schemes our Enemy, the Devil hurls our direction, *thanks be unto God who always causes us to triumph in Christ (2 Cor. 2:14).*

The following pages are the fruit of our three year journey. It is the fruit of the answer to my prayer requesting God to do a new work in my life. I present this work on "The Invisible War" to you with the prayer that through it our Lord will teach you to walk in His victory. It will be necessary for you to get your Bible and study the Scriptures as you read this book. When you come to the end of a section, meditate upon the Word of God and pray the Holy Spirit will use His Word to guide you into all truth. Our Lord will teach you in His Word how to live in His Victory. He came to set the captives free. He came to destroy the works of the Devil. Welcome to the "Invisible War."

Spiritual warfare is not about demons, although they are involved in the evil workings of the Enemy. Spiritual warfare is first and foremost about the work of the Holy Spirit in the Church and through the Church to accomplish His will on the earth as it is in Heaven. The Invisible War is not about the Devil or demons. It's about our mighty God who is Lord of all. The Invisible War is not about sin and sorrow. It is about the One who has given His life that all might be forgiven. The Invisible War is not about us, it's about Christ. It's all about Him. God created us for Him. We exist for Him. We live for Him. We preach for Him. Our song is about Him! We breathe for Him. He is Lord! He has come to set the captives free! He came to free us to Himself; free to do His will! Free to be what He has created! Praise His Holy Name!

All hail the power of Jesus' name! Let angels prostrate fall; Bring forth the royal diadem, And crown Him Lord of all!

Let every kindred, every tribe, On this terrestrial ball, To Him all majesty ascribe, And crown Him Lord of all!

O that with yonder sacred throng We at His feet may fall! We'll join the everlasting song, And crown Him Lord of all!

In any study of the supernatural, it is necessary that the terms used be clearly defined. There are words such as demon, blasphemy, cult, etc. that carry different meanings to different people. When you encounter such terms in this book, please refer to the glossary provided on page 273 in the back of the book. This list will give a clear understanding how these terms are being used in this study.

This book on "The Invisible War" should be studied not to duplicate as a program this or any specific approach as the only way to engage the Enemy. On the contrary, my prayer is that this book will so engage your heart to help you study the Word of God concerning these eternal matters. It is through the Word of God we learn the real truth concerning the invisible war. It is through the Word of God we learn how to engage the Enemy. It is in the Word of God we learn the TRUTHS that set men free. The Holy Spirit alone is our guide into all truth *(John 16:13)*. Through your study of His Word, may God develop in you a willingness to be led and used of Him as He comes to set the captives free.

# Introduction to the Second Edition of
# THE INVISIBLE WAR

What a holy privilege is mine to present to you this updated and expanded version of The Invisible War. In these four years since the first copy was printed, I have learned much about the great and all mighty God that has revealed Himself in Christ Jesus. If you had told me seven years ago that I would have taken this journey into helping folks walk in the freedom of Christ over the powers of darkness, I would have thought you had a case of delusion or an early problem with dementia. However, through the journey into the victory of our Lord Jesus, Christ has become even more precious to me than I could have ever imagined. In this new and expanded version of The Invisible War you will find even more help as you learn to pray for yourself and those you love.

There are those of you who have come to this book with a heavy heart and overwhelming sorrow concerning a loved one or maybe it is you who is still in bondage. My encouragement to you is to take the journey into spiritual cleansing. Each step of the way you will find the manifest power and presence of our Lord Jesus Christ. In the journey you will find God's wonderful blessing. Whatever you face, however terrifying and horrific, don't give up. Wherever the spiritual battles of life lead you, you will discover Jesus Christ is Lord. Even in the very Throne Room of Hell itself, Jesus Christ is Lord!

Many have asked, "How is your son?" (See Bob's story, page 13) Today our son is serving on ministry staff in a half-way house sponsored by a wonderful dynamic New Testament church. Daily he is ministering God's grace and healing to the wounded and discarded of broken humanity. The Word of God has proven to be true in each of our lives.

*Blessed be the God and Father of our Lord Jesus Christ, the Father of mercies and God of all comfort; who comforts us in all our affliction so that we may be able to comfort those who are in any affliction with the comfort with which we ourselves are comforted by God (2 Cor. 1:3-4).*

Each trial we have faced, each struggle and attack of the Enemy has become fertile ground for the ministry of healing to others. God has been so wonderfully good and faithful to the Randalls. May Christ alone be praised!

No one is better than anyone else. Each of us has stuff that needs to be cleaned up. I have come to understand, there are no nice families. All men everywhere have cooperated at some level with the powers of darkness through sin. Everyone is in desperate need of a savior. Praise His Holy Name, our Heavenly Father has given us that Savior in His only Son, Christ Jesus. Everyone needs to be saved from the stuff that seeks to enslave us. Everyone needs to be set free, to be delivered from everything in our lives that refuses to bow to Christ and exalt His name above all.

Although Christ has come to set us free, tragically there are those who continue to choose a life of bondage. The mere idea of a life of holiness and faith to Christ that God can use to produce His New Testament power is oddly foreign and unfamiliar. Many hold on to a false view of reality and twisted self identity that has been hammered through unhealed wounds and fused by the lies of the Enemy. Seemingly, more fearful are they of a life of freedom in Christ than of a life that continues its connections to the powers of darkness with its fears, subsequent bondages and ultimate death. Way too many of us have accepted a life without freedom built on the foundations of our compromises. Jesus came to give you a life that is free from the clutches and shackles of Satan. That's why He came.

*It was for freedom that Christ set us free; therefore keep standing firm and do not be subject again to a yoke of slavery (Galatians 5:1).*

It is our Lord's will for you and your loved ones to be free. Please, don't settle for anything less. May our Lord Jesus be your guide into all truth that can set you free.

It is my conviction that our unwillingness to receive the cleansing power of Christ is the primary reason revival continues to elude us. For the sake of souls, for the sake of the health of the body of Christ- His Church and for the sake of the eternity where men will live forever in either Heaven or a devil's Hell, please "pray it through" until your spiritual burdens are lifted. My prayer for you is that out of your journey into the cleansing power of our Lord Jesus, much praise to His wonderful name will come forth from your heart to which all the angels of Heaven will quickly add their voices.

> Fill this Temple with Your glory
> Fill my life with You now.
> May Christ be raised to His holy place.
> May all that is within me bow.
>                                     —*Rob Randall*

## Chapter 1

# The Discovery and Description of the Devil

*"Demonic activity and Satan worship are on the increase in all parts of the world. The Devil is alive and more at work than at any other time. The Bible says that he realizes his time is short, his activity will increase."*
                                                                 *–Billy Graham*

We read these words concerning the time prior to the coming of Christ:

*But the spirit explicitly says in the latter times some will fall away from the faith, paying attention to deceitful spirits and doctrines of demons, by means of the hypocrisy of liars seared in their own conscience as with a branding iron (I Timothy 4:1-5).*

There is clearly in the Word of God the time coming when men will not endure sound doctrine but believe the teachings of these teachers sent from Hell to confuse and ultimately destroy. In this Timothy passage we see an example of the kind of demonic teaching from the darkness. Does *"Forbidding to marry"* sound familiar? "It's O.K. for us to live together. We don't have to get married. We love each other. Why do we need a piece of paper anyway?" That's right, a doctrine of demons. We will discuss this matter in detail later in Chapter 2 concerning sex outside of marriage.

The Bible declares:

*For our struggle is not against flesh and blood, but against the rulers, against the powers, against the world forces of this darkness, against the spiritual forces of wickedness in the heavenly places (Eph. 6:12).*

It is necessary for us to understand that Jesus had to deal with the Devil, and if you and I are to be victorious, we too must deal with him.

Our son received a call one night from a long time friend who was in trouble and needed him to come. When he arrived he met him at the door with a loaded shotgun. Bobby told him to put it down, and he did. He began to pray for his friend in a way that he had just learned from a spiritual warfare conference he had attended with his mother just a few weeks before. In the middle of the prayer, a voice that was not his friend said, "You better stop praying like that. You don't know what you're doing." Bobby kept praying for his friend. The battle was on.

They knew they needed help. This situation was bigger than they knew how to handle. They called a local youth minister to come and help. When he arrived it soon became clear that he too did not know how to handle the situation. For hours they were in a battle with the forces of darkness in the bed of a pickup truck. Demons had been sent to kill this young man that night.

The result of the spiritual war that night was they knew they needed help. God wonderfully brought them the help that was needed. The young man was delivered from more than twenty five demons. Today he is studying for the gospel ministry and has a vibrant and fruitful youth ministry in a church in North Texas. He has turned into one of the finest soul-winners I have ever known.

The Bible says we don't wrestle with flesh and blood, but against spiritual forces of darkness. Is there a real Devil? Are there real demons? Or as some would suggest that evil is a matter of bad thoughts or personal presuppositions based upon outdated superstitions and a lack of good education. Some conclude that the matter of the Devil and the working of demons are for the emotionally charged charismatic world.

This book is written with the prayer that God's people will seek the truth with all their hearts. The Holy Spirit, who is our guide into all truth, will teach those who are willing to learn the way to complete victory through our Lord Jesus Christ.

There are many arguments as to why we don't study these matters. Time and space won't allow me to deal with all of them. However, here is a list of the most used objections to this kind of study.

## THE DEBATE ABOUT THE DEVIL
### Arguments Against the Study of The Invisible War

### ARGUMENT 1:
### "After Pentecost these demon manifestations are not seen again."

The argument follows since signs and wonders were only a sign to the Jews as to how they would recognize their Messiah, once the ministry of the Lord was finished on the earth, the day of signs and wonders ended. It is concluded that demon manifestations are linked to signs and wonders that have ceased for today.

Just a casual student of the Bible will find the Church involved in the practice of casting out demons after Pentecost *(Acts 16:16-18, 19:12-20)*.

## The Testimony of Church History

A careful study of church history reveals that the invisible war in the heavenlies has never ceased. The following is just a few examples from the Early Church Fathers concerning the matter of demons and how they dealt with the invisible war.

**Hermas** (A.D.100-150), perhaps is the earliest testimony of the effect demons had on believers. His writings reflect an early second century understanding in Roman Christianity. "He cannot oppress God's servants who hope in him with all their heart. The Devil can wrestle with them, but he cannot throw and pin them. So, if you resist him, he will be defeated and flee from you in disgrace. But those who are empty fear the Devil, as if he had power... So also the Devil comes to all God's servants to tempt them. All those who are full in the faith resist him mightily, and he leaves them alone, because he finds no place (topos) where he can gain entrance. So then he comes to those who are partially empty, and finding a place he enters them, and then he does what he wants with them, and they become enslaved to him" (Shepherd of Hermas, Mandate 12.5).[1]

**Clement** (A.D.96), a leader in the church at Rome. He admonishes healthy believers "to visit those who are harassed by evil spirits, and pray and pronounce exorcisms over them. In this way let us approach a brother or a sister who is sick. Let this man cast out demons and God will help him." The Clementine literature has much to say about the workings of evil spirits. "Therefore the demons themselves, knowing the amount of faith of those of whom they take possession, measure their stay proportionately. Wherefore they stay permanently with the unbelieving, tarry for a while with the weak in faith; but with those who thoroughly believe, and who do good, they cannot remain even for a moment… The labor, therefore of everyone is to be solicitous about the putting to flight of his own demon" (Clementine Homilies 9.11; see also Recognitions 4.17).[2]

**Tertullian** (A.D.160-230), a Roman theologian and apologist, the son of the Centurion, thoroughly educated. Converted in A.D.197, he became the most formidable defender of the faith in his day. In his apology as he addressed the rulers of the Roman Empire he said:

"Let a person be brought before your tribunals, who is plainly under the demoniacal possession. The wicked spirit forbidden to speak by a follower of Christ, will as readily make the truthful confession that he is a demon, as elsewhere he has falsely asserted that he is a God. Or if you will let there be produced one of the God-possessed and as they are supposed—if they do not confess, in their fear of lying to a Christian, that they are demons, then and there shed the blood of that most impudent follower of Christ.

All the authority and power we have over them is from our naming the name of Christ, and recalling to their memory the woes with which God threatens them at the hand of Christ their judge, and which they expect one day to overtake them. Fearing God in Christ and Christ in God, they become subject to God and Christ. So at one touch in breathing, overwhelmed by the thought and realization of those judgments fires, they leave at our command the bodies they have entered, unwilling and distressed and before your very eyes, put to an open shame."3

**Justin Martyr** (A.D.100-165), also a Christian apologist, sometimes called Justin the Philosopher. He opened a school of Christian philosophy at Rome and where he and some of his disciples were finally martyred under Marcus Aurelius. In his second apology, addressed to the Roman Senate, he says, "Numberless demoniacs throughout the whole world, and in your city, many of our Christian men, exorcising them and the name of Jesus Christ, who was crucified under Pontius Pilot, have healed and do heal, rendering helpless, and driving the possessing demon out of the man, though they could not be cured by all other exorcists, and those who use incantations and drugs."4

**Origen** (A.D.185-254), an important leader in Alexandria (Egypt) and then later in Caesarea (Palestine), actually mentions authority of believers to cast a demon out of themselves. He notes, "Anyone who vanquishes a demon in himself, e.g. the demon of lewdness, is put out of action; the demon is cast into the abyss, and cannot do any harm to anyone."5

**Cyprian** (A.D.207-258), a Father of the Church and Bishop of Carthage, expressed himself with equal confidence. He noted that it was evil spirits which inspired the false prophets of the Gentiles to deliver oracles by always mixing truth with falsehood in an effort to prove what they said. He adds: "Nevertheless these evil spirits adjured by the living God immediately obey us, submit to us, own our power, and are forced to come out of the bodies they possess."6

**Eusebius** (A.D.250), another early church historian, makes it clear that the ministry of deliverance was so important in the early church that he mentions a Roman bishop named Cornelius who says that there were fifty two exorcists serving in the church at this time (Eusebius, History of the Church, 6.43). He also gives similar testimony to the presence of exorcists in the churches of eastern Asia Minor and Syria during the time of the Emperor Diocletian (A.D.284-305), (Eusebius, History of the Church, 8.6).

Numerous other accounts and excerpts could be given from Christian leaders throughout the post-Nicene age, the Byzantine Empire, and from luminaries such as Thomas Aquinas, John Calvin, Martin Luther, and the Puritans.[7]

## *The Testimony from Revival History*

As we study the history of revivals and the great movements of God within this century, it is impossible to ignore the reports of demonic manifestations.

The great revival that is historically known as the "Shantung Revival" in the 1930s reported, "It may not be generally known that perhaps the greatest revival in the history of Southern Baptists in North China is now being experienced in many Chinese churches of our North China Mission. This has come as a result of earnest prayer, faith in God, Bible teaching, and much preaching on sin and kindred subjects. Numbers of Christians and churches are being revived; restitution of money is being made; tithes of the Lord held back are being brought forward; sins confessed to God and to those who have been wronged; sick are being healed; devils cast out; men and women, boys and girls are preaching with power hitherto not known; hundreds are crying for mercy and are being saved. The Devil is also at work, but there is great blessing and rejoicing in many places. Missionaries and Christians are marveling at the wonderful works of God."[8]

Also as one studies the reports of the "Welsh Revivals" one reads of the power of God over the powers of darkness. The Evangelist Evan Roberts writes in reflection of the moving of God in Wales, "The mistake at the time of the Revival in Wales in 1904 was to become occupied with the effects of Revival, and not to watch and pray in protecting and guarding the cause of Revival. The Spirit baptized souls, at present locked up in spirit, or side-tracked through satanic deceptions, are still those who would be the instruments through whom God could work, were they but set free. How, then, should the Lord's praying ones pray at the present time?  They should pray:

    1)    Against evil spirits now blocking and hindering Revival.

    2)    For the cleansing and delivering of those who became possessed through deception during the time of later Revivals.

3)      That when Revival is once more given it may be kept pure.

4)      For the preparation of instruments for Revival, trained and taught of God to guard against further inroads of the powers of darkness."[9]

## ARGUMENT 2:
### *"If you can't see it, touch it, feel it, taste it, It is not real."*

This argument is the result of a synthesis of several philosophies that have characterized much of western education in the past fifty years. These philosophies include Progressivism, Social Darwinism, and Pragmatism. This faulty logic is best seen in our "post modernity" culture in its most prevailing philosophy called relativism. Relativism is based on the presupposition there is no absolute truth or reality. Things can only be real if they can be verified by the physical realities as we define them. The Scientific Method is based upon this philosophy of relativism. Modern medical procedures and medicines have their foundation in this scientific method. The conclusions of "realities" are based upon experiments where the parameters are verifiable in strict laboratory conditions. This philosophy presupposes that if the results of such experiments draw the same conclusions the "majority" of the time then one can conclude truth on the basis of probability. The problem is that if the experiment fails only once then the conclusion of "truth" cannot be drawn. You see the nature of truth is not based in any way on relativism. Truth is always truth no matter what the circumstances. Truth is forever settled in Heaven:

*Forever, O, Lord, Thy Word is settled in Heaven (Psalm 119:89, Isaiah 40:8, John 17:17).*

Anywhere you go in the so called "Third World," (along with that one must add countries like France as well as the American Indian Tribes), people clearly understand the connection between the natural and the supernatural. They do not separate the two. From the worshiping of spirits and ancestors to sacrificial offerings for blessings and protection, it is a daily way of life for much of the world.

Man is created in the "image of God." We must understand that man is far more than merely natural; he is very much a supernatural being. Man will live somewhere forever. Man is able through the "New Birth" to know and fellowship with God. We must ask ourselves if our bodies are only natural, how is it that as Christians the Holy Spirit of God comes to dwell in us?

### ARGUMENT 3:
### "If we don't bother the Devil, He wont bother us."

How ridiculous is this notion. Look at our children. Look at our homes. Look at our institutions, our school boards. Look at our government officials. Look at our churches. Look at the pulpits across our land. Look at all the major denominations. Battle after battle, split after split, bondage upon bondage, spiritual defeat is more common than we want to admit. The Devil is bothering us. He is killing us. We must wake up to the battle before greater damage is done.

### ARGUMENT 4:
### It really isn't biblical,
### "It's some kind of emotional response to outdated superstitions of those who have not been well educated."

"This is charismatic teaching, this is for the holy rollers, not us we're Baptists. We're people of the Book."

C. Fred Dickason, while Head of the Theology Dept. at Moody Bible Institute, writes, "It is a significant testimony to the reality of demons that every writer of the New Testament, except the author of Hebrews, mentions demons or evil angels. Even Hebrews, however, directly names the Devil."[10]

When I began my own study of these matters, I was amazed at how much I didn't understand. Even in my theological training I had been exposed to so little of the biblical teaching. As a third generation evangelist, I had only heard stories. I had a few encounters with the supernatural darkness, but never understanding how to battle in the heavenlies. In all of my study as a preacher of the gospel very little time had been spent in the area of spiritual warfare. I hold degrees from the two largest Baptist institutions in the world. And yet, nothing was ever mentioned concerning this war in which we are all engaged. Just look at the Bible. *You shall know the truth, and the truth shall make you free (John 8:32).* We must study the Bible.

As I prayed seeking the truth, I told the Lord two things. 1) I would not go in the area of charismatic movement to be taught about this spiritual battle. Although I have great love and respect for our charismatic brothers for their zeal in evangelism, I believe way too much deception has characterized the most recent charismatic movements. 2) The Lord would have to teach me. I would look to Him alone for the guidance into the truth of spiritual warfare. So I began my study by taking the New Testament Scriptures and marking with a red highlighter every passage that spoke of the Devil, demons, dominion, the Evil One, freedom, victory, etc. I was amazed at the attention given by God's Word to these matters. Passage after passage, verse after verse, chapter after chapter, and book after book, there it was. From the beginning of Christ's ministry to the end of the ages this supernatural invisible war is ever present through all the New Testament. Jesus came to *set the captives free (Luke 4:18). The Son of God appeared for this purpose, that He might destroy the works of the Devil (I John 3:8).* To ignore the spiritual war in which we are engaged is to ignore the teachings of the Bible.

## ARGUMENT 5:
### *"Now that we are saved, we don't have to deal in these matters."*

"Doesn't the Bible say that we are to flee from the very appearance of Evil? No study of these matters is necessary. We shouldn't give the Devil that much attention. We ought to focus just on Jesus."

Although this argument sounds "spiritual" and "logical," the problem is that it ignores the fundamental reality that the Church is the primary target of the Enemy. Satan already owns the world *(I John 5:19, 2 Cor. 4:4).* It is only the church that is able to exalt and glorify the one true God. The Devil hates us with an undying wicked disdain. He tirelessly is scheming and setting vicious traps to destroy the children of God.

This is the same logic that says the thief that just came into my house is not really there. If I ignore him and just think happy thoughts, he'll go away and I won't have to deal with him. Dr. Timothy Warner, wrote an excellent book on Spiritual Warfare while a Professor in the School of World Mission and Evangelism at Trinity Evangelical Divinity School. The Professor says it best, "How RESIST got changed to IGNORE in so many segments of the church, I don't know. When it did however, Satan and his forces gained a great strategic advantage."[11]

I have found that a study of Spiritual Warfare is not a focus on the Devil, but rather it brings into focus our great and mighty God and what He has done for us on Calvary that we might live a victorious abundant Christian life. C.S. Lewis reminds us, "There are two equal and opposite errors into which our race can fall about devils, One is to disbelieve in their existence. The other is to believe, and to feel an excessive and unhealthy interest in them. They themselves are equally pleased by both errors."[12]

To say that now we are saved we don't need to study these matters is to ignore the teachings of Scripture. Every warning given in Scripture concerning this Spiritual Battle of life and death is given to the Church!

*Be sober, be vigilant; because your adversary the Devil, as a roaring lion, walketh about, seeking whom He may devour (I Peter 5:8, KJV).*

*For our struggle is not against flesh and blood, but against the rulers, against the powers, against the world forces of this darkness, against the spiritual forces of wickedness in the heavenly places (Eph. 6:12).*

*Put on the full armor of God, that you may be able to stand firm against the schemes of the Devil (Eph. 6:11).*

The only thing we have to fear is IGNORANCE:

*And you shall know the truth and the truth shall make you free (John 8:32).*

The Enemy hides behind ignorance and half-truths. My father used to say, "The problem with half-truths is that we always tend to believe the wrong half."

The Bible does not debate the existence of demons. The Bible assumes the reality of the spiritual battle we are in with the forces of darkness. A careful and prayerful study of God's eternal Word will help us understand the invisible war and the eternal victory that is ours in the Lord Jesus:

> *For though we walk in the flesh, we do not war according to the flesh, for the weapons of our warfare are not the flesh, but divinely powerful for the destruction of (strongholds) fortresses. We are destroying speculations and every lofty thing raised up against the knowledge of God, and we are taking every thought captive to the obedience of Christ (2 Cor. 10:3-5).*

## THE DISCOVERY OF THE DEVIL

Who is this one we call the Devil? Who is this one whose name is Satan? The Bible tells us that Satan's original name was Lucifer, Son of the Morning:

> *How art thou fallen from heaven, O Lucifer, son of the morning! How art thou cut to the ground, which didst weaken the nations! For thou hast said in thine heart, I will ascend into heaven, I will exalt my throne above the stars of God; I will sit also upon the mount of the congregation, in the sides of the north: I will ascend above the heights of the clouds; I will be like the most High. Yet thou shalt be brought down to hell, to the sides of the pit (Isaiah 14: 12-15, KJV).*

He was of the highest ranking cherubim. God's angelic kingdom is wonderfully and powerfully organized for God's purposes in His creation. It is organized in terms of rank and authority (power). We see in our own military a similar system of authority (power, responsibility) to accomplish its task.

Although Lucifer held the highest rank and possessed the greatest power and authority as an angel, he became envious of all the praise and glory going to God. Being an angel wasn't enough. Being responsible to God for great authority and power wasn't enough. He wanted it all. He wanted to be like God. In his heart, Satan decided to exalt himself to be worshiped like God was worshiped. *Ezekiel 28:12-19* refers to Satan. Without explaining how it happened, God says, *Iniquity was found in thee: vs. 15.* The only clue as to what occurred in Satan's mind is found in *verse 17: Your heart was lifted up because of your splendor* (KJV). His sin is obviously a proud heart and self-occupation. Reflecting upon his God-endowed beauty, he became enthralled with himself and was lifted up with pride *(I Tim. 3:6).*

He also perverted other angels from God's way. The words *merchandise (vs. 16)* and *traffick (vs. 18)* may refer to a soliciting to his evil cause a large group of fellow angels *(Matt. 25:41, Rev. 12:4, 9, Jude vs. 6).* His habitation was defiled by his sin also: *By the multitude of your iniquities, in the unrighteousness of your trade, you profaned your sanctuaries (vs. 18).*

Because of Satan's sin of arrogance and violence, God cast him from his privileged position (guarding) the throne of God *(out of the mountain of God, vs. 16).* He may have been cast to the earth after his original sin *(I cast you to the ground, vs. 17).* God accused him of flagrant and unwarranted rebellion and banished him from His presence. His ultimate punishment according to Christ is the lake of fire *(Matt. 25:41).*[13] God's Word reveals to us that all the angels that left their assignment given to them by God and joined Satan's rebellion against God are already doomed and damned:

> *And angels who did not keep their own domain, but abandoned their proper abode, He has kept in eternal bonds under darkness for the judgment of the great day (Jude vs. 6).*

Satan and all the angels that joined him in rebellion against God are under the judgment of God. And they know it! It's not just that one day they will be judged. They are under the judgment of God right now! Once God declares His Word, it is forever settled in Heaven. There is no taking it back. There is no getting around it. As the old timers used to say, "When God says it, that settles it!"

Some years back, I conducted a revival meeting in a small fishing town in the Gallatin Valley in Montana. While sharing a wonderful meal and sweet fellowship in the Lord with our host family around the table, the mother asked me to pray for their daughter. She told the pastor and me that she no longer recognized her daughter. That for a couple of years her daughter had lost control of her life. She had been involved in drugs, sex, and all manner of "rebellion" in the school, church, and in the home. When she said the word rebellion my spiritual ears came to attention. I told this sweet Christian couple that I would pray for their daughter. I expressed my concern. I told them I didn't want to spook or scare them, but I wanted to ask them a question. I asked, "Has your daughter ever been involved in witchcraft?" They looked at each other and then turned to me and said, "We don't think so. Not that we know about."

The next day I received a call and was asked to come back to their home. When I arrived the couple proceeded to tell me how they had pondered my question since I had left them the day before. They said that not until they began to discuss the possibility of their daughter's involvement in witchcraft did things become clear. They said that in a high school English class the teacher had assigned a term paper on casting spells and the class had ordered a book of spells and witchcraft for the class for this evil term project. As they began to recall the experiences of horrible changes in their daughter, they said it must have been the exposure to witchcraft that opened the door to evil in her life. She got a black cat named him Lucifer and began to live in rebellion. I told them what they were dealing with was far more than just their daughter. They needed to begin to pray for her deliverance from demonic forces.

***Rebellion is the sin of witchcraft*** *(I Samuel 15:23).* This is Satan's great sin. Rebellion against God, rebellion against God's authority is always a work of Satan. God has set forth in His kingdom a holy system of authority. This authority is carefully established in the Word of God, whether authority in the home *(Eph. 5:22-6:3),* community, government *(Romans 13:1-7),* or church *(Eph. 5:23, Eph. 1:22-23).* All authority has been ordained by God. Wherever you find rebellion, there you will find the working of the Enemy. You can count on it.

It is also extremely important to note *Isaiah 14:11.* In this amazing passage of Scripture, we find one of the most effective ways Satan is able to control and destroy God's creation. *Your pomp and music of your harps...* The King James Version says, *the noise of thy viols.* We get the word violin from this word. Here we see that Lucifer was a musician. The inference can clearly be made that since Lucifer was the highest in rank of all angels and since he was a musician, then Satan was personally involved in the praises and worship through music in heaven. Only Lucifer outside of God could know more about the power and importance of music in the heavenlies and subsequent war for dominion over God's creation.

It is through music that much of the working of the Enemy is done in our lives. Our young people can get CDs at most all major discount stores that enable them to commune with darkness and conjure evil spirits within their rooms. And all of this can be taking place in the presence of others through the ear phones and head sets of our children. The list of evil is inexhaustible within so much of the music that is targeted for our children. From hard rock to "gangsta" rock, from trance music to country music, the thoughts from Hell enter our minds without us even being aware of the dangers that are around the corner. Satan doesn't care what style of music it is. No style of music is more spiritual than any other. Style is about personal preference which ultimately comes down to the desires of the flesh. Even through so called "praise and worship" music much damage and division has come to the Church. Satan will use whatever music he can to destroy the work of Christ in our lives.

We would never allow someone to ride along with us in our cars and tell us to kill, to commit suicide, and to go and get stoned and drunk. Nor would we allow someone to try to talk us into being unfaithful to our wives and to get a divorce. But we will allow the same evil ideas to be poured into our hearts through an exciting beat, twang of a guitar, or melodious harmonies or melodies that pass through our conscious and are planted in our subconscious. These evil thoughts and ideas from music designed for the flesh are planted in our hearts until the day they bring forth their rotten and evil fruit of destruction.

## THE DESCRIPTION OF THE DEVIL

When the Bible records a name, there is far more known through that name than what we generally understand in the names of our culture. When a name is given in our day, it is usually no more than a family name handed down or a name that the mother and father personally liked. Not so in Scripture. Tied to every name given in the Bible a wealth of information is given concerning the one that bares that name. For example, Israel means "ruling with God." Isaac means "laughter," Isaiah "helper," Jesus "savior," Christ "the anointed one." So you see it is extremely revealing to know the name of a person in the Bible. So it is with the names given to the Devil in the Bible. Within the meaning of each name we learn not only who the Devil is but also his work and strategies against God and His creation.

There may be as many as 40 different titles referring to Satan. We will consider a few of the most significant so as to learn about God's Enemy and ours. To study Satan's names is helpful in the understanding of his schemes against God and His people.

GOD OF THIS WORLD- *(I John 5:19) ...the whole world lies in the power of the evil one (2 Cor. 4:4). ...the god of this world has blinded the minds of the unbelieving, that they might not see the light of the gospel of the glory of Christ..."* Prince or Ruler of this world *(John 12:31, 14:30, 16:11).* Make no mistake about it, Satan is ruling over this world and its systems of ungodliness and wickedness. As the old gospel song laments, "This world is not our home. We're just passing through." In the book of *Hebrews* the 11th Chapter and the 13th verse, we find the declaration that people of faith are *strangers* on the earth. One day Jesus will reign on David's Throne from Jerusalem in a time of great peace as King of Kings and Lord of Lords *(Isaiah 9:6-7, Luke 1:30-33, Isaiah 2:1-4, Revelation 19:11-16).* But who of us would be so foolish to believe that Jesus is ruling and reigning in our world? No, it is clear that the Evil One is ruling over the earth and its false kingdoms.

PRINCE OF THE POWER OF THE AIR- *...in which you formerly walked according to the course of this world, according to the prince of the power of the air, of the spirit that is now working in the sons of disobedience (Ephesians 2:2).* The Prince of the Aerial Host. There is a kingdom in the heavenlies that is highly organized and ruled by Satan. In that kingdom there are various areas and levels of authority. The headquarters of this kingdom are in the heavenly regions. That is a staggering fact, but it is quite clear. The fact that Satan heads a highly-organized kingdom astonishes some people, yet there are many clear indications of this in the Scriptures. In *Matt. 12:22-28,* this incident in the ministry of Jesus is recorded. Jesus had brought healing to a demon-possessed man who was blind and mute by driving out the evil spirit. *All the people were astonished and said, "Could this be the Son of David?" But when the Pharisees heard this they said, "It is only by Beelzebub, the prince of demons, that this fellow drives out demons."* Beelzebub means, literally, "lord of the flies." It is the title of Satan particularly as the ruler over demons. Jesus responds to the Pharisees in verse 25, *Jesus knew their thoughts and said to them, "Every kingdom divided against itself will be ruined, and every city or household divided against itself will not stand. If Satan drives out Satan, he is divided against himself. How then can his kingdom stand?"* (KJV) There is a clear implication that, first Satan has a kingdom. Second, it is not divided but highly organized. Third, it stands and has not been overthrown.[14] *

TEMPTER- *For this reason, when I could endure it no longer, I also sent to find out about your faith, for fear that the tempter might have tempted you, and our labor should be in vain (I Thess. 3:5).* Jesus was tempted by the Devil and so are we. All of the temptations of the Devil aimed at our Savior were targeted in the areas of vulnerability of man. These are listed in *I John 2:15-17 and Luke 4:1-13.*

The ultimate goal of the Enemy was to tempt Jesus to establish His life, His ministry, and His Kingdom short of going to the cross. It is also true in our lives. If Satan can get us to establish our lives, our families, our ministries, our music, our work short of the cross of Christ, he will win the invisible war for our souls. The glory of God for which we were created will be denied our Creator. He is tempter.

DEVIL, DIOBOLOS- *And not a new convert, lest he become conceited and fall into the condemnation incurred by the Devil. And he must have a good reputation with those outside the church, so that he may not fall into reproach and the snare of the Devil (I Tim. 3:6-7).* This name is the one most used in the New Testament. It means separator, slanderer: the one who divides through the use of lies and accusations. Implied is the name *The Accuser of the Brethren (Rev. 12:10).* How many churches and ministries have been destroyed because of a false accusation. How often has the work of Christ been stopped in a community because of a selfish accusation born in the pit of Hell. Look at all the many myriads of denominations claiming to be the only way to God. So much of our so called mission work is starting new churches through "organized splits" because God's people can't learn to work together and get along. How tragic in the light of Jesus prayer for His church in *that they may all be one; even as Thou, Father, art in Me, and I in Thee, that they also may be in Us; that the world may believe that thou didst send Me (John 17:13-21)*. Satan is Diobolos.

THE GREAT DRAGON, THE OLD SERPENT- *(Gen. 3, Rev. 12:3-4, 13:4)* Here we have the picture of Eden. The beguiling serpent bringing into God's paradise a challenge to his authority armed only with lies. Think of it, all that Satan has been able to do on this earth and in the heavenlies has been based on lies. That's right, nothing but lies.

I guess the most recognizable witch, fortune teller of our time is Jean Dixon. She claims to be a good witch. She claims that her prophetic gifts are from God. After all she is a faithful Catholic. However, in her biography, Jean Dixon tells of an experience without which "she would not have been able to interpret the more enlightening visions that were to follow." A snake crawled in bed with her. She says, "As a snake gradually entwined itself around my chest I could see its head but not its eyes. While I watched, it slowly turned its eyes and gazed into mine. In them was the all-knowing wisdom of the ages. I sensed that it was telling me that if my faith was great enough I could penetrate some of this divine wisdom."[15] That's right, the Old Serpent, the Great Dragon has a name. His name is Satan.

DECEIVER- *(Rev. 12:9, 13:14, 20:3) And he deceives those who dwell on the earth because of the signs which it was given him to perform in the presence of the beast,...* This deception involves a wide range of scheming from hiding his own existence to actively promoting false philosophies, religions, and outright perversions of behavior and morals *(Col. 2:8-10)*.

THE EVIL ONE- This name refers to one intrinsically wicked who is not content to be corrupt in himself but must seek to corrupt others. The article limits the name to a specific person who is well known, not just the concept of evil. Christ prayed that believers might be kept from the power of the Evil One *(John 17:15)*, in which the whole world lies *(I John 5:19)*.

SATAN- *(Zec. 3:1, Rev. 12:9)* This common title is used fifty-two times in the Bible. It means adversary or one who opposes. It designates this person as a self-proposed rival of God whose purpose it is to set up a counterfeit and rival kingdom. In his opposition to God, he also opposes God's people *(Zec 3:1-2, Luke 22:31-32)*. However, our Advocate, Christ the Lord, defends us against him successfully.

ANGEL OF LIGHT- *(2 Cor. 11:14) And no wonder, for even Satan disguises himself as an angel of light.* He can appear as beautiful and powerful, even as a messenger of the true God, an angel of light. My father-in-law has often said that Satan's will is so close to God's will that only one who is walking in the Spirit of Christ will be able to discern the difference. How true and how sobering it is to think that we must be walking in Christ when we encounter this Angel of Light.

LIAR, FATHER OF LIES- *(John 8:44) You are of your father the Devil, and you want to do the desires of your father. He was a murderer from the beginning, and does not stand in the truth, because there is no truth in him. Whenever he speaks a lie, he speaks from his own nature; for he is a liar, and the father of lies.* It is in this name we see the true nature of the spiritual battle in which we struggle. Spiritual warfare in its essence is the conflict between the truth of God and the lies of Satan. Our freedom comes from knowing and believing the truth of God. *And you shall know the truth and the truth shall make you free (John 8:32).*

ROARING LION- *(I Peter 5:8) Be of sober spirit, be on the alert. Your adversary, the Devil, prowls about like a roaring lion, seeking someone to devour.* What a picture of the Enemy. Scheming and hunting like a hungry lion. His goal is not to irritate you; he wants to gobble you up. Satan is not trying to eat your lunch; he wants to eat you for lunch.

THIEF- *(John 10:10) The Thief comes only to steal, kill, and destroy; I came that they might have life, and might have it abundantly.*

It is past time for the Church to wake up spiritually. It is as though we have been drugged into a trance state of ignorance. It's time to plug in our I B Ms, (ITTY-BITTY MINDS). It is time we stop resting in our ignorance and join the battle that is destroying our churches, our homes, and our children. When we see something in our children's lives that comes to steal from them, kill them, and to destroy them, it comes from the Thief, the Devil himself.

How do I know that liquor is from the Devil? That's right; it will kill you and destroy your life. How do we know that sex outside of marriage is a scheme of the Enemy to steal, kill, and destroy? Because it does steal, kill and destroy! I believe the Greek word is "DUH"! How do I know that abortion is a work of the Devil? That's right; it kills and destroys a precious innocent life as well as destroying the joy and peace of the mother. How do I know that drugs are from the Devil? They KILL and DESTROY! We must wake up from our spiritual slumber. We must join the battle lest we all are destroyed in it. We find the same clear logic within the Word of God concerning the works of the Enemy:

> Does a fountain send out from the same opening both fresh and bitter water? Can a fig tree, by brethren, produce olives, or a vine produce figs? Neither can salt water produce fresh (James 3:11-12).

You see where there is bitter fruit there is a bitter root! The Thief comes to steal, kill, and destroy!

We must conclude from the study of the Word of God we have a formidable adversary. The Devil is real and must be encountered in a fierce battle of life and death for the souls of men. Satan has a highly organized kingdom that has been set up as a counterfeit to the Kingdom of God. The kingdom of darkness is carefully structured to deceive man from knowing and glorifying the one true and living God. The Devil is doing all he can as long as he can (which is a bunch) to either rule as God or destroy all that God created for His rule. Satan and all rebellious angels have been severely judged by God and have been defeated through the work of Jesus Christ on Calvary. Victory in the invisible war only comes through our union in the Lord Jesus.

Chapter 2

# The Dangers of the Devil

*"His (Satan's) craft and power are great, and armed with cruel hate, on earth is not his equal."*
*—Martin Luther*

No good soldier would ever go into battle without knowing all he can about his enemy. We have a formidable enemy in Satan and His forces of darkness. He is more cunning and wicked than human minds can imagine. My father used to say, "Son, you can't get up early enough to out think a thief." How true this is when we speak of the Arch-deceiver, Satan. Paul tells us *in order that no advantage be taken of us by Satan; for we are not ignorant of his schemes (2 Cor. 2:11)*. To be effective in battle, the Church must understand the dangerous schemes of the Enemy. This Chapter is divided into four main sections. They are 1) The Deception of the Devil. 2) The Division caused by the Devil. 3) The Diversion caused by the Devil. 4) The Damnation that accompanies the Devil.

## THE DECEPTION OF THE DEVIL

Satan is about deception. All that he does, all his schemes are to cause you and me to believe his lies instead of the truth of God. Remember, *you shall know the truth and the truth shall make you free (John 8:32)*. Satan knows that if you and I believe the truth of God, he doesn't stand a chance to win the battle for control of our lives.

Jesus said of the Devil:

*You are of your father the Devil, and you want to do the desires of your father. He was a murderer from the beginning, and does not stand in the truth, because there is no truth in him. Whenever he speaks a lie, he speaks from his own nature; for he is a liar, and the father of lies (John 8:44).*

It is deception that is his main strategy of control. In the Book of *Colossians* we find these words of great warning in the *2nd Chapter, vs. 8-10*:

*See to it that no one takes you captive through philosophy and empty deception, according to the tradition of men, according to the elementary principles of the world, rather than according to Christ. For in Him all the fullness of the deity dwells in bodily form, and in Him you have been made complete, and He is the head over all rule and authority.*

The word "philosophy" means the love of wisdom; however, in this context Paul is clearly defining the word as the love of the world's wisdom. Empty deception and the traditions of men clearly indicate the dangers of being deceived by the wisdom and thought processes of the world.

## *The Vulnerability of Man*
(See Illustration A, Man's Area of Vulnerability and His Victory in Christ on page 86)

The Scripture tells us:

*Do not love the world nor the things of the world. If anyone loves the world, the love of the Father is not in him. For all that is in the world, the lust of the flesh and the lust of the eyes and the boastful pride of life, is not from the Father, but is from the world (I John 2:15-17).*

The three areas of vulnerability to the schemes of the enemy in our lives are 1) The Pride of Life 2) The Lust of the Eyes 3) The Lust of the

Flesh. Here are the areas in which Satan is looking for a foothold so he can ultimately establish a stronghold in our lives. Think of it, Satan has done all that he has done to rule the world through lies. That's right, nothing but lies. From the very beginning of his relationship with man in the Garden of Eden until today all of it is based on deception.

We see the vulnerability of man as we study the temptations of Christ in *Luke, Chapter 4:*

## THE LUST OF THE FLESH

*And Jesus, full of the Holy Spirit, returned from the Jordan and was led bout by the Spirit in the wilderness for forty days, being tempted by the Devil. And He ate nothing during those days; and when they had ended, He became hungry. And the Devil said to Him, "If You are the Son of God, tell this stone to become bread."*

## THE LUST OF THE EYES

*And he led Him up and showed Him all the kingdoms of the world in a moment of time. And the Devil said to Him, "I will give You all this domain and its glory for it has been handed over to me, and I give it to whomever I wish. Therefore if You worship before me, it shall all be Yours."*

## THE PRIDE OF LIFE

*And he led Him to Jerusalem and had Him stand on the pinnacle of the temple and said to Him, "If you are the Son of God, throw Yourself down from here; for it is written, He will give His angels charge concerning You to guard You, and on their hands they will bear You up, lest you strike Your foot against a stone."*

All temptations are designed to get man to establish his life, his family, his ministry, his walk in this world short of the cross of Christ. Satan was and is defeated at the Cross *(Col. 2:13-15)*!

Spiritual warfare is the encounter of TRUTH in the midst of the lies of the Enemy. Neil Anderson, while Chairman of the Practical Theology Department of Talbot School of Theology, put it this way, "Freedom from spiritual conflicts and bondage is not a power encounter; it's a truth encounter. God's power is in His truth. Satan is a deceiver, and he will work undercover at all costs. But the truth of God's Word exposes him and his lie. Satan's power is in the lie, and when his lie is exposed by the truth, his plans are foiled."[1] He can do nothing about your position in Christ, but if he can deceive you into believing his lies about you and God he wins the battle of control. In the spiritual battle for control, truth is the liberating agent. The power of Satan is in his lies. The power of the believer is in knowing the truth. Anderson continues, "We are to pursue truth, not power."[2]

## *Philosophies, Empty Deceptions, Traditions of Men Elementary Principles of the World (Col. 2:8)*

What are these traditions of men and elementary principles of the world that the Enemy so readily uses to deceive us? Have you ever thought, "I can't help it, that's just the way God made me." "My mother (or Father) was this way, so I'm going to be this way." "It's just our family trait to be stingy." "My Father was a tight-wad, so I'm going to be a tight-wad." So many ways the Enemy deceives us to believe his lies. What is the truth? God created us in His image. He created us to be holy even as He is holy:

> *...but like the Holy One who called you, be holy yourselves also in all your behavior; because it is written, you shall be holy, for I am holy (I Peter 1:15-16).*

Have you every heard this one? "God helps those who help themselves." My grandfather put it this way, "Faith is fine. You can't eat faith; you got to have that cracker." My uncle used to put it this way, "You can live by faith, but you can't live on faith." Although these "wise old sayings" might sound good (to the flesh), they're simply not true when one looks at the truth of the Word of God. How many churches have been severely damaged spiritually because decisions were made on the basis of the philosophies of the world rather than the Word of God?

> *...for whatsoever is not of faith is sin (Romans 14:23, KJV).*
> *And without faith it is impossible to please Him (Heb.11:6).*
> *And my God shall supply all your needs according to His riches*

*in glory in Christ Jesus (Phil.4:19).*

*For whoever wishes to save his life shall lose it, but whoever loses his life for My sake, he is the one who will save it. For what is a man profited if he gains the whole world, and loses or forfeits himself (Luke 9:24-25)?*

Satan uses these worldly philosophies to keep us from the freedom in Christ that God has given to us through the finished work of Christ on Calvary. If it wasn't a good lie, it wouldn't be of the Devil. There are many ways we are deceived. The schemes of the Devil are as numerous as those he is attempting to deceive. Here are some of the Devil's schemes of deception with which the Bible warns us.

1. The man is *deceived* if he is a hearer, and not a DOER of the Word of God  *(James 1:22).*
2. He is *deceived* if he says he has no sin *(I John 1:8).*
3. He is *deceived* when he thinks himself to be "something" when he is nothing *(Gal. 6:3).*
4. He is *deceived* when he thinks himself to be wise with the wisdom of this world *(I Cor. 3:18).*
5. He is *deceived* by seeming to be religious, when an unbridled tongue reveals his true condition *(James 1:26).*
6. He is *deceived* if he thinks he will sow, and not reap what he sows *(Gal.6:7).*
7. He is *deceived* if he thinks the unrighteous will inherit the Kingdom of God *(I Cor. 6:9).*
8. He is *deceived* if he thinks that contact with sin will not have its effect upon him *(I Cor. 15:33).*[3]

Satan's main weapon is deception. He does all that he does to oppose God through manipulating man with his lies. He never stops. He will never quit trying to get you and me to believe his lies. At the moment we believe the Devil's lie, we have stopped believing God and God's Word. Here lies Satan's ultimate goal. He does all that he does to oppose and destroy the work and Word of God. Why? Because he is defeated by it. Even in the Great Tribulation, the time of God's great judgment on a Christ-rejecting world, the Devil continues his work of deception:

*That is, the one whose coming is in accord with the activity of
Satan, with all power and signs and false wonders, and with all
the deception of wickedness for those who perish, because they
did not receive the love of the truth so as to be saved (2 Thess.
2:9-10).*

## The Danger of Legalism

A word must be said here concerning the hideous dangers of legalism. There may be no more deceptive scheme of the Enemy than legalism. Obeying Christ is not legalism. Trusting the Word of God is not
legalism. True Christianity must not ever be confused with legalism.
Legalism is the attempt by man to set up his own "moral" standards to
gain the approval of men or of God. The approval of God is only gained
through what Jesus did for us on Calvary. That's why legalism is such
an attack on the Gospel. Legalism sets up its own laws only to focus on
the keeping (or not keeping) of those laws. No matter what laws man
sets up for himself, he can in return break those laws.

In many Christian schools and churches, legalism often becomes a
catalyst in destroying so many of our children. Laws or rules are set up
to control a child's behavior. Certainly the Christian walk is a life of
discipline. But as we teach our children discipline, the rules that we set
up for them should not be allowed to confuse them with the rules and
approval of God. Their hair styles, uniforms, and the like are not to be
classified in their minds as the Christian way of living. Although my
children attended Christian schools, I have watched legalism infect its
deadly poison in the life of young children only to ultimately confuse
them concerning Christ's claim for their lives. Legalism is NOT
Christianity.

These man-made rules so often accomplish just the opposite for
which they were intended. For instance, as soon as the school bell
rings, most all the boys will pull their shirt tails out in defiance of the
rules. You see, the rule for tucked in shirt tails doesn't change their
behavior at all. All it does is cause them to rebel against the rules.

Marilyn Manson is a teenage rock star idol of rebellion. He is proud
of the fact that he has demons. Making no apology, he wants to get your

children involved in the darkness. To look at him is to wonder how in the world anyone could be so confused. Although a boy, he looks as if he is confused about his gender. When you hear him speak, nothing but confusion comes out of his mouth. You guessed it; he grew up in a so-called Christian school. That's right, legalism likely caused this young man to reject true Christianity. Listen to his own words from his own autobiography concerning the Christian school he attended. "At Christian Heritage School it didn't take much to rebel. The place was built on rules and conformity. Everything was regimented and ritualistic. Gradually, I began to resent Christian school and doubt everything I was told. The seeds of who I am now had been planted."[4] Through the rules set up in the name of Christianity, he was never able to distinguish the difference between the teachings of Christ and these man-made rules. Legalism sets up the rules for the purpose of acceptance. Man in his fallen nature always looks to how he can break the rules so as to be his own master.

It is amazing to note how many of the boys and girls in a Christian school become sexually active. Many girls are not able to finish before becoming pregnant. One cannot ignore the overwhelming drug and alcohol problem among our children in Christian schools. The reason is clear to me. We have taught them to live by the rules, all the while neglecting teaching them how to walk with the Savior.

Sin is not an issue of breaking man's rules. Sin is breaking God's laws. Christianity is not a way of life based upon not smoking, drinking, carousing, cursing and the like. If it is, then a man that doesn't do these things can think he's pretty good. As long as I provide for my family, as long as I am faithful to my wife, as long as I do my best, God will be pleased with me. The Bible says:

*All our righteousness is like filthy rags (Isaiah 64:6, KJV).*

*There is none righteous, no not one (Romans 3:10, KJV).*

Don't misunderstand me. I am not a proponent of antinomianism. That is, against all law. Some say, "Now you are saved, anything goes." God's grace becomes a license for all kinds of disobedience. Jesus did not come to abolish the law, but to fulfill it *(Matt. 5:17).*

*What shall we say then? Are we to continue in sin that grace might increase? May it never be! How shall we who died to sin still live in it (Romans 6:1-2)?*

It is not the rules that keep us doing the right thing. It is our walk with Holy God as we daily die to sin that enables us to live holy and righteous lives.

It is in Christ alone that the law of God has been fulfilled. It is only in the new birth, through this new relationship with the Holy Spirit that the Christian is able to "live out" God's will. God's will is not done by meeting standards set up by men in the so-called name of Christ. No matter how we set up rules by which to live, only the righteousness of Christ in us and through us can bring true Christianity. Legalism is NOT Christianity! The authority, as we shall see, has been set in the heavens. Sin is an attitude of challenging the one true authority, God's Word, not man-made rules.

## THE DIVISION OF THE DEVIL

Of all the names given to Satan in the Scriptures, the one most often used is Diobolos. The word means the one who separates or the one who slanders for the sake of separating. We find these words in *Romans 16:17-20:*

*Now I urge you, brethren, keep your eye on those who cause dissensions and hindrances contrary to the teaching which you learned, and turn away from them. For such men are slaves, not of our Lord Christ but of their own appetites; and by their smooth and flattering speech they deceive the hearts of the unsuspecting. For the report of your obedience has reached to all; therefore I am rejoicing over you, but I want you to be wise in what is good, and innocent in what is evil. And the God of peace will soon crush Satan under your feet.*

Have you ever heard a rumor in the church that later caused the church to splinter and divide? The rumor was an accusation that some wanted to believe, but was never verified. People took sides according to what they thought happened, what they thought was said or done.

But no one ever really knew for sure what happened. When it happens it is easy to smell the foul stench of the Devil:

*...for the accuser of our brethren has been thrown down, who accuses them before our God day and night (Rev. 12:10).*

As I have traveled as an evangelist, I have seen this happen all across Christendom. The Apostle Paul writing to the church in Corinth writes:

*Now I exhort you, brethren, by the name of the Lord Jesus Christ, that you all agree, and there be no divisions among you, but you be made complete in the same mind and in the same judgment (I Cor. 1:10).*

How important is the unity of the Body of Christ? How critical is the union that is ours in the Lord Jesus? There is great power in prayer as we will discuss in the Chapter 5. There is greater power in corporate prayer:

*Again I say to you, that if two of you agree on earth about any-thing that they may ask, it shall be done for them by My Father who is in heaven. For where two or three have gathered togeth-er in My name, there I am in their midst (Matt. 18:19-20).*

Is it any wonder that the Devil is about dividing churches, dividing families, dividing friends, dividing believers? We are weaker in the spiritual battle when we are separate. Oh how we need to remember:

*For our struggle is not against flesh and blood, but against the rulers, against the powers, against the world forces of this dark-ness, against the spiritual forces of wickedness in the heavenly places (Eph. 6:12).*

Have you ever thought that someone in the church was your enemy? Have you ever been so full of personal resentment that you were consumed with personal hurt and anger? Have you ever been so angry at something someone did or said to you that you wanted to seek revenge and judgment? I have. Well, guess what? According to the

Word of God at that moment you and I fell into one of Satan's lying traps. Our enemy is Satan. Our fight is with the Devil. People in the church are our brothers and sisters in Christ. That's why we find these words of warnings in the Word of God:

*Pursue peace with all men, and the sanctification without which no one will see the Lord. See to it that no one comes short of the grace of God; that no root of bitterness springing up causes trouble, and by it many be defiled (Heb. 12:14-15).*

As we look back at church history, the one scheme of the Enemy that has been continually effective in the church is division. Oh, that the Church would stop believing the Devil's lies and come to understand he and he alone is our real enemy. We must stop fighting one another and join hands and hearts to fight our common enemy, Satan. You see, if our attention is on one another, then we will not focus on the battle with Satan.

Listen to the heart beat of our Savior as He is praying for His Church:

*...that they may all be one; even as Thou, Father art in Me, and I in Thee, that they also may be in Us; that the world may believe that Thou didst send Me (John 17:21).*

How critical is the spiritual unity of the church? How important is it that we work together for the cause of Christ? The world will not come to know our Savior apart from the spiritual cooperation within the Church. Satan has already won the battle in millions of lives because of the disobedience within the Church. We must learn to recognize and reject the Enemy's efforts to divide the Church of the Living God. To join in any word or any effort that would cause a schism within the Church, however noble it may seem at the time, is to join in the rebellion against God and His Word's authority in our lives. If you have been a part of anything that resulted in the dividing of God's Church, you must confess it today. If you continue in your disobedience to the Word of God, you will allow Satan a foothold, a stronghold not only in your life but in the life of your family. Repent now!

Not only is the Devil about dividing the Church, he also is about dividing our families. Wherever Satan finds the authority of God, the Church, the home, etc., he is at work in tearing down the structures through which resides God's authority. More marriages are destroyed by anger and bitterness than probably any other single cause.

## THE EVIL OF BITTERNESS

Bitterness is one of the great tools of Satan to control our lives. Like a slow growing cancerous tumor, ignoring it will not save us from its ultimate destruction. Be certain if you allow bitterness to remain at any time in your life, Satan will use it to his benefit to rob you of your joy, faith, and ultimately your life. We find the clear warning in *Eph. 4:26-27:*

> *Be angry, and yet do not sin; do not let the sun go down on your anger, and do not give the Devil an opportunity.*

The word translated opportunity is *topos*. We get our word topography from this root word. It literally means ground or a place for the Devil to work in our lives. Look at Chapter 3 for a more extensive study of the ways we give the Devil areas to control our lives.

How did Jesus teach us to pray? One of His requests in His "model" prayer was:

> *And forgive us our debts, as we forgive our debtors (Matt. 6:12).*

We must forgive with the same heart of obedience as our Lord has given to us by forgiving us our sins. What is at stake is our fellowship with Him:

> *For if you forgive men for their transgressions, your heavenly Father will also forgive you. But if you do not forgive men, then your Father will not forgive your transgressions (Matt. 6:14-15).*

Forgiveness is necessary in our lives to be able to receive the work of God. Any and all bitterness plugs up the flow of the power of God in and through our lives.

For many years my family and I have attended an old cowboy camp meeting in the Davis Mountains way out in West Texas. The meeting was established by an old circuit riding Presbyterian preacher by the name of Bloys. For over a century thousands of people who have their family ties to the West Texas ranches, come to worship and fellowship around the things of the Lord. Well, it was an afternoon meeting I chose to attend while most of those in the camp were taking a nap. Of the four preachers preaching that week, the Methodist preacher had been chosen for this afternoon service underneath the old tabernacle. His text was:

*As you therefore have received Christ Jesus the Lord, so walk in Him (Col. 2:6).*

God spoke to me that afternoon through that wonderful Methodist preacher. He gave me a word that has forever changed my life. His last word was, "If you have been saved by grace, why can't you learn to be gracious to others?" Wow, what a word! I have come to understand that the "litmus test" of authentic Christianity is grace, the willingness to give as our Lord has given. Forgiving those who have hurt you, the same way our Lord has forgiven us.

Bitterness is in its root form rebellion against God. You see, God's Word says:

*Never take your own revenge, beloved, but leave room for the wrath of God, for it is written, vengeance is Mine, I will repay says the Lord (Romans 12:19).*

The only one who has the right to judge is our Lord. He is righteous. He is just. He will make all things right one day. All will face Him in judgment. God sent His only Son to die for all sin. Jesus became the supreme sacrifice that God has declared is sufficient for all sin, even the sin of the one who has hurt you.

If you and I decide that we must help God out to bring judgment upon our enemies, we have joined the rebellion against God. You see, God can handle these matters all by Himself. He has shed His perfect Son's blood that all sin might be cleansed and forgiven. To remain bitter is to become a heretic. Please hear me out. To allow bitterness any place in our lives is to act as though Jesus' shed blood was not enough to cover the sins of the person who hurt you. Bitterness demands more blood. Isn't it true that Jesus blood is the full payment for your sins and for all the sins of the people who have hurt you. Stop listening to the lies. Jesus' blood is enough for all ALL sin!

*But when Christ appeared as a high priest of the good things to come, He entered through the greater and more perfect taber-nacle, not made with hands, that is to say not of this creation; and not through the blood of goats and calves, but through His own blood, He entered the holy place ONCE FOR ALL, having obtained eternal redemption (Heb. 9:11-12). But He, having offered ONE sacrifice for sins FOR ALL TIME (Heb. 10:12).*

Resentment that results in bitterness is the full blown manifestation of pure selfishness. It freezes the one who is the object of our anger in time. Let me explain. We expect others to allow us to grow and move on. However, when we hold a grudge, when we enter into the judgment of another we are refusing to let them grow and move on from the evil event. You see bitterness ties the person to that event. Essentially we are saying, "I'm not willing to allow that person to grow in the Lord and be forgiven."

If you want others to forgive you, then you must offer them the same forgiveness. To hold on to our un-forgiveness and bitterness is not to allow others the same grace that has been given to us. Bitterness is simply changing the rules on the playing field. If you expect others to forgive you then my brother or sister you must let others move on from the evil that happened in the past.

Don't allow bitterness to be only about you. Allow what has hap-pened to bring everybody involved to the Cross of Christ where His mercy, forgiveness and healing are limitless. Praise His Holy Name that His blood was shed for you and me, and for all those who have caused hurt and pain in our lives. Let's leave it with Jesus. Take your burdens to His cross and leave them there. He can handle it!

Bitterness is also a rejection of God's work in our lives. It is through suffering that God's purifying process is accomplished in our lives. Now I don't like this any more than you do. However, it's still true:

*Therefore, since Christ has suffered in the flesh, arm your-*
*selves with the same purpose, because he who has suffered in*
*the flesh has ceased from sin, so as to live the rest of the time*
*in the flesh no longer for the lusts of men, but for the will of*
*God (I Pet. 4:1-2).*

I know this flies in the face of so much of the false self-centered preaching of self gratification we hear today. The false preachers declare when you get saved, everything is going to be wonderful. Christians and non-Christians go through the same life experiences, with one big difference. God's people don't have to go through their suffering alone. When Jesus died on the cross, the darkness surrounded Him and He cried out in agony. Jesus went through His darkness all alone so that I don't have to go through my darkness alone.[5] Jesus did not come to make us happy. He came to make us HOLY!

*For to you it has been granted for Christ's sake, not only to*
*believe in Him, but also to suffer for His sake (Phil. 1:29).*

God's Word is full of teaching concerning suffering and its purpose in our lives.

Bitterness is making God accountable to me. It's also an affront to His sovereignty. In effect, we're saying, "God, I don't like what You're doing and I want You to know it. You didn't ask my permission or check with me ahead of time and I'm angry."[6] When my parents' marriage ended in divorce, the hurt and pain was overwhelming. I was just entering my teen years. Since my Father was a famous preacher, the hurt was even greater than you can imagine. Instead of humbling myself before God, I shook my fist in the face of God and said, "If you're the kind of God that would allow this kind of pain in my life, the deal is off. Everything I have promised, You can forget it."

Although I had been saved and called to preach, it was at that point I gave the Devil a place to work in and through my life. The result of that anger against God was I became sexually active. I became a thief. My life quickly became full of trash. My mouth became filthy because my heart became filthy. I joined others in playing the music of rebellion. My young life began to spiral out of control. God showed me through the unfailing love of others that His love never fails. My heart was broken and I returned to Him in repentance. You see, my bitterness didn't help my parents get back together. My bitterness didn't keep the Lord from loving me. His love for me stayed the same. All my bitterness did was to divide me from the love and power of the cross that would have healed my hurts and sorrows:

*Surely our griefs He Himself bore, And our sorrows He carried; Yet we ourselves esteemed Him stricken, smitten of God and afflicted. But He was pierced through for our transgressions, He was crushed for our iniquities; The chastening for our well-being fell upon Him, and by His scourging we are healed (Isaiah 53:4-5).*

After some years of walking in the grace and forgiveness that the Lord had given me, His working in my life concerning my parents' divorce was not over yet. While an undergraduate student at Baylor University, in the midst of studying in the library for an upcoming exam, God told me to go home to Dallas and tell my mother I loved her. The last thing I wanted to do was to tell her I loved her. I didn't even like her. Oh, I loved her generally as my mother, but I was embarrassed by the way she acted through the divorce. Well, the Lord had spoken to me very few times as clearly as He did that day. I knew I had to go.

When I found my mother, I began to tremble. This was the hardest thing I had ever had to do. But in obedience to our Lord, I did it. I told her that I loved her. I can't begin to tell you the burden that was lifted from my life that day. I am certain had I been disobedient to God's word to me that day in Waco, I would never have had the ministry He has given me today. Forgiveness is a choice, not a feeling. It is an act of obedience. Oh, dear friend, take back the ground given to the Devil in your life through bitterness and anger by asking God to forgive you for hanging on to bitterness and anger. The Enemy has done enough to divide and destroy. Oh, dear friend, LET IT GO! God can handle your hurts and sorrows. Jesus bore them in His body on Calvary when He shed His blood for us.

## *THE DIVERSION OF THE DEVIL*

One of the great dangers and pitfalls of the Devil's schemes is his diversionary tactics:

*And no wonder, for even Satan disguises himself as an angel of light (2 Cor. 11:14)*

The Devil's disguises are amazingly effective. He can appear as an angel of light. Think of it, he can appear as an angel of the true and living God. It is a counterfeit; but like so much of what the Devil does, it is a good counterfeit.

This counterfeiter has had centuries to perfect his disguises and to study his prey's weaknesses. As he considered Job, the Devil considers God's faithful to determine the most vulnerable place to bring his attack. Charles Spurgeon put it well when he said, "The Enemy, like a veteran fisherman, watches his fish, adapts his bait to his prey, and knows in what seasons and times the fish are most likely to bite. This hunter of souls comes secretly. Satan knows, however, just where to smite each of us. Our position, our capabilities, our education, our standing in society, our calling, all may be doors through which he may attack us."[7]

All of these diversionary efforts of our Enemy are to hinder us from knowing and doing God's will. Paul, Silas, and Timothy were very desirous to visit the church at Thessalonica, but they were unable to do so for the singular reason announced in this text, namely, *Satan hindered us (I Thess. 2:18)*. When Moses stood before Pharaoh and said, *"Thus saith the Lord, Let my people go, that they may serve me" (Exodus 8:1)*. A sign was required. The rod was cast upon the ground, and it became a serpent. In *II Timothy 3:8* we find an interesting reference to this event in Egypt. We read that the magicians did the same thing with their witchcraft. They did the Devil's work, and they did it well, for Pharaoh's heart was hardened when he saw that the magicians apparently produced the same miracles as Moses. God's will was hindered.

We read an amazing story of Satan's power to hinder even the Word of God through God's prophet Daniel. The Book of Daniel has a specific example of spiritual warfare. In fact, it describes a battle of angels. In Chapter 10, Daniel describes how he set himself to pray and seek God for a revelation concerning the future of His people Israel. For three weeks he devoted himself with special intensity to prayer and waiting on God. At the end of the three weeks, an angel from heaven came to Daniel with the answer to his prayer. Satan's angels kept the angel of God three weeks on the journey. Somewhere in the journey from the heaven of God to earth, the angel was required to go through

Satan's kingdom in the heavenlies. There he was opposed by evil angels who tried to prevent him from getting through with a message to Daniel.[8] The angel of the Lord was accompanied by the archangel Michael. Although hindered by Satan's forces, God's Word was revealed to Daniel.

Satan's hindrances are carefully designed counterfeits of God's true work. He hinders so many to keep them from true worship by offering them counterfeit religions. So-called "priests" today claim to offer daily sacrifice at the place they call an altar. They claim to have power to forgive sin, saying to sick and dying persons, "by authority committed unto me, I absolve you from all your sins." All this in the face of the truth of the Word of God that Jesus *offered one sacrifice for sins for ever, sat down on the right hand of God (Heb. 10:12-14)*. This is the great hindrance to the propagation of the Gospel.[9]

The diversionary tactics of the Devil are designed to get you and me to accept something noble, something good, all the while missing God's best. Have you ever heard the saying "Well, if we are going to err on one side or the other, we ought to err on _____?" Why do we accept the notion we must err at all? It's nothing but Satan's diversion to keep us from the truth of God. Satan's schemes are about helping us miss God and His will for our lives. If he can divert our attention from the truth of God's Word, Satan's work is well accomplished.

## *THE DAMNATION OF THE DEVIL*
### *Spiritual Curses*

As certain as you put your hand on a hot stove you will be burned, if you follow the Devil a heavy price will be levied on your soul. It is impossible for someone to entreat Satan without bringing upon themselves the judgment of God. If a person continues in sin, when you and I continue to willfully disobey God's Word, serious spiritual consequences will follow. The Word of God gives warning after warning concerning involvement in the ways of darkness.

## *Warning Concerning Sex Outside of Marriage*

*All because of the many harlotries of the harlot, the charming one, the mistress of sorceries, who sells nations by her harlotries and families by her sorceries. "Behold, I am against you," declares the Lord of hosts; "And I will lift up your skirts over your face, and show to the nations your nakedness and to the kingdoms your disgrace. I will throw filth on you and make you vile, and set you up as a spectacle" (Nahum 3:4-6).*

*And if a man seduces a virgin who is not engaged, and lies with her, he must pay a dowry for her to be his wife. If her father absolutely refuses to give her to him, he shall pay money equal to the dowry for virgins. You shall not allow a sorceress to live (Exodus 22:16-18).*

Also in the New Testament we find a clear warning concerning the eternal consequences of having sex outside of marriage.

*Do you not know that your bodies are member of Christ? Shall I then take away the members of Christ and make them member of a harlot? May it never be! Or do you not know that the one who joins himself to a harlot is one body with her: For He says, "The two will become one flesh" (I Cor. 6:15-16).*

Sex is not merely a physical act. It is a spiritual act. The Bible equates having sex with someone outside of the spiritual bonds of marriage, witchcraft. As we will study in Chapter 4 on Dominion and the Devil, the issue in spiritual warfare is control. When someone has sex with another, he/she has given control of himself or herself to that person. As long as the Lord is in charge of the union, it is holy and wonderful. When the Lord is left out, Satan takes advantage by helping us into disobedience to God and His Word. What has happened is that our bond of fellowship with God is broken when we sin. Neil Anderson points out that in its place, people form all kinds of unnatural bondings. We call them "soul ties." These soul ties can be incredibly powerful. That's why a woman will go back time and again to a man who beats her. There's some kind of an unnatural tie to that person that has to be broken by the power of God. Remember what Proverbs 5:22 says? *He shall be holden with the cords of his sins.* There are people who have God's life in them, but they are bound up with all kinds of sins. Somehow, when it is sexual it seems to be worse.[10]

## Warning Concerning Witchcraft, Divination

*There shall not be found among you anyone who makes his son or his daughter pass through the fire, one who uses divination, one who practices witchcraft, or one who interprets omens, or a sorcerer, or one who casts a spell, or a medium, or a spiritist, or one who calls up the dead. For whoever does these things is detestable to the Lord; and because of these detestable things the Lord your God will drive them out before you (Deut. 18:10-12).*

*Do not turn to mediums or spiritists; do not seek them out to be defiled by them. I am the Lord your God (Lev. 19:31).*
*And when they say to you, "Consult the mediums and the spiritists who whisper and mutter," should not a people consult their God? Should they consult the dead on behalf of the living (Isaiah 8:19)?*

God's Word is clear concerning witchcraft. He doesn't like it. Why? Because God wants us to trust only Him. We are to seek Him. We are to believe only Him. We are created to do His will. If the Enemy can get us to trust anyone or anything other than God, he wins the battle. Therefore all witchcraft is an abomination to the Lord:

*If a prophet or a dreamer of dreams arises among you and gives you a sign or a wonder, and the sign or the wonder comes true, concerning which he spoke to you, saying, Let us go after other gods (whom you have not known) and let us serve them, you shall not listen to the words of that prophet or that dreamer of dreams; for the Lord your God is testing you to find out if you love the Lord your God with all your heart and with all your soul (Deut. 13:1-3).*

Some years ago in a revival meeting in Northeast Texas, after I had preached a strong message entitled, "Six Reasons I Don't Want to Go to Hell," I had a young mother with two beautiful daughters approach me. She said, "I noticed you gave a warning tonight concerning those who are involved in witchcraft." She said, "I am a witch." But she hastened to say, "I am a good witch, I am a white witch. I do what I do to help people. I believe what I have in telling the future is from God. My aunt who also had this gift laid hands on me as a little girl and gave me her gift of fortune telling." I could tell she was sincere, although sincerely wrong in her beliefs. I asked her if she had ever been wrong in her fortune telling. She told me that she had been wrong on occasion. However, she said, "No witch is 100% correct all the time." I showed her the Word of God:

> *But the prophet who shall speak a word presumptuously in My name which I have not commanded him to speak, or which he shall speak in the name of other gods, that prophet shall die. And you may say in your heart, "How shall we know the word which the Lord has spoken?" When a prophet speaks in the name of the Lord, if the thing does not come about or come true, that is the thing which the Lord has not spoken (Deut. 18:20-22).*

I begged her to repudiate her involvement in witchcraft. I pleaded with her to give her life to the Lord and serve Him. She never came back to the meeting. I have often prayed for her and her daughters.

Dabbling in witchcraft is not just a fanciful game. Witchcraft is a practice of rebellion against God. Hollywood may couch it in comedic clothes, but make no doubt about it the stakes of witchcraft are eternally high. God will not tolerate those who practice it. Speaking of the judgment, God's Word says:

> *But the cowardly and unbelieving and abominable and murderers and immoral person and sorcerers and idolaters and all liars, their part will be in the lake that burns with fire and brimstone, which is the second death (Rev. 21:8).*

What a picture of the roll call of Hell. You don't want any part of the anger of God in the judgment. Leave witchcraft alone. Tarot Cards, Crystal Balls, Tea leaves, Palm readings, psychic hotlines, fortune tellers, charming, clairvoyance, fetishes, fire-walking, omens, spiritism, superstition, telepathy, seeking tongues, transference, yoga and transcendental meditation, astral projection, divining, channeling, have nothing to do with any of it. If you have been involved, right now ask the Lord to forgive you for not trusting in Him. Ask Him to forgive you of your sin of witchcraft. Don't wait, the cost is too high. Repent and confess your sin against God now. (For a more complete list of the dangers of evil practices read: *The Devil's Alphabet* by Kurt Koch, Kregel Publications, Grand Rapids, MI, n.d.).

## The Sins of the Fathers, Generational Curses
*Our Fathers sinned and are no more.*
*It is we who bear their punishment. (Lamentations 5:7)*

When one speaks of generational curses, we have much in the Bible to study. The Scriptures are not silent concerning the matter of the sins of the fathers. We would do well to believe what the Bible says concerning these matters. To ignore the teachings of Scripture for the sake of convenient comfort is to allow Satan an advantage in the invisible war. All who are born are under the curse of sin:

*Therefore, just as through one man sin entered into the world, and death through sin, and so death spread to all men, because all sinned (Romans 5:12).*

David cried unto the Lord:

*"Behold, I was brought forth in iniquity, and in sin my mother conceived me" (Psalm 51:5).*

It is clear from the teachings of Scripture that man is born a sinner separated from God. Man's sinful nature brings the judgment of God (death- separation from God who is life, *Romans 6:23*) upon us as the result of Adam and Eve, our first parents' sin and disobedience. Herein lies the biblical basis of the generational curse.

It must be said that with just a casual handling of the matter of generational curses, one comes to be confused at best. It is necessary to carefully study the Word of God concerning these eternal matters:

*You shall not worship them or serve them; for I, the Lord your God, am a jealous God, visiting the iniquity of the fathers on the children, on the third and the fourth generations of those who hate Me, but showing lovingkindness to thousands, to those who love Me and keep My commandments (Exodus 20:5).*

*The Lord is slow to anger and abundant in lovingkindness, forgiving iniquity and transgression; but He will by no means clear the guilty, visiting the iniquity of the fathers on the children to the third and fourth generations (Numbers 14:18).*

*...who showest lovingkindness to thousands, but repayest the iniquity of fathers into the bosom of their children after them (Jeremiah 32:18).*

*Our fathers sinned, and are no more; it is we who have borne their iniquities (Lamentations 5:7).*

Even in the New Testament we find the understanding of the teaching of the sins of the fathers and generational curses:

*And His disciples asked Him, saying, Rabbi, who sinned, this man or his parents, that he should be born blind (John 9:2)?*

At first glance the quick conclusion of this matter is, "That's not fair. How could God be fair and allow children to bear the consequences of the sins of their fathers?" A deeper study into the Scriptures will bring forth a greater understanding. There are two statements that must be made here. 1) The Devil doesn't play fair. Fairness is a concept only known in our Lord. 2) Since sin is ultimately against God, the consequences of sin are eternal in nature. Therefore a supernatural eternal solution for sin is needed; God's solution.

God is just and right in all that He does. The ways of our Lord are many times mysterious and beyond human understanding:

*For as the heavens are higher than the earth, so are my ways higher than your ways, and my thoughts than your thoughts (Isaiah 55:9).*

The problem is we don't want God to do those things we don't understand. How arrogant can we be?

*Far be it from Thee! Shall not the Judge of all the earth deal justly (Gen. 18:25)?*

We may never come to understand all God does in His perfect as well as His permissive will. We may never be able to understand what my wonderful Pastor, the late Dr. W.A. Criswell, called, "the imponderables of God."

One thing we must conclude, God never makes a mistake. His character demands that He will deal with man in justice and righteousness. To put God on "trial" is to question his sovereign place in our lives. To do so is to join the rebellion of the Enemy. Remember Jesus taught:

*But Jesus answered and said to them, "You are mistaken, not understanding the Scriptures, or the power of God" (Matt. 22:29).*

When the Bible speaks concerning anything, we would do well to believe it. For it is truth. When the Bible is silent concerning a matter, we must leave it by faith in the hands of the Lord.

Since sin is ultimately against God, the consequences of sin are eternal. David says in Psalm 51:

*And my sin is ever before me. Against Thee, Thee only I have sinned.*

Since sin is committed against the Lord, He is the only one who can forgive our sin. He has chosen to forgive all our sins through the shed blood of His only begotten Son, Jesus. It is only through this substitutionary work of Christ on Calvary dying for our sin, that sin and its curse was forgiven and broken:

*And not through the blood of goats and calves, but through His own blood, He entered the Holy Place once for all, having obtained eternal redemption (Heb. 9:12).*

*You see, without shedding of blood there is no forgiveness of sin (Heb. 9:22).*

It must be shouted from the housetops that God's will is blessing for His people! The blessing contract of God with His people is corporate. Abraham, Isaac, and Jacob are the ancestors of many nations; and the covenant making of God, one-sided though it be, is designed to bring corporate blessing to many if it is obeyed *(Gen. 17:4, 18:18, Psalm 112, Prov. 20:7).*

Now Satan, the great counterfeiter and exploiter, views this blessing as something to corrupt and then to exploit as corporate curses. The command, "thou shalt have no other gods before Me," has a penalty attached to it; violate it and be cursed, even to the third and forth generation *(Exodus 20:5, Numbers 14:18). Leviticus 26* and *Deuteronomy 28* are graphic in their description of the results of blessing for obedience and curses for disobedience. *Leviticus 26:39* says the descendants rot away because of their forefather's sin. *Isaiah 65:6-7* puts it in context of idolatry. *Jeremiah 32* is a forceful statement on the consequences of forsaking God and law breaking in general. God promises blessing for obedience and the benefits thereof, to a thousand generations *(Exodus 20, Deut. 5).* He limits the curses to four generations except for unkindness shown to Israel, and also to the illegitimate birth of children where it's indicated that the curse goes to ten generations *(Deut. 23:2-3).*[11]

The Devil works through man's disobedience to bring his destruction and ruin upon God's creation. Satan doesn't bring the curse upon us. He exploits the curse that man has brought upon himself. Satan doesn't separate us from God. Our sin separates us from Holy God. All Satan does is scheme ways to encourage our disobedience to God, which joins us to his rebellion against God. Then he is able to exploit these sins against God to his fullest vile evil intentions.

But you say, "Rob, I'm saved. I accepted Christ as my Savior. All sin and its curses have been broken at Calvary. And I'm in Christ. Therefore these generational matters don't apply to me." Please listen carefully. Although saved, we still have the capacity to sin against God. The spirit that is now reborn wars against the flesh, and the flesh wars against the spirit. So much of the time the flesh wins the battle and the result is sin against God. *(Romans 6-8).* All sin carries serious spiritual consequences that can ultimately lead to spiritual bondage. Now that you have been saved, the right to be free is now available to you in Christ. Forgiveness of sin is now your birthright in your union with Christ. However, if we do not walk in this freedom through repentance and the confession of our sin before God, spiritual defeat is certain and the generational curses continue.

Please understand it is not the confession of sin that cleanses sin. Only the blood of Jesus can cleanse me from my sin. Although the work of God in Christ to forgive all sin is finished, the confession of my sin places me in right relationship to God so that His blood is applied and His wonderful faithful cleansing is able to take place:

*If we confess our sins, He is faithful and righteous to forgive us our sins and to cleanse us from all unrighteousness (I John 1:9).*

It is common in the counselor's room to see children who are the victims of the sins of their parents. In the area of emotions through all kinds of abuse, it is readily understood that through no fault of their own children are victims of their parent's sins. Mothers addicted to crack will bear children that are called crack babies because they too are addicted to this deadly cocaine. AIDS is past from one unfaithful marriage partner to another and on to unborn children, again through no fault of their own. The result of death and sorrow is still the tragic result. It is a well known fact that abused children tend to become abusive parents if the consequences of that abuse are not healed in their own lives.

The same principle applies in the spiritual. Demons claim that if a parent was giving them ground through unconfessed sin in his or her life, they have the right to harass the offspring of that person. The Bible calls them familiar spirits. This does NOT make the child guilty of the sins of the parents; everyone is responsible for his or her own sins. But the consequences of sin are still present and must be dealt with.[12]

No matter what you and I do to try to fix our sins, only Jesus' death on the Cross is God's remedy. We can't ignore it and it go away. We can't excuse and justify it in our own minds and it go away. We can't erase our sin by trying to forget it. It simply will not go away. God's Word says that sin is a spiritual problem. Thanks be to God that He sent His Son to die for all sin and through His blood the spiritual problem of sin is forever fixed.

Even death does not stop sin's evil destruction. When we die without the cleansing of the specific sins the Holy Spirit has brought before us, we have left an open door of disobedience the Enemy can exploit in our families. Since the sin and disobedience was not dealt with through the only way it can be absolved, through confession and repentance, through the washing of the blood of Christ on Calvary; the consequences of those unconfessed sins continue a path of destruction through our generations. Generational sin is sin judgment which moves through the family line. It is called by various other names such as transference, inheritance, or familial sin. The Word of God gives divine warnings that the sins of parents can have potentially devastating consequences on their children. The context in which these warnings are given is very clear. Heads of families, usually males, have rebelled against God. God says they hate Him *(Exodus 20:5)*. What is implied is a deliberate turning away from God. Usually, if not always, it involves serving other gods, denying God the love and obedience which His singular and absolute Lordship demands *(Exodus 20:5-6, Deut. 5:9-10, 18:9-14)*.[13]

Have you ever wondered why it is that an alcoholic father will have an alcoholic son? Have you ever wondered why it is that drug addiction (prescription or illegal) runs in certain families? Why a stingy, tightwad father or mother will produce selfish and self-centered children? Those of us in ministry have seen over and over again the results of generational curses at work, even though many times we didn't know what to call it. A teenage girl becomes sexually active and gets pregnant before marriage. After learning about her family, her mother and grandmother did too. Why? There are spiritual realities at work through generational curses on the family.

Does that mean that a person is not free to choose righteousness and the way of the Lord? No! It's not a question of free choice. The Bible defuses the notion that we can blame our fathers for our sin *(Jeremiah 31:29-30)*. Each of us is responsible for his or her own sin before God. However, there are spiritual weaknesses and vulnerabilities passed down from the unconfessed sins of our forefathers. It's a matter of what psychiatrists and the medical community call genetic predisposition. There is an unholy programming toward destruction allowed by the disobedience of our forefathers. Ground given to the Enemy in families is exploited to the fullest extent of Satan's purposes. Until the sin ground is acknowledged and given back to God through repentance and confession, this evil programming (the generational curse) continues in the family.

How many of us know for sure that no one in the last four generations (120 years) of our family lineage has made a promise or pact with the Devil? Agreements someone may have made for the sake of fame, money, healing, love and the like. How many know for sure that our great, great grandfather didn't call upon the Wicked One to give him what he wanted? Who knows what false gods have been sought and worshiped by those who have gone before. From the eastern religions practiced in the 1960s, Indian worship of spirits and ancestors, to the secret oaths made in unholy rituals in secret lodges, how many of us know for sure? We don't, but the Devil does. And our Lord does. Our Lord was there when the sin and blasphemy was committed against Him *(Lev. 17:7, Deut. 32:17, Psalm 106:37, I Cor. 10:20-21)*. He knows all about it. There are no secrets in Heaven *(Psalm 90:8)*. My dear friend, the act of disobedience does not go away without bringing it to the Cross of Christ. Death doesn't cover or hide sin. Sin has eternal consequences, because sin is against God.

In Chapter 6, we will look at how to break these generational curses. However, it must be concluded that there is a great danger of destruction coming through our families' disobedience and rebellion against God. Many are in bondage today because they have not allowed the Lord to deal with the sins of their fathers and their consequences that have been passed to them. I may not like the reality of the "sins of the fathers," however, I best accept it because the Bible teaches it. And if we are to become free from the certain curse of sins committed against God, we can't ignore it. The sins of our fathers must be dealt with at the Cross of Christ. Without the cleansing of these sins in our lives, we will continue the legacy of sorrow and death to our children and to our grandchildren according to Scripture to the third and forth generation. It is an eternally grave matter that we walk in holiness and righteousness before the Lord. Confess your sin against God today and be cleansed by His blood. All sin curses can only be broken through the blood of Christ. It is through the confession of our sin (agreeing with God) that the blood of Christ is appropriated and we are cleansed from all unrighteousness *(I John 1:9)*.

## Chapter 3

# Demonization and the Believer
## "Saved, But not Safe"

*"Thus, for you who honor God most, Satan will struggle very sternly. He wants to pluck God's jewels from His crown, if he can, and take the Redeemer's precious stones even from the breastplate itself."*
*–Charles H. Spurgeon*

It's amazing how the subject of Christians and their relationship to the darkness becomes a point of contention within the church. It would seem to me that if there was ever an area where we would work toward a biblical agreement, it would be this one. The Enemy knows if we stay in the area of argument and division, we won't look for the truth that can set people free. So the reality is, instead of studying for the sake of truth, we draw our self-centered conclusions and wrap them up in our "spiritual platitudes" and scurry to the nearest place of so-called personal safety. All the while in our willing ignorance those we love around us continue bound up in darkness.

The issue of the Christian and demonic activity is a hot button. But that doesn't mean we can ignore it or retreat to the safety of the standard answers. It is interesting to note that man has an innate fear of demons. We speak of the Devil or Satan regularly; however, when one mentions demons, fear begins to enter the conversation. Many believers have adapted the fallacious idea that if they ignore Satan and his strategies, he will ignore them. Scripturally, such a position is indefensible.[1] Remember, Paul says, *"in order that no advantage be taken of us by Satan; for we are not ignorant of his schemes"* (2 Cor. 2:11). Paul may have not been ignorant of Satan's schemes, but I must admit, I was. I simply had not studied the matter biblically.

All of us can make a long and painful list of those in ministry that have had to forsake their ministries because of attacks of the Enemy. Only eternity will reveal the number of believers who have led unproductive, frustrated lives of spiritual defeat. This happens in spite of the fact that the New Testament warnings concerning demonic activity are all addressed to believers.

The schemes of the Enemy to attack and ultimately control the believer are totally different than how he controls the nonbeliever. Although the results of destruction look the same in the believer as well as the nonbeliever, the process, which led to that destruction, is very different. When it comes to God's people, evil spirits are spirits of influence. That's not true for unbelievers in the world. They're held firmly in Satan's grasp, under his control, blinded in their hearts and minds and utterly dead to spiritual truth until quickened by the Holy Spirit. They're members of his kingdom of darkness *(Ephesians 2:2)*.

Christians are already "possessed" (owned) by the Holy Spirit, so demonic possession in the sense of ownership is not the issue. Rather, the issue is the influence the Evil One can exert on us. We quickly underestimate the powerful influence Satan can have in the life of a believer. In discussing demonic spiritual warfare on the personal level, Dr. Scott Moreau, Assistant Professor of Missions in Intercultural Studies at Wheaton Graduate School, explains, "One general principle must be noted on the onset: demons can only influence believers to the extent that we allow them to do so. The act of giving or allowing Satan to take any amount of control in our life is referred to as giving ground" *(Eph. 4:27)*.[2]

Dr. Clinton Arnold, Professor of New Testament Language and Literature and Director of the Th.M. program at Talbot School of Theology, describes the process and how to resist this way: it is likely that any sinful activity that the believer does not deal with by the power of the Holy Spirit can be exploited by the Devil and turned into a means of control over a believer's life. Therefore, Christians need to resist. For Paul there is no middle ground. There's no nominal Christianity. Believers either resist the influence of the Evil One who works through the flesh and the world, or they relinquish control of their lives to the power of darkness. Giving in to those temptations does not just confirm the weakness of the flesh; it opens up the lives of believers to the control of the Devil and his powers. We need to recognize the supernatural nature of temptation and be prepared to face it.[3]

It is critical that Christians understand their vulnerability to demonic influence, so they may have an adequate biblical answer for any situation they face. Those who don't understand their vulnerability will likely blame themselves or God for their problems. If we blame ourselves, we feel hopeless because we can't do anything to stop what we're doing. If we blame God, our confidence in Him as our benevolent Father is shattered. Either way, we have no chance to gain the victory that the Bible promises us. Then there is the tendency of the church in the Western world to attribute all of Satan's activities to the flesh. This also leaves us with no way to resolve spiritual conflicts.[4]

Whole books have been written on this subject. Let me refer you to a complete work on this subject by C. Fred Dickason entitled *Demon Possession and the Christian*, Crossway Books, Wheaton, Ill., 1987. To come to a consistent biblical view, we must study the Scriptures carefully and prayerfully. When I first seriously considered the question of Christians and demonization, I, like so many, could not understand how this could be. There were two conclusions I had drawn in my mind that I believed to be theologically correct. Through faulty deductive reasoning, I had drawn my conclusions. Then working from my comfortable conclusions, I worked backwards to prove them. We must resist the temptation to resolve the conflict intellectually without resolving it spiritually and biblically. Spiritual problems demand spiritual answers. In our willing ignorance many believers remain in defeat and are never helped to walk in the victory of our Lord. Ignorance, however comfortable, is not bliss especially in the invisible war. My conclusions were the same as so many today who reject the possibility that Christians can have a demon.

These arguments state: 1. Demons cannot be in the same place with the Holy Spirit. 2. Once bought by the blood of Jesus, the believer becomes God's own personal possession. Therefore, a Christian cannot be possessed (owned) by any devil. Let's take each one and study the Word of God thoroughly.

Demons cannot be in the same place with the Holy Spirit. This is a theological presupposition, not a biblical certainty based on scriptural exegesis. Not a single verse of Scripture states that the Holy Spirit cannot or will not dwell in a human body or any other area, where demons are present.[5] The argument is based more upon a syllogism of logic rather than sound biblical interpretation. Although, this argument seems logical, is it biblical? The following syllogism represents this argument.

> **The major premise**: Every Christian is indwelt by the Holy Spirit.
> **The minor premise**: The Holy Spirit cannot dwell with demons.
> **Conclusion**: Christians cannot have demons.

In any syllogism, if any premise is false then the conclusion cannot be true. The verses of Scripture that are most often quoted are *2 Corinthians 6:14-18* and *James 3:11-13*. But when taken in context of the rest of Scripture it is clear that neither of these verses teaches that the Holy Spirit cannot or will not dwell in the same location with a demon. My Father taught me as a boy, "Text without context can be pretext."

Earnest B. Rockstad for many years was a pioneer in the area of warfare counseling. He poured out his life ministering to the spiritual sick and afflicted. He and his precious wife opened up their home to many of the "castaways" of society. Through trial and error, the Lord used Rockstad to bring deliverance to the captives. Out of the crucible and encounters with the darkness, came a careful study of these matters. Through his taped memoirs and teaching outlines we are able to learn much concerning the realities and relationship between the Christian and demons. He states, "It rather amazes me that men can be so sure that the Holy Spirit will not dwell in the same body with an evil spirit. They must have a higher estimate of the human nature in themselves and others than what the Bible teaches. The depravity of the human heart is such that it is difficult to see how the Holy Spirit deigns to enter in the first place. And think what He has been subjected to in the life of every one of us!"[6] Let's face it, the Holy Spirit dwells within us, and according to the Scriptures, *the heart is deceitful above all things and desperately wicked, who can know it (Jeremiah 17:9, KJV).*

We also find in the Scriptures many occasions when the Devil is in the presence of Holy God. In the study of Job we see that Satan is summoned by God into His presence. As we have seen, one of his names is "Accuser of the Brethren." Satan spends much of his time in the presence of God accusing Christians before God, the Righteous Judge.

Satan is the god of this world and *"the prince of the power of the air" (Eph. 2:2).* Thus Satan and his demons are present in the atmosphere of this world, but so is the omnipresent Holy Spirit. This means that they must coexist.[7] Sound biblical interpretation demands that Scripture must be taken in light of all Scripture.

Let's look at the second argument. Once bought by the blood of Jesus, a Christian cannot be owned or "possessed" by a devil. The difficulty is the presupposition based on the definition of the King James translation "possessed or possession." Once again I had drawn my conclusion and sought to prove it on the basis of my presupposition.

The word "possession" clearly implies ownership. And the Scriptures do clearly teach ownership of the believer through the purchasing of the blood sacrifice of Christ:

*Be on guard for yourselves and for all the flock, among which the Holy Spirit has made you overseers, to shepherd the church of God which He purchased with His own blood (Acts 20:28).*

*In Him, you also, after listening to the message of truth, the gospel of your salvation having also believed, you were sealed in Him with the Holy Spirit of promise, who is given as a pledge of our inheritance, with a view of possession, to the praise of His glory (Eph. 1:13-14).*

Clearly one cannot mistake the truth of the Scriptures that once a person has been saved he or she becomes God's personal possession. It is here we have our dilemma. The word in the New Testament is "daimon." In fact, the very term "demon possession" itself is a part of the problem. It is used in most English versions of the Bible to translate a single Greek word-and it may not be the best translation at all.

Dr. Timothy Warner writes, "The use of the word possession to translate the expressions used in the Greek New Testament to indicate the relationship between demons and people is unfortunate, if not unwarranted. We obtain our English word demons by translating the Greek word daimon. We should have done the same with the Greek word daimonizomai a verb form of the same Greek root. It would then come into English as demonize and we could then speak of the degree to which a person could be demonized rather than being limited to either-or options imposed by the possessed-not possessed view."[8]

I believe Warner is correct when he concludes, "spiritual possession clearly implies ownership and would seem to include the control of one's eternal destiny. It would be impossible to be owned and controlled by Satan and have a saving relationship with Christ at the same time." So if the question is, Can a Christian be demon possessed? The answer is clearly, NO![9] A born again, born of the Spirit Christian CANNOT BE POSSESSED by the Devil! The question is not, Can a Christian be possessed, but rather, Can a Christian be DEMONIZED?

## What the Bible has to say concerning Demonization and the Believer

Let's look at the Word of God together. The following is a list of just a few scriptural examples of God's people being demonized. It is necessary to look at all of the Word of God to glean the eternal truth of this most serious matter.

1. Case of King Saul *(I Sam. 9-31)*. He was a true Old Testament believer. He was filled by the Holy Spirit on more than one occasion. On three occasions an evil spirit entered his life, causing dramatic personality changes when the demon was in manifestation.

2. Case of Israel as a rebellious nation *(Hos. 2:13,17)*. It is altogether possible that most of the adult Jews who had given themselves to gross spirit-idol worship were demonized when God sent them into captivity. The prophets describe in shocking detail their total surrender to the spirit world. Israel united the cult of Baal with the worship of Jehovah. The result was a deplorable syncretism, which soon led Israel to reject the Law of her God. She was, in turn, rejected by God *(Hos. 4:1-10)*. Israel had become ensnared by the Devil. The people became as demonized as the Baal worshippers they had joined *(Hos. 9:1,7-10, 15-10:2* with *I Cor. 10:18-22; I Tim. 3:6-7, 2 Tim. 2:26)*.

3. In the New Testament we have vivid case studies of Jews, regular synagogue attendees, who were severely demonized *(Mark 1:21-28;39)*.

4. The case of the demonized daughter of Abraham (Abraham- The Father of the Faithful) *(Luke 13:10-17; see John 8:33-35; Gal.*

*3:29).* She was a true Jewish believer. Her sickness was caused by an evil spirit from which Jesus set her free.

5. The case of the demonization of Peter *(Matt. 16:23, Mark 8:33, Luke 4:8).* Notice Jesus does not rebuke Peter by name. He rebukes Satan who was able to so invade Peter that his mind and voice were used for evil.

6. The case of the early church being demonized *(Acts. 5:1-10).* It is clear that Ananias and Sapphira were true believers, but Satan filled the heart of Ananias. To fill is to control, the same expression used for the filling of the Holy Spirit.

7. Paul's thorn in the flesh in *2 Cor. 12:7.* He refers to the source of it as a *messenger of Satan.* This word is *aggelos* or better translated *angel.* Most of the time this word is translated in the New Testament as angel.

### Warnings of the New Testament given to the Church:

1. Paul cautions against the potential demonization of bishops, elders, and pastors *(I Tim. 3:6-7),* Bible teachers, preachers, and prophets *(2 Cor. 11:3-4, 13-15; I Tim. 1:19-20* with *2 Tim. 2:14-26; 1 Tim. 4:1, I John 4:1-4).* There is the enigma of demonized "deaconesses *(I Tim. 5:9-15),* and the danger of demonized gifted Christian leaders and miracle workers *(I John 4:1-4* with *Matt. 7:13-29; 2 Thess. 2:1-17; Rev. 13).*

2. The two wisdoms available to every believer. Bitter, jealous, selfish, ambitious, arrogant, lying, and cursing believers who receive this unholy wisdom can become demonized *(James 3:9-15).*

3. Paul's concern of his new converts *receiving another spirit (2 Cor. 11:4).*

4. *Neither give place to the Devil (Eph. 4:27,* KJV). The warning to Christians about the danger of giving an area of their lives (knowingly or unknowingly) over to the occupancy by Satan.

5. In the study of the Armor of God, a warning is clearly implied that a Christian without the Lord's armor can be penetrated by Satan *(Eph. 6:10-18)*.

6. In the passage that warns the Christian of the danger of Satan as a *roaring lion,* it is also implied that the believer can be destroyed or "gobbled up" by his adversary, Satan *(I Peter 5:8)*.

Dr. Neal Anderson observes, "The fact that a Christian can be influenced to one degree or another by the God of this world is a New Testament given. If not, then why are we instructed to put on armor of God and stand firm *(Ephesians 6:10)*, to take every thought captive to the obedience of Christ *(2 Corinthians 10)*, and to resist the Devil *(James 4:7)?* And what if we don't put on the armor of God, stand firm, assume responsibility for what we think; And what if we fail to resist the Devil? Then what? We're easy prey for the Enemy of our souls."[10]

*Be sober, be vigilant for your adversary the Devil is like a roaring lion seeking whom he may devour (1 Peter 5:8, KJV).*

What does it mean to be devoured by Satan? Why is God warning us of that if it's not a possibility? The word *devour* means to gobble down quickly. The Bible clearly states that the Devil was a murderer from the beginning. *The thief comes only to steal, kill, and destroy (John 10:10)*. Satan is not trying only to irritate or intimidate us; He is trying to kill us.

It is clear that all of the warnings given in the New Testament concerning the dangers and potential destruction by the Enemy are given to the Church. In the light of this, the believer must understand that although our victory is secure in the finished work of our Lord Jesus at Calvary *(Col. 2:13-15)*, we are in a fierce battle *(Eph. 6:13-18)*. The battle is from without and sometimes from within. In the same way we can lose our peace, love, joy, etc. (although we possess it in Christ). We can lose the victory if we continue in sin and rebellion against God and the working of His Holy Spirit within us. The habitual ignoring of the work of the Holy Spirit in the believer's life will lead to habitual sin and rebellion against God. Any rebellion against God joins the believer to Satan's rebellion and can allow a *stronghold ("topos" Eph. 4:27,* a place for the Enemy to work) in the believer's life. This stronghold will ultimately render the believer hopeless and powerless in the battle and can bring ultimate defeat.

There are two primary ways by which a believer can become demonized. First, they were demonized before their conversion. All demons do not always automatically leave the body of demonized unbelievers when they turn to Christ. While most of us have been taught that they will, the New Testament nowhere teaches such a doctrine. To affirm otherwise is a theological presupposition, not a biblical certainty. Second, believers become demonized after their conversion by traumatic blasphemous sins they commit or these most serious sins committed against them. Satan and his evil spirits will attach themselves to sin areas of a believer's life. They will work continually to increase their control over these areas. That control is only partial, however, never total. Thus, demonized believers are able and responsible to turn against the demons attached to their lives.

If these believers do not learn the way to victory in the warfare for their thought life, they will begin to form evil habits of imagination and fantasy. This, in turn, leads to the beginning of loss of control over their thought life. Over a period of time, loss of thought control inevitably leads to bondage to evil fantasies, which soon leads to evil actions. The end can be almost total control by certain compulsive forms of sin.[11] Remember, *as a man thinketh in his heart, so is he (Prov. 23:7, KJV).*

Usually demonically troubled believers battle in four primary sin areas:

1. Illicit sexual practices or fantasies out of control.

2. Deep-seated anger, bitterness, hatred, rage and rebellion, often leading to destructive and/or self-destructive impulses (Preoccupation with Rock Music).

3. A sense of rejection, guilt, poor self-esteem, unworthiness, and shame (Alcohol and or drug abuse).

4. Strange attraction to the occult and to the spirit world, often, but not always, with a desire for elicit power over circumstances and other people.[12]

After many years of careful study of the Word of God and his experiences in praying with those in darkness, Dr. Chuck Swindoll weighed in on the subject, "Can a Christian be Demonized?" "For a number of years I questioned this, but I am now convinced it can occur. If a 'ground of entrance' has been granted the power of darkness (such as trafficking in the occult, a continual unforgiving spirit, a habitual state of carnality, etc.), the demon(s) sees this as a green light—okay to proceed.

Wicked forces are not discriminating with regard to which body they may inhabit. I have worked personally with troubled, anguished Christians for many years. On a few occasions I have assisted in the painful process of relieving them of demons.[13]

There is also the matter of generational sin. The believer is most vulnerable in the area of familial sin. (See Chapter 2, pgs. 67-73) Generational sin is sin judgment which moves through the family line. It is called by various other names such as transference, inheritance, or familial sin. An ancestor who gives place to Satan is not only hurting himself, but he is opening the door of grave harm to his children, grandchildren, and on down the line. This ground of transference would seem to account for little children having to endure this invasion of the powers of darkness.[14] Satan and his demons are "legalists." That is, they do not have to leave unless the covenant or contract made with the Devil is broken. Only the blood of Jesus, which is the New Covenant, has the power to cancel out the covenant of sin and death (I Cor. 11:25). The ground that the Enemy has taken through generational sin must be discovered and denounced. A clear commitment to Christ through confession of these specific sins brings the blood covenant of the Lord Jesus to bear. Once the ground has been taken back through confession, demons must leave, for they have no other place to go within the life of the believer.

Also there is an area that is extremely controversial within some circles. However, it is an area that is widely being discussed and accepted in the area of clinical psychology. That is the matter of "alters" or what is known as multiple personality disorder (MPD). Some in this complex world of Christian counseling call the splitting of the personality "fragments." Multiple personality disorder usually begins in childhood because, unlike adults, children can't run from abuse. The only place they can hide is inside their heads. As the victim grows older, the separate personalities become ever more autonomous, and each has its own special way of functioning in the everyday world.[15]

Wherever one finds the fragmentation of a personality, you will always find the work of the Enemy. The personality of the believer can be split or fractured because of unhealed damage. Our Lord wonderfully has created every human whole, not fragmented. Alter egos or fragments are the work of the Enemy. Whenever you find a personality that has been split through emotional or physical trauma, you will find demons. When dealing with fragments, one must not only have deliverance from evil spirits that have attached themselves to the different personalities, but there must also be a work of healing and restoration. Jesus offers wholeness as well as healing *(John 5:1-6)*.

## *The Believer's Vulnerability*
## *To the work of the Enemy in the Invisible War*

The Believer finds himself in an evil environment. He is surrounded by the forces of darkness all around him: The WORLD– *(I John 5:19)* The FLESH– *(Romans 7:18)* The DEVIL– *(2 Cor. 4:4)*. Through Christ alone can man join in the victory that has been won through Calvary. Jesus has overcome the world *(John 16:33, I John 5:4)*. This world is so wicked and full of unrighteousness that God tells us in His Word He is going to destroy all that is and create a New Heaven and a New Earth *(2 Pet. 3:10)*. Jesus has overcome the flesh *(John 17:2)*. In the resurrection Jesus became the first fruit from the dead, which means there is going to be more resurrection fruit. Those in Christ will also rise from the dead. He has overcome the flesh *(I Cor. 15:51-55)*. Jesus also has overcome the Devil. Satan was disarmed and defeated at Calvary *(Col. 2:13-15)*. His ultimate destruction is declared in Heaven and recorded forever in God's Word *(Rev. 20:10-15)*. In Christ we are victorious over all evil environment. Victory is ours in our union with Christ.

To understand the Christian's vulnerability to the work of the Enemy, we must look at the complex makeup of man. There is an inherent danger in discussing man in his complexity. There can be a paralysis of the analysis. However, it is helpful to understand that although man is whole, he is made up of three parts: The Spirit, the Body or Flesh, and the Soul:

# THE INVISIBLE WAR

## MAN'S AREAS OF VULNERABILITY AND HIS VICTORY IN CHRIST
### (Illustration A)

Man's environment:
  World- I John 5:19,
  Flesh- Romans 7:18
  the Devil- 2 Cor. 4:4
Jesus has overcome the World:
  John 16:33, 2 Pet. 3:13  New Heaven and New Earth-only righteousness
Jesus has overcome the Flesh:
  John 17:2,  Resurrection- I Cor. 15
Jesus has overcome the Devil:
  Col. 2:13-15-His defeat, Rev. 20:10- His Destruction

## SPIRIT
John 3:3  Born of the Spirit
John 4:24 God is Spirit...worship Him in Spirit...

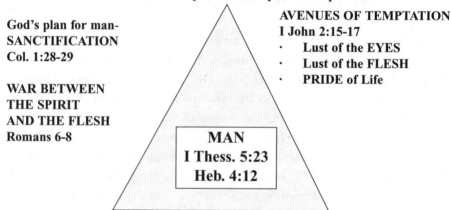

God's plan for man-
SANCTIFICATION
Col. 1:28-29

WAR BETWEEN
THE SPIRIT
AND THE FLESH
Romans 6-8

AVENUES OF TEMPTATION
I John 2:15-17
  ·   Lust of the EYES
  ·   Lust of the FLESH
  ·   PRIDE of Life

**MAN**
**I Thess. 5:23**
**Heb. 4:12**

## BODY
### FLESH
Gal. 6:18   Shall reap corruption
Gal. 5:19-21 Works of the Flesh:
Romans 7:18 No good thing

Romans 12:1-2  Present Your Bodies
I Cor. 6:12-20  You are not your own...
Glorify Christ in your body...

## SOUL
### THE "PERSONALITY"
MIND- Prov. 23:7, 2 Cor. 4:4-5,
  II Cor. 10:3-5, Romans 12:2
Phil. 4:8- Think on these things
  Two Wisdoms: James 3:13-15
EMOTIONS- Eph. 4:26-27, Anger...
  Isaiah 53:4-5 Griefs, Sorrows, Wounds,
WILL- Phil. 2:13 Both to will and to do...

Our ONLY hope for VICTORY is in CHRIST'S FINISHED WORK ON
CALVARY....Col. 2:13-15
Our ONLY hope for VICTORY is in our UNION with the
Resurrected Christ... Eph. 2:4-6
THE ARMOR OF GOD Eph. 6:10-18

*Now may the God of peace Himself sanctify you entirely; and may your **spirit** and **soul** and **body** be preserved complete, without blame at the coming of our Lord Jesus Christ (I Thess. 5:23).*

*For the word of God is living and active and sharper than any two-edged sword, and piercing as far as the division of **soul** and **spirit**, and of both **joints** and **marrow**, and able to judge the thoughts and intentions of the heart (Heb. 4:12).*

God's goal for man is perfection by means of sanctification. That is the process by which we become like Jesus in every area of life:

*And we proclaim Him, admonishing every man and teaching every man with all wisdom, that we may present every man complete in Christ (Col. 1:29).*

God's will for every man, women, boy, girl, or young person is that they might become holy even as God is holy *(I Pet. 1:16)*. This completeness, this wholeness, this holiness is a work of our Lord. The process of transformation begins when a person is reborn spiritually. This spiritual rebirth takes place when a person accepts by faith the death of Christ for the forgiveness of his/her sin *(John 3:3)*. Until the new birth of the spirit takes place, a person is dead spiritually *(Eph. 2:1)*.

The regeneration and rebirth of the spirit of man is an instantaneous miracle that takes place the moment he believes. As I understand it, the spirit is as reborn at the moment of a person's conversion as it will ever be. His full soul and body transformation into the likeness of Christ, however, is a lifelong process and will only finally be complete when he receives his resurrected, glorified body. Transformation requires the involvement and active participation of his mind, his will, his emotions, and his body. The combination of faith in God's provisions and processes, and submission to the Holy Spirit is necessary to this ongoing process of transformation.[16]

Let me ask you, when you were saved, what part of you was saved.? The quick answer is all of me. And that's right. Jesus' sacrifice of Himself on Calvary paid the price for you and me to be totally saved. Amen! Let's look at it a little closer though. When we are saved we become born of the spirit. The regeneration of our spirit from death to life allows the living Lord Jesus through the person of the Holy Spirit to come to dwell and make His home, His dwelling in the life of the believer. Therefore the re-birthed spirit is not vulnerable to the attacks of the Enemy. What about your body or your flesh? Is it totally saved yet? It will be in the resurrection but not completely yet.

There is a war that is ongoing in the life of every believer between the spirit and the flesh. We find the description and details of this battle in the book of Romans (*Romans 6-8*). Even the Apostle Paul laments concerning his battle of the flesh:

*Wretched man that I am! Who will set me free from the body of this death (Romans 7:24)?*

The process by which the body or flesh is perfected is not yet completed:

*For I know that nothing good dwells in me, that is, in my flesh; for the wishing is present in me, but the doing of the good is not (Romans 7:18).*

The flesh in the life of the believer is still vulnerable to the schemes of the Enemy.

We see in the avenues of temptations used by the Enemy against God's children, the areas of vulnerability in the life of the believer:

*For all that is in the world, the LUST of the FLESH and the LUST of the EYES and the boastful PRIDE of LIFE, is not from the Father, but is from the world (I John 2:16).*

Since Jesus was fully man as well as fully God, He too was tempted in all these areas, yet without ever falling into sin. (See Chapter 2, pg. 49) If the Enemy tried to get Jesus to fall into sin by using these three areas of temptation, how can we neglect the battle in these areas in our lives, without falling into sin *(Heb. 4:15)?*

We are directed by God's Word to *present your bodies a living and holy sacrifice, acceptable to God, which is your spiritual service of worship (Romans 12:1).* What is the result if we don't obey the Word of God? What happens then? That's right, we lose our victory. The victory in the invisible war. Our bodies become avenues of the workings and schemes of the Enemy. Instead of God's will being done in and through our bodies, Satan's will is accomplished through the believer. Notice verse two:

*And do not be conformed to this world, but be transformed by the renewing of your mind, that you may prove what the will of God is, that which is good and acceptable and perfect (Romans 12:2).*

The believer who stays conformed to this world can be used to thwart God's permissive will.

The other area of vulnerability for the believer in the invisible war, in which we are engaged, is the area of the soul. The soul is the part of man that houses the personality. If momma has fixed "soul food" she has fixed it with her love. Her personality is part of the preparation of the food. The soul is that which makes me different from you. In the personality or soul reside the **mind**, the **emotions**, and the **will**. As we shall see in Chapter 5, the battle for the control of our lives is in the mind. The Scriptures speak clearly of the relationship between what we think and what we do.

What a man thinks is ultimately what he will do:

*For as a man thinketh in his heart, so is he (Prov. 23:7, KJV).*

*The weapons of our warfare are not of the flesh, but divinely powerful for the destruction of fortresses We are destroying speculations and every lofty thing raised up against the knowledge of God, and we are taking every thought captive to the obedience of Christ (2 Cor. 4:3-5).*

God's Word tells us what we should think about:

*Finally, brethren, whatever is true, whatever is honorable, whatever is right, whatever is pure, whatever is lovely, whatever is of good repute, if there is any excellence and if anything worthy of praise, let your mind dwell on these things (Phil. 4:8).*

It is clear from the teachings of Scripture that the battle for the control of our lives is in the mind. There are two wisdoms mentioned in

*James 3:13-15.* One, which is earthly and demonic, and one that is from heaven. The believer is capable of being infected by one or the other.

The soul of man is also made up of his emotions. This too is an area of vulnerability to the schemes of the Enemy to control our lives:

> *Be angry, and yet do not sin; do not let the sun go down on your anger, and do not give the Devil an opportunity (Eph. 4:26-27).*

What is the result of getting angry and allowing that anger to continue in our lives? The Scripture says we will give the Devil a place (topos- ground) to work in our lives. Remember this warning is written to believers. Only God knows the damage the Enemy has caused in the lives of so many believers because they could not control their emotions. They were not willing to allow Jesus to heal them of these hurts, pains, and sorrows:

> *Surely our griefs He Himself bore, And our sorrows He carried; Yet we ourselves esteemed Him stricken, Smitten of God, and afflicted. But He was pierced through for our transgressions, He was crushed for our iniquities; The chastening for our well-being fell upon Him, And by His scourging we are healed (Isaiah 53:4-5).*

If our Lord has carried our sorrows, griefs, pains, and wounds, then for the believer to carry them is tantamount to rebellion and unbelief. To not allow Jesus to do His work of forgiving and healing in our lives, allows the Enemy an open door to do his evil work of destruction.

The soul also houses the will. You are who you are because of the decisions you have made in your life. I am who I am because of the schooling I decided to accomplish. I am who I am because of the girl I decided to marry. Life is simply one decision after another. My Father used to say that the paradox of life is that we have to make so many decisions that will form the rest of our lives before most of us are mature enough to make those decisions. But isn't God good in His sovereign grace. He guides us even when we aren't aware of it. You see, as we yield our lives to the Lordship of Christ, God is at work in us to do His will:

*For it is God who is at work in you, both to will and work for His good pleasure (Phil. 2:13).*

Think of it, God not only gives us the desire to do His will, but He also empowers us to do His will. Praise His Name!

My question once again is, when you were saved what part of this wonderful salvation was finished? Has your body been made like Jesus yet? Is your mind completely sanctified yet? Is the work of God making your emotions like Jesus' completed yet? Is your will totally like Jesus' yet? The answer is obviously no. One only has to drive by the nearest cemetery to discover the truth that the body of the Christian is not saved yet. But praise His Holy Name! Jesus payment of my sin on the cross of Calvary entitles me to everything God did for Jesus. He got a new body. I'm going to get a new body. He conquered sin. In Jesus, I too can conquer sin in my life. He came to destroy the works of the Devil. In my union with Christ, I too can be used of Him to destroy the works of the Devil.

Jesus went to be with the Father in Heaven *(Acts 1)*. Just think of it. Everyone who comes to put their faith and trust in Christ alone for the forgiveness of their sins will one day enter into the home that our Heavenly Father has prepared for those who love Him *(John 14:2)*. In the mean time we are in a fierce battle with an enemy who wants to kill us. Each area of our lives that is not under the authority of our Lord Jesus can become an open door for the work of the Enemy not only to ultimately control our lives, but also gives him the opportunity to destroy our lives.

## *"The Devil made me do it?"*
## *The Relationship between the Flesh and Demons*

A longtime friend and wonderful Bible teacher has raised the important question concerning the relationship between the flesh and demons. He said, "Rob, how do you know it's a demon, when it may just be the work of the flesh?" "Surely," he said, "you wouldn't want to attribute the works of the flesh to demons. Then no one would take responsibility for their actions. All you would be left with is 'the Devil made me do it.'"

What about this evil all about us, is it all the result of the work of demons or is some of it just natural humanism or just natural flesh? Is it not possible that you just do something because it is the flesh and demons don't have anything to do with it? Read this carefully! You cannot do anything in the flesh or of the flesh that a demon does not activate his work of deception and destruction in your life! Let's study it together:

> *Let no one say when he is tempted, I am being tempted by God; for God cannot be tempted by evil, and He Himself does not tempt anyone. But each one is tempted when he is carried away and enticed by his own lust (James 1:13-14).*

Since God says that evil temptation is not what He does. Then when we are tempted, why and how are we tempted? I am never tempted to go get a bottle of liquor and get drunk. It would never cross my mind. I would never go to the horse races and bet on the horses. The wicked thought would never come into my mind. Why? Because those things are settled and the demons of hell know where I am strong in the Lord and where I am vulnerable. But I do have temptations and so do you. These are the areas in which we must fortify ourselves in the invisible war. You see these are the areas where demons are at work in our lives.

God says when a man is tempted he is *"drawn away."* Now, to be drawn away there has to be a force field and God said, "I'm not doing it." So that leaves just one. That has to be evil and all evil comes from the Devil and we have already learned in *Eph. 6* that our wrestling match is not just against the Devil, but also against demons. So we are "drawn" away. The phrase "of our own lust" is the key to understanding how demons work on and through the flesh. The Greek word "lust" simply means a "selfish desire." It doesn't mean some horrible dark sexual perversion. It's just a word that indicates a desire of the flesh. You see what James is saying? When you are tempted of evil, it is because of your own selfishness. Anytime you get selfish, demons go to work in your life.

Why do you think God says, *"Mortify the deeds of the flesh?"* Why do you think God says, *"Say no to the ungodly deeds of the flesh?"* Why do you think God says *Crucify your flesh?* Why does the Word of God teach us to *"die to self?"* Why does the Word of God point out those parts of our disposition that are wrong? Why does God tell us in His Word how we are to feel and act? God tells us what's evil and what's holy; God tells us what to avoid and what to cling to for our benefit because God knows that if you and I live selfishly and if we allow in our lives, dispositional sins, sins of attitude, sins of personality, the demons are going to take advantage of it! Whatever you and I do of a selfish nature is an open door for demons to begin to draw us away from God's will for our lives. You can depend on them to come through that open door!

It is impossible for you to be selfish in any area of your life without demons taking note of it and coming against you to try their best to establish a stronghold in your life. I'm not saying that every time you sin you become demonized. However, it is through continual sin that sinful habits are developed. If these habitual sins continue, demonization will certainly follow. Sin is the highway demons travel. Demonization takes place when the believer continues in sin and rebellion against the convicting power of the Holy Spirit within his life. Rebellion against God joins us to Satan's rebellion. Remember as we have studied, rebellion against God is the sin of witchcraft *(I Sam.15:23)*. Jesus created you and saved you for His glory! Anything less than total submission to the Lordship of Christ in your life can and will be exploited by the Enemy. Our basic sinful nature is what allows a demon to draw us away! That is what the spirit-filled life is. Rev. Johnny Jackson from Little Rock, Arkansas, a long-time family friend and one of my personal counselors, said it best. "The Spirit-filled life is when the Spirit tells the flesh what to do instead of the flesh telling the spiritual man what to do."

Here is the truth we must understand. Whatever part of your life is not under the control of our Lord Jesus is an opportunity for demons to take control. That's why the Word of God says:

*Whatsoever you do in word or deed do all for the glory of God (I Cor. 10:31, KJV).*

Why? Because if we are not doing what you are doing for the glory of God, we are going to come under the control of a demon. When we get selfish, they will go to work on us and they will establish a beachhead, then a stronghold, and they will bring that one point of our lives under control! Demons are anxious to get control in just one area. I mean just one, just one little area in your life. The Bible calls it our besetting sin, *the sin that so easily entangles us (Heb. 12:1).* If they can just get one area under their control and can manipulate you in that area, they will then branch out and make it worse.[17] The Devil is looking for anything to rule. When we are filled with the Spirit of God, we become invulnerable to the attack of the Enemy. Why? Because the flesh is not in control. The Enemy can only exploit the believer who is walking and being controlled by his flesh.

The Enemy doesn't play fair. Fairness is a concept only known to our God. Satan is an opportunist. He will take whatever ground he can exploit for his thieving murdering strategies. He beats up on the helpless. He looks for the hurting, the sorrowful, and the wounded to play out his evil deeds of destruction. Children are probably the most vulnerable of all to Satan's schemes. Unless parents are faithful to walk in holiness before the Lord and to pray for a covering for their children, even the Christian and his family is vulnerable to Satan's attacks. The difference is, as we shall study, the believer has the victory in Christ Jesus in this invisible war in which we are engaged.

One of the best illustrations of how the Enemy takes advantage of the helpless and most vulnerable is the experience that was recorded in a biography of the late great Bible preacher and world famous pastor Donald Grey Barnhouse. The great preacher was for many years the pastor of the Tenth Presbyterian Church in Philadelphia, Pennsylvania. He served two terms as commissioner of the General Assembly of the Presbyterian Church in the U.S.A. His outreach far exceeded this congregation however. He was the founder of the Evangelical Foundation and for many years the radio voice of Bible Study Hour and Editor of *Eternity* magazine. He is probably best known for his faithful preaching of the gospel on national radio for over thirty years. After his homegoing his wife, Margarate N. Barnhouse, wrote a book on his life and ministry. The title of her book about her late husband is *That Man, Barnhouse*.

The great preacher, Barnhouse, wrote one of the great classics on spiritual warfare entitled *The Invisible War, the Panorama of the Continuing Conflict Between Good and Evil*. In this wonderful work on spiritual warfare, he draws the conclusion, "Even though Satan may travel with the speed of thought and even though he be overlord to a vast host of subordinates that report to him, he can never be on the throne of God nor can he ever come inside the body of being of one who has been born again and whose body has become the temple of the Holy Spirit. There are temptations upon the soul that come directly and personally from Satan, but even though there are possibilities of enemy action, there is no possibility that the Devil can possess the soul or body of the one who has been born again."[18] Although he came to the traditional evangelical conclusion that a Christian cannot be demonized, read carefully what happened to the preacher as he was dying. His widow writes about an incident while her husband was dying with a brain tumor.

"The Thursday before the last cobalt treatment was due; I had a strange conversation with Donald. His eyes were moving back and forth as if he were planning something, thinking deeply about it. I sat beside him and asked, 'What are you thinking about?' 'I'm writing a show.' 'Oh', I asked, 'Is this for TV, Movies or a play or what?' 'Oh, any of them', He said. His voice was not at all his normal voice, it sounded strange and sly. I asked, 'What's it about?' 'Deceit.' 'Deceit?' 'Yes, the deceitfulness of the deceit.' 'Tell me about it.' 'It is to teach deceivers how to deceive.'" All the while he had been looking directly at me, as if by holding my eyes he could keep me from seeing him working his fingers under the bandage holding the nose tube in place, a thing forbidden.

With a start, I recognized the strange, sly voice, because at one time that same voice had spoken through me. When I was in my teens, I used to read palms, as a parlor game. I became so good at it; I was quite in demand at parties. For some reason I could see in a person's palm things I had no way of knowing. At times like that I was aware that the voice saying these things through me was not my voice-and the voice coming from Donald sounded just like it. After I knew Jesus as my Savior, The Holy Spirit convinced me that I had been dabbling in the occult, and that the voice speaking through mine could be that of a demon. I renounced the whole thing in Jesus' name.

I took both of Donald's hands and began to pray. I claimed Jesus own request from the Father in his high priestly prayer of *John 17:15*.

*I pray not that they should take them out of the world, but that you might keep them from the evil one.*

Immediately I was aware of the invisible warfare. Satan had spoken through the Apostle Peter's vocal cords and Jesus had rebuked him. I prayed to Jesus that this thing should likewise be rebuked and leave Donald. Satan works through subtle suggestion and Donald's mind was so vulnerable at this point. I was relieved to see the sly look vanish and the expression of his eyes return to normal."[19]

"But that's not fair," you say. You're right; it's not fair. The Devil is that wicked and more. Now you know why his judgment is so severe. In your most wicked moment it would be impossible for you to conceive the depth of the wickedness of our Enemy. Man is not able to imagine the wicked schemes of Satan. The good news is that our great God and Savior, Jesus Christ has challenged and won the fierce battle against all sin and wickedness.

The conclusion must be made that the believer is the central target of Satan. Only the Christian can glorify and magnify our Lord Jesus. Possibly the greatest Baptist preacher of all time was Charles H. Spurgeon. I guess no one has said it better. "Those of us who are called to the work of the ministry must expect from our position to be selected as the special objects of his (Satan's) consideration. When the magnifying glass is at the eye of that dreadful warrior, he is sure to look out for those who by their uniforms are discovered to be the officers, and he tells his sharpshooters to be very careful to aim at these. 'For,' he says, 'If the standard-bearer falls, then the victory will be more readily gained for our side, and our opponents will be easily put to flight.' If you are more generous than other believers, if you live nearer to God than others, as the birds peck most at the ripest fruit, so may you expect Satan to be the busiest against you. Who cares to contend for a province covered with stones and barren rocks, and ice-bound by frozen seas? But in all times there is sure to be a contention after the fertile valleys where the crops are plenteous and where the farmer's toil is well rewarded. Thus, for you who honor God most, Satan will struggle very sternly. He wants to pluck God's jewels from His crown, if he can, and take the Redeemer's precious stones even from the breastplate itself."[20]

But Rob, if the battle is already won, why do we have to fight? At first, I confess I didn't understand it either. Why are we called to fight a battle that is already won? Here it is. Don't miss it. Without the battle, there is no crown. The Bible Speaks of a victor's crown *(I Cor. 9:25-27)*. Oh, how I want to gain it so I can give it to my wonderful Savior *(Rev. 4)*. If we didn't have to learn to trust the Lord and live by faith *(the evidence of things not seen, Heb. 11:1,* KJV) in the invisible war, we never would. Without faith, God's purposes in Heaven won't be done in us and through us on the earth *(Heb. 11:6)*. Always remember, we do not fight TOWARD victory, we fight FROM victory! The victory is yours my brother and sister in Christ. Claim it, trust it, and walk in it. Reclaim the surrendered ground in your life. Victory is ours in the Lord Jesus! Praise His Holy Name!

## Chapter 4

# Dominion and the Devil

*"Satan is aflame with desire for unlimited dominion over the human family; and whenever that evil ambition is challenged by the Spirit of God, he invariably retaliates with savage fury."*

–A.W. Tozer

## *The Problem of Sin*

All sin is an authority problem. The problem of sin at its core is a problem with authority. As simple and this is, we must come to understand sin in the light of its challenge to authority. Remember, the Devil's great sin was to challenge the authority of God by setting himself up to be worshiped as God. Rebellion is the challenge to authority. Note this carefully, God's Word is His perfect standard of truth and righteousness. Sin then must be defined as the attitude, the unwillingness to submit ourselves to what God has said. In His Word our Lord has told us how to live. He has told us how to love our wives, how to raise our children, and how to handle our financial affairs. He has laid out for us how to treat other believers, how to relate to unbelievers, and how to trust Him in every area of our lives. He has given us His system of authority in all matters of life. All will be judged according to the Word of God. I will be judged by the same Word of God by which my children will be judged. We don't judge the Word of God, the Word of God judges us!

The Father is to be the spiritual head of the home *(Eph. 5:23)*. The

Pastor, the overseer, is the spiritual authority in the church:

> *Be on guard for yourselves and for all the flock, among which the Holy Spirit has made you overseers, to shepherd the church of God which He purchased with His own blood (Acts. 20:28).*

> *Obey your leaders, and submit to them; for they keep watch over your souls, as those who will give an account (Heb. 13:17).*

Sheep don't lead sheep without serious consequences! These places of authority have been so ordered by God *(Romans 13:1-2)*. It must be understood that all authority set up by God is under His sovereign rule. His rule has been established for His glory. Therefore to reject these places of God's established jurisdiction is not only to reject the purposes of God, but also it is to rob God of His glory. To discount and disbelieve the Word of God is to join oneself to the spiritual rebellion of Lucifer. Sin with all its many facets in its essence is an authority problem.

What is it that makes a theological liberal, that which makes an infidel of the faith? Is it a liberal school or a bad teacher? No! That which makes a heretic within the church is unbelief, which results in disobedience to the Word of God. Anyone who does not bow to "thus saith the Lord" becomes an infidel. Sin is an issue of authority. Behind every theological infidel, you will find some unconfessed sin and disobedience within their lives. They have decided to justify themselves instead of being justified by the finished work of Christ on Calvary:

> *Who will bring a charge against God's elect? God is the one who justifies (Romans 8:33).*

Their unbelief whatever its root, ties them to spiritual rebellion in the heavens. And remember, any rebellion against God joins us to Satan's rebellion *(I Sam. 15:23)*.

## *The Purpose of Creation*

> *For by Him all things were created, both in the heavens and on earth, visible and invisible, whether thrones or dominions or*

*rulers or authorities— all things have been created by Him and for Him (Col. 1:16).*

Those who are confused as to the creator of all things and to the purpose of His creation stay in their confusion in the face of the truth of God's Word:

*All things came into being by Him, and apart from Him nothing came into being that has come into being (John 1:3).*

My dear friend, God did it. All that is, seen and unseen, has been created by God. The air we breathe. The warmth of the Sun we enjoy. All the planets, all the stars and their galaxies, everything you see, everything you don't see, God created it. Not only all things were made by God, but all things were created for Him. As my Father used to say in his sermons, "this preposition is a proposition." All has been created for the glory of God. That's why when a church ceases to glorify God in all it does, it becomes spiritually sick and unfruitful. When a family ceases to glorify God, it becomes tragically dysfunctional. The purpose of creation comes into focus in light of the spiritual warfare in which we find ourselves.

All things were made for the purpose of the sovereign rule of the Lord Jesus. Christ is ultimately in control of all things. All things are under His control for His glory:

*To the only God our Savior, through Jesus Christ our Lord, be glory, majesty, dominion and authority, before all time and now and forever, Amen (Jude 25).*

*To Him be honor and eternal dominion! Amen (I Tim. 6:16).*

The key word here is DOMINION. The word in the original language is "kratos" in some places it is translated "might, force, or strength." The word is derived from a root "kra," which means to perfect or complete. The idea of creator is no doubt connected. In *I Tim. 6:16* and *Hebrews 2:14* it is translated *"power."*[1]

So what we know for certain is that God created all things by His power for His power. All things were made by God for His power and rule:

*Whoever speaks, let him speak, as it were, the utterances of God; whoever serves, let him do so as by the strength which God supplies; so that in all things God may be glorified through Jesus Christ, to whom belongs the glory and dominion forever and ever. Amen (I Peter 4:11).*

*To Him (Christ) be dominion forever and ever. Amen (I Peter 5:11).*

Often the Scriptures use the concept of dominion in the same phrase with authority. Authority is also implied in the use of dominion. All things visible and invisible, all principalities and powers, all rulers and authorities, all mankind, and everything that is, has been created for the sole rule of its creator. God has created all things for the purpose of His absolute rule and authority that He might be glorified in all His creation. Only Jesus has the right to rule over God's creation.

## The Plan of the Enemy

It is here we begin to understand the purpose of the rebellion in the heavens. Remember the Devil set himself up to be worshiped as God. He decided to rule as God and therefore take God's glory away from Him. Satan tried to steal away from God His dominion. The Devil's attack was for the purpose of stealing from God His sole sovereign right to rule *(Isaiah 14:12-15)*. The Devil is a thief. He comes to steal anything that he can take from the rule of the Lord Jesus. Satan's attack against God in the heavens was an attack on His Lordship. Because of the Devil's rebellion, he and the angels who joined the rebellion, have been severely judged by God. They carry God's curse and they know it. They just don't want us to know it. There is no possibility for the Devil and his demons to repent. And they know it:

*And angels who did not keep their own domain, but abandoned their proper abode, He has kept in eternal bonds under darkness for the judgment of the great day (Jude vs.6).*

All of Satan's schemes are an attempt to steal from the Lord anything which rightfully belongs to Him. Through lies, deception, and all manner of evil, the Devil is working tirelessly to take anything which rightfully belongs to the one true God. Satan is aflame with desire for unlimited dominion over the human family; and whenever that evil ambition is challenged by the Spirit of God, he invariably retaliates with savage fury.[2]

As we look again to the concept given to us in Ephesians, we begin to understand the basis of the invisible war. *And do not give the Devil a place (Eph.4:27, KJV)*. The word translated place is the word *topos*. As we have stated, "topos" is the word from which we get the word *topography*. It literally means the ground or the place given to the Devil for him to rule. Don't give the Devil a place to stand. Don't give him the territory that belongs to the only true God. Through disobedience and unbelief we give the Enemy a place to work in our lives. Since all things have been created for the rule and dominion of God alone, not trusting the Lord is to give that area of unbelief over to the Devil.

We see this echoed in Paul's letter to the Corinthian church:

*For though we walk in the flesh, we do not war according to the flesh, for the weapons of our warfare are not of the flesh, but divinely powerful for the destruction of fortresses. We are destroying speculations and every lofty thing raised up against the knowledge of God, and we are taking every thought captive to the obedience of Christ (2 Cor. 10:3-5).*

King James Version of the Bible calls these fortresses *strongholds*. What are these strongholds we are to destroy? What are these fortresses we are to pull down? They are the "toposes," the places given over to the Devil through sin and unbelief. Notice in the last of this verse the word "captive" is used. You and I are to hold every thought captive to the Holy Spirit. When one is held captive he/she is under the authority and rule of the one who has him/her captive. Our lives are to be under the sole rule of the Lord Jesus. When you and I decide not to believe what God says, we are allowing the Enemy to build a stronghold, a place to rule in our lives.

Why is this so serious? Because the Devil doesn't have the right to rule any place. No one does unless it is so ordained by God for His holy purposes and for the glory of God alone. Satan wants to rule any ground or area. Any attitude, any habit, any bitterness Satan wants to control. Any business, any family, any life Satan wants to control. Any school, any class, any student Satan wants to control. Any city, any town, any community Satan wants to control. Any denomination, any association or mission, any church Satan wants to control. To do so he must steal it from the one true Lord, the Lord Jesus Christ. He does so by getting us to join His rebellion against God through our unbelief. At the moment man refuses to believe what God has said is true, he gives the Devil the unlawful right to rule and control these areas.

## *The Purpose of Christ*

Why did Jesus come? Why was Jesus born of a virgin named Mary? Why did God go to all the trouble of sending His only Son to die on an old Roman cross in a place of sorrow and humility called Calvary? What is this all about? Did Jesus come to make us happy? Did Jesus come to give us all that we want? Is Jesus our cosmic Santa Claus who exists only to bring us happiness? The Bible gives us at least three specific reasons why Jesus came.

1. *For the Son of Man has come to seek and to save that which was lost (Luke 19:10).* All men without Christ are lost according to the Word of God. They are lost as a lost sheep to a shepherd. They are lost as a lost coin to a laborer. They are as a lost son to a brokenhearted parent *(Luke 15).* Jesus came that all mankind that is lost would be found and given back to the rightful owner, our Heavenly Father.

2. *I came that they might have life, and might have it more abundantly (John 10:10,* KJV*).* God's Word declares that in Jesus we have life. *He that has the Son has life, and He who does not have the Son has not life (I John 5:12).* Back in the "Jesus Movement" of the early 1970s we used to hear and sing a song by Andre' Crouch called, "Without Jesus, You Ain't Livin!" Jesus came to give life. The life that Jesus bought with His blood is abundant life. In *John 3* we find that this abundant life has two wonderful realities, eternal life and everlasting life. One is quantitative and one is qualitative.

The life that Christ offers all those who will trust Him is a life that will last forever. That's right, never ending life, everlasting life. Even if our life on this earth ends in death, we will live with Christ forever in the place God has prepared for those who love Him. *I am the resurrection and the life; he who believes in Me shall live even if he dies, and everyone who lives and believes in Me shall never die (John 11:25-26).* Think of it life without end. Wow! He also offers every man eternal life. Eternal life is God's life. Eternal life is God's kind of life here and now. That's right, God's peace, God's joy, God's purpose in our lives everyday we live. What an offer. Abundant life is possible through faith in Christ's offering of Himself for our sin.

3. *The Son of Man appeared for this purpose, that He might destroy the works of the Devil (I John 3:8, KJV).* We find the same thing echoed in *Luke 4:*

> *The Spirit of the Lord is upon me, because He anointed Me to preach the gospel to the poor, He has sent Me to proclaim RELEASE TO THE CAPTIVES, and recovery of sight to the blind, to SET FREE those who are downtrodden, to proclaim the favorable year of the Lord.*

Jesus came into this old sin sick world. He was born in a cattle stall in a little shepherd's town called Bethlehem. He lived a perfect life:

> *One who has been tempted in all things as we are, yet without sin (Heb. 4:15).*

Jesus was offered up as the final sacrifice for all sin:

> *He made Him who knew no sin to be sin on our behalf, that we might become the righteousness of God in Him (2 Cor. 5:21).*

Jesus endured the death of a common criminal. Jesus received in His body the payment for all sin for all time:

> *And not through the blood of goats and calves, but through His own blood, He entered the holy place once for all, having obtained eternal redemption (Heb. 9:12).*

Why all of this? Why is this salvation so important for everyone? Don't miss it. Here it is. Satan came to steal the work of the Lord from you. He came to steal you from the Father who created you for His glory. He came to steal anyone or anything from its rightful creator and owner, the one true Lord and ruler of all creation. God sent His Son into the world to redeem, to buy back through the purchase price of His blood all that the Devil has stolen from God. That's why Jesus came. He came to destroy the works of the Devil.

## *The Position of Christ*

After having lived a perfect life, Jesus died for our sins. Three days later after Jesus was buried in a borrowed tomb, He was raised from the dead. For forty days and forty nights he walked and talked among his disciples. He taught them many truths concerning the kingdom of God. At the end of these forty days, we find Jesus and His disciples on a mountain called Olivet:

*To these He also presented Himself alive, after His suffering, by many convincing proofs, appearing to them over a period of forty days, and speaking of the things concerning the kingdom of God. And gathering them together, He commanded them not to leave Jerusalem, but to wait for what the Father had promised, "Which" He said, "you heard of from Me" (Acts 1:3-4).*

As our Lord was giving His last words to His disciples concerning the work that his disciples would be doing. He explained to them that before they would be able to do this work of the kingdom they would receive a supernatural power. This power from heaven would enable them to accomplish this holy task of reaching the ends of the earth with His life changing message of truth and love. Then, in an instant, He disappeared from them into the clouds:

*And after He had said these things, He was lifted up while they were looking on, and a cloud received Him out of their sight (Acts. 1:9).*

Where did He go? Where did Jesus disappear to?

*And what is the surpassing greatness of His power toward us who believe. These are in accordance with the working of the strength of His might which He brought about in Christ when He raised Him from the dead, and seated Him at His right hand in the heavenly places, far above all rule and AUTHORITY and POWER and DOMINION, and every name that is named, not only in this age, but also in the one to come (Eph. 1:19-23).*

Jesus is now at the right hand of God the Father in heaven, the place of authority. Jesus rules over all. All other names are under His rule. All power is under His power. All things are under the Lordship of Christ. Jesus is now LORD!

*Therefore also God highly exalted Him, and bestowed on Him the name which is ABOVE every name, that at the name of Jesus every knee should bow, of those who are in heaven, and on earth, and under the earth, and that every tongue should confess that Jesus Christ is LORD, to the glory of God the Father (Phil. 2:9-11).*

*And He is the radiance of His glory and the exact representation of His nature, and upholds all things by the word of His power. When He had made purification of sins, He sat down at the right hand of the Majesty on high; having become as much better than the angels, as He has inherited a more excellent name than they (Heb. 1:3-4).*

Do you see it? Jesus is master of all! His rule is above all rule and all authority. The Bible exclaims that *there is ONE LORD, ONE FAITH, ONE BAPTISM, ONE GOD AND FATHER OF ALL WHO IS OVER ALL AND THROUGH ALL AND IN ALL  (Eph. 4:5-6)!* All others who claim to be Lord are impostors. All other so-called lords or gods are liars. The Word of God calls them *NO GODS* and refers to them as demons *(Lev. 17:7, Deuteronomy 32:17, Psalm 106:37, I Cor. 10:20-21).* Whether the world recognizes it or not, Jesus is Lord. One day when Jesus comes back all will recognize Him as Lord:

*And from His mouth comes a sharp sword, so that with it He may smite the nations; and He will rule them with a rod of iron; and He treads the wine press of the fierce wrath of God, the Almighty. And on His robe and on His thigh He has a name written "KING OF KINGS, AND LORD OF LORDS" (Rev. 19:15-16).*

Jesus is Lord of all. All authority is His. Jesus said:

*"All authority has been given to Me in heaven and on earth" (Matt. 28:18).*

JESUS IS LORD OF ALL!

## *The Position of the Believer*

*But God, being rich in mercy, because of His great love with which He loved us, even when we were dead in our transgressions, made us alive together with Christ (by grace you have been saved), and raised us up with Him, and seated us with Him in the heavenly places, in Christ Jesus (Eph. 2:4-6).*

Think of it. In our union with Christ, we have been seated in the place of authority with Him in the heavenlies. This truth is so amazing that few believers ever come to understand the position we have in the Lord Jesus. In this holy union that is ours through the blood covenant of Christ Jesus we have now been joined with Christ. That's why Jesus taught:

*I will give you the keys of the kingdom of heaven; and whatever you shall bind on earth shall be bound in Heaven; and whatever you loose on earth shall be loosed in Heaven (Matt. 16:19).*

*Again I say to you, that if two of you agree on earth about anything that they may ask, it shall be done for them by My Father who is in heaven. For where two or three have gathered together in My name, there I am in their midst (Matt. 18:19-20).*

Did Jesus really mean what He said? Are we really able to join with

Him to see God's will done? He even taught us to pray, *Thy will be done on earth as it is in heaven (Matt. 6:10).* Since Jesus came to destroy the works of the Devil, in our union with Him we too share in His work of destroying the works of the Devil. The power we have over demons is Christ's power. The understanding we have of the supernatural and the invisible world comes from Christ. The power to cast out demons is only in Jesus.

In the Book of Acts, we find an amazing story of how some Jewish exorcists went out to take on demons without the power of God. They had learned that the name of Jesus was powerful over demons. But they did not have a personal union with Christ through the New Covenant in His blood.

*But also some of the Jewish exorcists, who went from place to place, attempted to name over those who had the evil spirits the name of the Lord Jesus, saying, "I adjure you by Jesus whom Paul preaches." And seven sons of one Sceva, a Jewish chief priest, were doing this. And the evil spirit answered and said to them, "I recognize Jesus, and I know about Paul, but who are you?" And the man, in whom was the evil spirit, leaped on them and subdued all of them and overpowered them, so that they fled out of that house naked and wounded (Acts 19:13-16).*

The protection against demons is only through the blood covenant in the Lord Jesus. It is at Calvary they have been defeated. It is through the blood of the Lord Jesus that Satan's demons are exposed and expelled.

It must be noted that only Christ's power is sufficient in dealing in the invisible war. Only Jesus has won the victory over sin and death. Our faith is in Him. Our victory is in Him. Our union in the heavens is only through the Lord Jesus. The believer's authority is a delegated authority. In *Luke 10* Jesus gives total authority over all dimensions of evil supernaturalism to all of His disciples, not just the twelve apostles *(Luke 10:1, 17-19).* [3]

The power and authority over evil spirits has been given to the believer in his union with Christ. The following story from the missionary ministry of George and Mary Birch illustrates this truth. "It was in Pontianak, the equator city, in Kalimantan Barat (West Borneo) that

I had my first opportunity to be involved in such a ministry. While ministering there in the Chinese church, other leaders and myself received an invitation from a heathen home asking us to come and cast a demon out of the wife of a well-to-do merchant. Her name was Virtue. Her mother had been a sorceress for twenty-five years. Her husband used to consult this spirit for advice regarding his business ventures, but now the spirit would not let Virtue eat. She was in bed, very weak and troubled. A relative advised the family to ask the Christians to come and cast out the demon."[4] Even the heathen understood that only a Christian could cast out the demon. Any believer trusting in Christ's power will do. As we trust God for His work in and through our lives, God's will is accomplished. It is in our union with Christ that the captives are set free:

> *And whatever you ask in My name, that will I do, that the Father may be glorified in the Son. If you ask Me anything in My name, I will do it (John 14:13-14).*

> *Now to Him who is able to do exceeding abundantly beyond all that we ask or think, according to the power that works within us, to Him be the glory in the church and in Christ Jesus to all generations forever and ever. Amen (Eph. 3:20-21).*

What an awesome God we serve. What an awesome responsibility He has given to the church. We can see God's will done. We can know that God is at work. We can know God's power. We are *workers together with Him (2 Cor. 6:1).* In our union with Christ we share in the work of God. Through Christ's dominion, through His Lordship God's will is done. In Christ we are joined to the authority of heaven and earth. In the union that is ours in Christ, the power of God is given to set the captives free.

## Chapter 5

# Defending Against the Devil
## The Armor of God

*"Christ might have repulsed Satan with a word, or by commanding him to silence, as He to whom all power was given in heaven and earth; but it pleased His mercy to teach us how to use the sword of the Holy Ghost, which is the Word of God, in battle against our spiritual enemy."*

*–John Knox*

*Finally, be strong in the Lord, and in the strength of His might. Put on the full armor of God, that you may be able to stand firm against the schemes of the Devil. For our struggle is not against flesh and blood, but against the rulers, against the powers, against the world forces of this darkness, against the spiritual forces of wickedness in the heavenly places. Therefore, take up the full armor of God, that you may be able to resist in the evil day, and having done everything, to stand firm. Stand firm therefore, having girded your loins with truth, and having put on the breastplate of righteousness, and having shod your feet with the preparation of the gospel of peace; in addition to all, taking up the shield of faith with which you will be able to extinguish all the flaming missiles of the Evil One. And take the helmet of salvation, and the sword of the Spirit, which is the Word of God. With all prayer and petition pray at all times in the Spirit, and with this in view, be on the alert with all perseverance and petition for all the saints (Eph. 6:10-18).*

God has provided for the believer all the equipment needed to be victorious in the invisible war. Using the imagery of the armor of the Roman soldier preparing for battle, the Holy Spirit gives a precise insight into the areas of the believer's vulnerability in this intense spiritual war. As we have already studied in Chapter 3, the Christian though saved is the target of Satan's schemes. The believer is targeted for destruction. Although the Devil can never separate us from the love of God in Christ Jesus *(Romans 8:38-39),* he can so wound us in battle to render the believer powerless in his life and witness for Christ.

Charles H. Spurgeon said it so well. "Like the Spartans, every Christian is born a warrior. It is his destiny to be assaulted; it is his duty to attack. Part of his life will be occupied with defensive warfare. He will have to defend earnestly the faith once delivered to the saints, he will have to resist the Devil, he will have to stand against all his wiles; and having done all, still to stand. He will, however, be but a sorry Christian if he acts only on the defensive. He must be one who goes against his foes, as well as stands still to receive their advance. He must be able to say with David, 'I come against thee in the name of the Lord of hosts, the God of the armies of Israel whom thou hast defied.' He must wrestle not with flesh and blood, but against principalities and powers. He must have weapons for his warfare—not carnal-but mighty through God to the pulling down of strongholds. He must go forth to attack the castles of the Enemy, and to put them down, to drive the Canaanite out of the land."[1]

When God saves, He delivers man from the domain of darkness *(Col. 1:13).* But as long as you and I are in a mortal body, we remain in Enemy territory *(I John 5:19).* If you are a Christian who is unaware of being involved in an intense spiritual conflict, you are very likely a prisoner of war! If you know you are a child of God but are incapacitated in any way in the Lord's service, you are a battle casualty.[2]

Before we study each piece of the armor, there are some general realities that must be understood concerning the armor provided to the child of God by our Heavenly Father while in this intense spiritual warfare. They are:

## *The Necessity of the Armor*

*Put on the full armor of God, that you may be able to stand against the schemes of the Devil.* There is a clear order from our Lord for the Christian to put on the armor of God. In the invisible war, the child of God is to obey his commander. Here is implied that the believer is called to militant action. The believer is responsible for preparing for battle with the Enemy. From the text it is clear that without the armor of God, the believer cannot stand in this spiritual war of life and death. There is no substitute for the armor of God. It is impossible to outwit the Devil. It is impossible to out strategize him. All of education will never keep us from falling in the invisible war. It is impossible for man to even understand the depth of the wicked schemes of the Evil One. In the words of Martin Luther's hymn, "His craft and power are great, and armed with cruel hate, on earth is not his equal."

The whole armor of God is a necessity for the believer to be able to stand in warfare. Charles Spurgeon wrote of the Devil, "He will attack you sometimes by force and sometimes by fraud. By might or by slight he will seek to overcome you and no unarmed man can stand against him. Never go out without your armor on, for you can never tell where you may meet the Devil. He is not omnipresent, but nobody can tell where he is not, for he and his troops of devils appear to be found everywhere on this earth."[3] I've often heard it said, "I put on my armor every morning when I get up to start the day." My question is, "Why in the world did you take it off?" Don't ever take off your armor. Don't even go to bed without your armor. Don't ever consider taking the Lord's armor off. You can't survive in the invisible war without it! Whatever you do, put it on and leave it on!

## The Totality of the Armor

*Put on the WHOLE armor of God. Therefore, take up the FULL armor of God, that you may be able to resist in the evil day, and having done everything, to stand firm.* Twice in the text, we are told not to leave off a single piece of our armor. Every piece of the armor is necessary for the believer to be able to stand in the evil day. Any piece of the armor that is left out of the battle is the very area in which the believer will be attacked and ultimately defeated. One piece will not do. The Christian is to wear all the armor in battle. There are some professing Christians who only in part obey the injunction given here, but it is no use to wear a part of the Christian armor, and to leave the rest of the body unarmed. A little leak will sink a ship, and the absence of one piece of the armor of God can cost a man his life and witness. No good soldier would ever go into battle without all of his armor. Each piece is essential in battle. If these instructions are not obeyed, tragic defeat will be the result.

## The Personality in the Armor

*Be strong IN THE LORD, and in the strength of HIS MIGHT. Put on the full armor OF GOD.* To understand the armor of God, we must first understand that this armor is a person. His name is our Lord Jesus Christ:

*Let us therefore cast off the works of darkness, and let up put on the armor of light...put ye on the Lord Jesus Christ" (Romans 13:12,14).*

To understand the armor one must come to understand the armor of God is Jesus:

*Whosoever among you have been baptized into Christ, have clothed yourself with Christ (Gal. 3:27).*

This links the cross and the armor together. Cast off darkness! Put on Christ as Light! Be planted into Christ on the cross, and you become clothed with Christ, the armor of Light.[4] Each piece of the Christian's spiritual armor represents the presence and power of our Lord Jesus. Jesus is truth. Jesus is righteousness. Jesus is the gospel of peace. Jesus is salvation. Jesus is faith. It's all about Jesus. Our armor in spiritual battle is in our union with the Lord Jesus. Jesus is the armor in battle.

## The Victory in the Armor

The victory in this spiritual battle is certain. The Bible declares that:

*But in all these things we overwhelmingly conquer through Him who loved us (Romans 8:37).*

*But thanks be to God, who always leads us in His triumph in Christ (2 Cor. 2:14).*

In the early 1970s, while a student at Baylor University, we experienced a time of great revival on our campus. People were getting right with God through confession of their sin. All around us was the moving of God among His people. Many were coming to faith in Christ during the days we called "The Jesus Movement." In the midst of this great movement of God, I was exposed to some of the spiritual truths concerning the invisible war. Although I was just learning about spiritual warfare, I came to understand that our victory was already won in Jesus. I learned that whenever I was called on to confront the powers of darkness, I needed to be armed with the Word of God. I came to put my trust while in battle in the truth of the Word of God. Any time I was faced with demonic presence, I would quote out loud what Jesus has done for us on Calvary:

*And when you were dead in your transgressions and the uncircumcision of your flesh, He made you alive together with Him, having forgiven us all our transgressions, having canceled out the certificate of debt consisting of decrees against us and which was hostile to us; and He has taken it out of the way, having nailed it to the cross. When He had disarmed the rulers and authorities, He made a public display of them, having triumphed over them through Him (Col. 2:13-15).*

Every time I would quote these powerful verses, the evil presence would leave. My dear brother and sister in Christ, the victory is certain. Satan is defeated through the blood of Calvary. In our union with Christ, we now share in this eternal victory over the powers of darkness. The outcome of the battle in your life may be in question because of sin and disobedience, but the outcome of the war is certain. Jesus is Lord! Satan is defeated! His doom is settled in Heaven:

*...into the eternal fire which has been prepared for the Devil and his angels (Matt. 25:41).*

*And angels who did not keep their own domain, but abandoned their proper abode, He has kept in eternal bonds under darkness for the judgment of the great day (Jude vs. 6).*

The judgment of God on all the powers of darkness is certain. Satan's ultimate defeat and destruction is forever settled:

*And the Devil who deceived them was thrown into the lake of fire and brimstone, where the beast and the false prophet are also; and they will be tormented day and night forever and ever (Rev. 20:10).*

Herein lies the great tragedy of the invisible war. There is no need for anyone to be destroyed and defeated by the schemes of the Devil. Our Lord Jesus has conquered his archenemy on Calvary's Cross. The victory is settled and secured in the blood of Jesus. Always remember, we don't fight **Toward Victory,** we fight **From Victory.**

## The Believer's Posture in Victory

*Even so consider yourselves to be dead to sin, but alive to God in Christ Jesus. Therefore do not let sin reign in your mortal body that you should obey its lusts (Romans 6:11-12).*

Here is the posture of victory for the believer in spiritual warfare.

**1. Know what you are in Christ.** We are dead to sin but alive to God in Christ Jesus. Our life comes from Christ's work on Calvary. In and of the flesh there is no good thing. *For I know that nothing good dwells in me, that is in my flesh (Romans 7:18).*

**2. Count on what you are in Christ** *(Col. 2:10).* To share in the victory of Christ, the believer must come to understand that he must reckon himself dead to the flesh. If we fight the spiritual war in the flesh, defeat is certain. If we fight from our position in Christ, victory is certain. The Enemy will test the believer at every point to see if he or she is certain and confident of his/her victory in Christ. Remember, it was at Calvary our victory was won and secured. It is in our union with Christ that victory is certain.

**3. Act what you are in Christ.** It's not enough just to know these Bible facts. The believer must put them into action by faith. If we are victors in Christ Jesus, then we must act like victors. If we are more than conquerors through Him who loved us, then we must go into battle knowing that the victory is certain. Jesus now has the keys to Hell and death. Jesus has disarmed the rulers and authorities. Jesus' name is above all other names. Jesus is right now seated at the right hand of God the Father. Do you believe it? Do you know it? Then my dear brother and sister in Christ act on it!

## *Gird Your Loins with TRUTH*

It is not surprising that our Lord begins with TRUTH in explaining the armor that He has provided each believer in spiritual warfare. Remember, it is the Devil who is the father of lies. He is the archdeceiver. All that he has done and will ever do is based upon man's willingness to believe his lies. The only remedy for a lie is the truth. In our western mindset and worldview, the concept of truth is often determined by nothing more than individual philosophy and/or opinion. We live in a postmodern western mindset where the prevailing philosophy in American education is relativism. That is, there is no absolute truth. Truth is defined and practiced as that which you determine in your relative world to be true. That's why we have the problem of parents killing their children through selfish barbarism called abortion. That's why so many marriages end in divorce, leaving our children alone and easy prey for the Enemy. That's why our churches are full of self-seeking, self-centered, self-acclaimed lords ruling over their own kingdoms. So many today believe they can create their own realities, their own truth. They build their lives on the assumptions of their self-imposed truths instead of on the foundation of the Word of God.

Let the deception end! There is a truth that can never change. What God has said is forever settled in Heaven *(Psalm 119:89)*. Mark Bubeck, in his bestseller "The Adversary," helps us in understanding the significance of truth in the invisible war. As we study his wonderful outline of truth, we will glean much help in the invisible war.

**1. The Word of God is the word of TRUTH.** In *2 Tim. 2:15*, NIV, we read:

*"Do your best to present yourself to God as one approved, a workman who does not need to be ashamed and who correctly handles the word of truth." He chose to give us birth through*

*the word of truth, that we might be a kind of first fruits of all He created (James 1:18, NIV).*

The Psalmist prays:

*"Then I shall answer the one who taunts me, for I trust in your word. Do not snatch the word of truth from my mouth, for I have put my hope in your laws" (Psalm 119:42-43, NIV).*[5]

Through all of Scripture we find the Bible claiming or inferring to be the word of TRUTH.

For there to be victory in spiritual warfare one must come to believe that what God has said is truth. The Bible doesn't just contain the Word of God; it is the Word of God! It is not coincidental that every major denomination has fought a fierce battle over the issue of the inerrancy and authority of the Bible. You see, if you take the authority of the Word of God out of the battle, you lose. We must see that *"the world through its wisdom did not come to know God" (I Cor. 1:21).* TRUTH comes through God's revelation. This is how we know where to stand; it is written in the Word of God. This is what we use to fight the Enemy, the Bible.

I have always had a high view of Scripture. Anyone who knows the life and ministry of Rob Randall knows that I have never been confused as to the authority of God's Word. However, let me say that through my experiences in spiritual warfare, I have come to a greater respect and reverence for the Word of God than ever before. The authority of Scripture might be debated in the classrooms of our universities and seminaries. The authority of Scripture might be disbelieved in the everyday programs of the church. But please hear me when I say, Demons have a HIGH view of Scripture! They tremble in the presence of "Thus saith the Lord." You see it is in the Word that they are judged. It is in the Word of God that they are doomed and damned, and they know it. They are constantly looking for those who are confused about the Word of God to bring their evil agenda into the world.

Truth exposes the work of the Enemy. Everything he does is in the darkness covered in lies. Truth shines the light into the darkness and exposes his lies and deception.

**2. The Holy Spirit is the Spirit of TRUTH.** The Holy Spirit is the One who illumines and opens the word of truth to our understanding.

*The Spirit searches all things, even the deep things of God. For who among men knows the thoughts of a man except the man's spirit within him (I Cor. 2:10, NIV)?* It is the Holy Spirit who guides us into all truth. *But when He, the Spirit of truth, comes, He will guide you into all the truth (John 16:13).*

**3. The Church is the pillar and foundation of TRUTH.** The apostle Paul in his instruction to young Timothy wrote:

*"Although I hope to come to you soon, I am writing you these instructions so that, if I am delayed, you will know how people ought to conduct themselves in God's household, which is the church of the living God, the pillar and foundation of the TRUTH" (I Tim. 3:14-15, NIV).*

Here the local church is of great importance in the plan and purpose of God. A local church is called "God's household" and "the Church of the living God." Every believer is always to be related closely to a sound, Bible-centered, Christ-exalting local Church. He is to submit himself to the disciplines, the checks and balances that God in His sovereignty builds into that local Church. When believers rally to pray, protect, and encourage, the Enemy is put to flight.[6] As an itinerate evangelist, I have always understood that I needed the accountability of my Church. My family needed the discipline and accountability of a Bible believing, soul saving, Christ honoring Church. I would not attempt to do what I do as an evangelist without the spiritual covering of my Church.

To be victorious in spiritual warfare we must:

**1. Face the TRUTH!** No matter how painful the truth is, only the lies will kill you. My father used to say, "Son, live your life as an open book. So, if anyone were to see any part of your life, you wouldn't be ashamed."

**2. Tell the TRUTH!** Confess your sins *(I John 1:9).* Keep your sins hidden and the Enemy will stay at work in your life. My parents were of a generation that didn't talk. They never admitted their problems. It somehow showed a lack of manners to discuss those things that were disturbing. In no small way was my parent's unwillingness to face the truth, a catalyst for the destruction of their marriage. Dear friend, however challenging to the flesh it may be, tell the TRUTH! Remember, they overcame the Devil, *by the word of their testimony (Rev. 12:11).* They told the truth. Satan can't handle the truth. All he does is through lies. Tell the truth!

**3. Believe the TRUTH!** There is no freedom in Christ where there is unbelief.

*But let him ask in faith without any doubting, for the one who doubts is like the surf of the sea driven and tossed by the wind. For let not that man expect that he will receive anything from the Lord, being a double minded man unstable in all his ways (James 1:6-7).*

**4. Trust the TRUTH!** *You shall know the TRUTH and the TRUTH shall make you free (John 8:32).* The only thing we have to fear in the invisible war is ignorance. We must trust the TRUTH of God if we are to be free.

**5. Live the TRUTH.** Whatever God says, do it. So discipline your life to live in the truth of the Word of God. *Thy word have I hidden in my heart, that I might not sin against Thee (Psalm 119:11).* Freedom in Christ comes through the TRUTH of God.

Let me share with you a part of my life and testimony of what God has done for me. This illustrates how putting on the belt of TRUTH protects us against the schemes of the Devil. When I was entering my teen years, my parents ended their twenty years of marriage with a bitter and painful divorce. As a son of a famous preacher, the pain of my parents' divorce was a load I could not carry. Although I had been saved and had surrendered my life to the Gospel ministry, I became mad at God. I told Him that if He was the kind of God that would allow this kind of pain, the deal was off. I would not follow Him anymore. I would not seek

Him or His will in my life anymore. I entered my teen years an angry young man.

Everything I knew that was wrong, I jumped in headlong. I was the kid you would not have wanted to run with your kids. I was the kid you would not have wanted to date your daughters. I was full of hurt and anger. The Enemy's work was in full force in my life. I was miserable and I wanted everyone else to share my misery. I just didn't care anymore. I became preoccupied with Rock and Roll. My band became the best band in our city through the process of elimination called the "battle of the bands." I was lead singer, lead guitar of the top band at 15 years old. That brought to my life everything my young teenage flesh could possibly want; plenty of money, praise, and plenty of girls. Spiraling downward toward destruction, I became a thief. Stealing everything I wanted to, including the self-respect of young girls. That's right, I became sexually active.

Through the wonderful grace of our Lord, He showed me how much He always loved me. No matter how angry I was at the Lord, He never stopped loving me. When I needed to see the real Jesus, He showed Himself to me through the finest Christian I have ever known, LeeRoy Till. God showed me how much He loved me when He forgave my sins. It broke my heart and led me to the place of repentance. And although it was a long way back, every day on the road back to "the Father's house" was blessed with the presence of our Lord.

Everywhere I have preached these 33 years I have shared the work of God in my life during those difficult teen years. As I have shared my testimony of those years and the work that the Lord has done in my life, everyone has heard the truth. I have held nothing back. Some few years ago, a prominent lady in our church that knew me "back when" came to me and asked if she could talk to me. I said, "Sure." To my shock, she proceeded to tell me how through her counseling she had run into a girl that had never been able to trust men because I had been sexually active in those teen years with her. I asked the concerned lady the name of this person I had supposedly hurt. She said that she wouldn't tell me. I told her that I knew the work of the Enemy, "the Accuser of the Brethren" and this smelled like him. I told her that if she was not willing to tell me who it was she was referring to that this conversation was over.

Reluctantly she told me the name of the girl. I was shocked. Our relationship was never as she described. When I proceeded to tell her the truth, she told me that I needed to seek out this person and make reconciliation for the things we had done. I told her that I would pray about it and I would gladly do as the Lord would lead me.

With much fear and trembling, I told my wife to pray for me as I approached this old acquaintance from my wayward teen years. It was like going into an old graveyard digging up old nasty bones. It was awful. However, I wanted to make certain that I was not being a stumbling block to anyone. So I humbled myself and made the phone call. When she answered the phone, boy was she surprised to hear my voice. I told her that I was taping the conversation for her protection and mine. She said, "O.K." I told her of the conversation I had just had with a mutual acquaintance. How this lady said that because of our relationship, she had not been able to ever trust men.

She began to be angry. She said, "Who does this _____ think she is? I never told her that. Of all the relationships I have had with men, ours was one of the few good ones. You treated me like a lady. I'm not ashamed of anything we did." Man, was I relieved. I told her that I was sorry to bother her, but I needed to clear the air of this false accusation. Her memory confirmed the truth.

Here is what I want you to see. If I had kept the truth hidden concerning my teen years, the Enemy would have had a field day in my life. I would have been overwhelmed with guilt and insecurity. This spiritual attack could have easily caused spiritual immobility in my life and ministry. You see, since I had told the truth concerning those days, since I had allowed the Lord Jesus to cleanse me and heal me of those horrible days in my early teens, when the Devil's accusations came, they didn't stick. When you put on the Belt of TRUTH, the Enemy and his evil plans to destroy are defeated.

D.M. Lloyd Jones says it best concerning the Belt of TRUTH. "The Authorized Version Translation in this instance is not as good as it might be; it is misleading in the sense that it puts it in a passive way instead of an active manner. Instead of reading, 'Stand therefore, having your loins girt with truth,' as if someone else did it for you, a better translation is, 'Stand therefore, having girded your loins with truth,' In other words; it is we who have to do this. The girdle is not put on us, we have to put it on; and we have to put it firmly into position."[7] The verb in the middle voice means the Christian must gird himself with the truth.

## *The BREASTPLATE of RIGHTEOUSNESS*

The Breastplate of Righteousness is the next condition of victory. This may be briefly said to be a "conscience void of offense toward God and men." It is only when our heart does not condemn us that we have boldness toward God. The Adversary knows this and so is the "Accuser of the Brethren" seeking to bring the believer into condemnation before God.[8] It is impossible to survive in the invisible war without the Breastplate of Righteousness.

How righteous are you? How do you measure up spiritually? The Bible declares:

*For all of us have become like one who is unclean, and all our righteous deeds are like a filthy garment (Isaiah 64:6).*

*As it is written, There is none righteous not even one (Romans 3:10).*

Oh, how the flesh hates this truth. Do you see it? You and I will never be good enough to survive the onslaught of Satan. The righteousness that is needed in spiritual battle is not our righteousness but the righteousness of our Lord.

The Lord saved us not because of our righteousness, but because He loved us:

*He saved us, not on the basis of deeds which we have done in righteousness, but according to His mercy, by the washing of regeneration and renewing by the Holy Spirit (Titus 3:5).*

The righteousness needed to be victorious in spiritual conflict is the righteousness of Christ. Everyone who has truly trusted in the Lord Jesus Christ has a perfect standing before God, because Christ is his righteousness.

*But by His doing you are in Christ Jesus, who became to us wisdom from God, and righteousness and sanctification, and redemption, that, just as it is written, "Let him who boasts, boast in the Lord" (I Cor. 1:30-31).*

God declares righteous the ungodly person who believes in Him, and he reckons that person's faith as righteousness *(Romans 4:5)*. Every true believer has this righteousness as a bestowment of God, and the only sense in which he needs to put it on as his breastplate is to rest confidently in it at all times. He must stand on the fact that there is no condemnation for him because he is in Christ Jesus *(Romans 8:1).*[9]

"But Rob, what about when I sin, don't I lose my righteousness?" No, absolutely not! Your standing in Christ can never change because Christ is your righteousness. He always keeps the record clear at the Throne of Grace:

> *if anyone sins, we have an Advocate with the Father, Jesus Christ the righteous (I John 2:1-2).*

In theological terms the righteousness of God has two wonderful facets. The righteousness of our Lord is that which has been IMPUTED and that which has been IMPARTED to the believer. Imputed righteous is what Christ has given to us by way of the new covenant in His blood. Webster defines impute as the act of crediting by way of transferal. Another helpful translation of the word is reckoned. What a wonderful picture of truth. The believer has been made righteous through his union with Christ, paid for with the blood of Jesus. The righteousness of God is a gift given to all who will receive Christ as their savior:

> *And the Scripture was fulfilled which says, "And Abraham believed God, and it was reckoned to him as righteousness" (James 2:23).*

Imparted righteousness is the work of God in our lives through the ministry of the Holy Spirit that has come to dwell in the life of every believer. It is the holy desire to be right with God and to be right with men. The Holy Spirit never allows the believer to rest until he is walking in holiness. He gives every believer a holy desire and the strength to do the right thing.

> *In view of this, I also do my best to maintain always a blameless conscience both before God and before men (Acts. 24:16).*

When we sin, the Holy Spirit immediately brings conviction of that sin to our hearts. We have the choice to cooperate with the Holy Spirit through confession. Our standing with the Lord is secure. But our fellowship with Him can be damaged through unconfessed sin.

*If we say that we have no sin, we are deceiving ourselves, and the truth is not in us. If we confess our sins, He is faithful and righteous to forgive us our sins and to cleanse us from all unrighteousness (I John 1:8-9).*

Positionally, the believer has been made right with God through his union with the Lord Jesus. All that the Christian needs to walk right before man and God has been made possible through the union he now has with Christ.

In spiritual warfare the believer's relationship with our Heavenly Father is never in question. The issue is our walk with the Lord in submission and obedience. Our fellowship with the Lord Jesus must be maintained through confession of sin. Remember, He is the HOLY Spirit. Sin always separates us from the power and work of God in and through our lives. We will discuss this in greater depth in the next chapter on the steps toward deliverance. The Psalmist says it best:

*O Lord, lead me in Thy righteousness because of my foes (Psalm 5:8).*

The righteousness of God is not only our position before Holy God but it is also the working of the Lord in our lives to make us like Jesus in all of life. Imparted righteousness is the cleansing work of the Holy Spirit bringing about holiness and righteousness in our lives. No one can survive the accusations of the Accuser unless he/she has on our Lord's Breastplate of Righteousness.

## *Your Feet Shod with the PREPARATION of the GOSPEL of PEACE*

The feet shod with the preparation of the Gospel of Peace, or "shod as ready messengers of the glad tidings" is the next vital piece of armor in spiritual conflict with the Enemy. The feet represent the believer's walk on earth. The shoes Roman Legionaries usually wore were strong, heavy sandals with thongs to keep them in place. These sandals enabled the warrior to march long distances quickly. It made him available to his commander at the time and the place where he was needed in the battle. Think of these shoes as providing mobility and availability to your commander, the Lord Jesus Christ.[10] Following the Belt of Truth and the Breastplate of Righteousness, we see that a life of truth and fellowship with God is bound to result in testimony. The one who dwells with Christ in the heavenlies walks on earth for the one and only purpose of being a ready messenger for Him.[11]

The feet must be shod with the preparation, which is always ready to go, to do, and to suffer. This means no slow movements or reluctant doing of God's will. Being off guard creates a general lack of readiness for life or death, for earth or heaven, for sacrifice or service, for doing and suffering. It cuts the nerve of Christian valor and lays us open to surprises and crushing defeats. Being ready to move precedes victory. Wakeful vigilance assures us of victory against the Devil.[12] Let us make preparation today through commitment, sacrifice, and study. So that when our Lord calls us to go and represent Him, we will say, "Yes Sir, here am I your servant reporting for duty ready to be used of you in the battle." Whether on the street corner or the White House, whether in the creek bottoms or the county seats, whether before our families or before our enemies, we must stand ready to be used of God to bring His message of peace.

For this part of the armor to be overlooked will mean defeat for the believer. Wherever he is called to go, the believer is ready to obey bearing the message of the Lord. This message of our Lord is a message of peace. Peace with God through our Lord Jesus Christ and peace with men through humility and the working of God through our lives. There is one thing certain about peace. You can't administer peace unless you have peace. You can't give away what you don't have.

There are three aspects of this peace that is of God that must be noted.

**1. Peace with God** *There is therefore now no condemnation for those who are in Christ Jesus (Romans 8:1).* The free gift of salvation brings peace with God through the Lord Jesus Christ.

**2. Peace of God**  *And let the PEACE of Christ rule in your hearts (Col. 3:15). PEACE I leave with you; My PEACE I give to you; not as the world gives, do I give to you. Let not your heart be troubled, not let it be fearful (John 14:27). Be anxious for nothing, but in everything by prayer and supplication with thanksgiving let your requests be made known to God. And the PEACE of God, which surpasses all comprehension, shall guard your hearts and your minds in Christ Jesus (Phil. 4:7-8).*

**3. Peace with all Men**  *If possible, so far as it depends on you, be at PEACE with all men (Romans 12:18). ...being diligent to preserve the unity of the Spirit in the bond of PEACE (Eph. 4:3).* The believer is to pursue diligently each aspect of God's peace in his life. To leave any area undone is to be unprepared in the invisible war of life and death. To leave off this vital part of the spiritual armor of God is to give the Enemy a distinct advantage in the battle.

## In addition to all, Taking up the SHIELD OF FAITH

Now we come to the part of the armor provided to the Christian warrior by our Lord that is a protection of all the other armor, the Shield of Faith. Each piece of the armor is spiritually related to all other parts of the armor. The Shield of Faith is the armor for the armor. The Shield of Faith protects the armor as well as the warrior. After naming certain various pieces of the armor, he says, "Above all." Though these pieces are all part of the armor, the shield is not only a defense for him, but also a defense for his defenses.

The Roman shield was more like a door. This shield covered the soldier completely. As the shield enveloped the entire man, so we see that our faith envelops the entire man, and protects him from all missiles wherever they may be aimed against him. There has never been a battle planned by Hell's most gifted strategist that can conquer faith. All his flaming and terrible darts fall harmless as they strike against the Shield of Faith.[13]

What is faith? Is faith the unyielding desire to see or feel something from God? Is faith a trigger by which I can manipulate God to do my bidding? Is faith an exercise of mental weakness by which we ignore all matters of science and education? What is faith?

Faith is not subjective. For faith to be true biblical faith it must be objective. That is, faith does not begin with us. Faith is the response to what God has said. The writer of Hebrews put it this way:

*Now faith is the assurance of things hoped for, the conviction of things not seen (Hebrews 11:1).*

Look carefully with me at the words "assurance" and "conviction." What is this assurance in? Conviction in what? Faith is the assurance and conviction that what God has said He will do. In each example given of biblical faith in the *eleventh Chapter of Hebrews*, God spoke first before these "superstars" of faith could become faithful. Then you must see to it that your faith is that which rests only upon truth, for if there be any error or false notion in the fashioning of it, that shall be a joint in it which the spear can pierce. You must take care that your faith is agreeable to God's Word, that you depend upon true and real promises, upon the sure word of testimony and not upon the fictions and fancies and dreams of men.[14]

Note carefully the three aspects of true biblical faith.

**1. Revelation-** For there to be authentic faith, it must respond to "Thus saith the Lord." God must speak before faith can exist. Faith is simply, believing what God has said is true. *By faith Noah, **being warned by God about things not yet seen**, in reverence prepared an ark for the salvation of his household (Heb. 11:7).* Faith is the response to the revelation of God. Faith is believing what God says.

**2. Decision-** Before faith can be born a decision must be made in our hearts. That decision is whether or not to accept what God has said is true. The active will is necessary for faith to have its rightful place in the life of the believer. *By faith even Sarah herself received ability to conceive, even beyond the proper time of life, since **she considered Him faithful who had promised** (Heb. 11:11).*

**3. Action-** After God has spoken, and after the decision is made to believe what God has said, the believer still has not entered into faith. Faith is the action based upon belief in what God has said. I like what one evangelist friend has said, "What you believe is what you do, everything else is just talk." *By faith Abraham, when he was called, obeyed by going out to a place which he was to receive for an inheritance; **and he went out**, not knowing where he was going (Heb. 11:8).* Faith is not just a belief in a doctrine or teaching. Faith is responding to what God has said to the extent of ordering our lives of the basis of His revelation.

Herein lies the invisible war. Do you see it? Even if I don't see demons, if God says they exist, then they exist. Even if I don't see the waging spiritual war around me, if God says there is one, then there is one. If I don't see this spiritual armor by which to engage the Enemy, if God says put it on, then I best put it on. If I don't see the victory that is mine in the Lord Jesus, if God says the victory is already won, then I best trust Him for His victory. Faith is the evidence and conviction of things not seen. As the old-time cowboy evangelist used to say, "If God says it, then that settles it!" Our belief doesn't make the Word of God true. The Word of God is true whether we believe it or not. Our belief in the truth of the Word of God enables us to share in the work of the Lord in and through our lives.

The flaming missiles of Satan are not fired aimlessly at the believer. The Devil doesn't waste his arrows. At the end of each arrow is a tip set on fire from Hell. This messenger from the pit is aimed at the weakest place of our lives. Any area of unbelief, unconfessed sin, or disobedience is the one place where the Enemy will strike his deadly blow. The Enemy has studied the weaknesses of your family for generations. He knows the areas of vulnerability in every family. Jim Logan who serves on the staff of the International Center for Biblical Counseling in Sioux City, Iowa has said it well, "Whatever you have done; you are capable of doing again." These are the areas in which you will be attacked by the Enemy. My weak places are not necessarily your weak places, but we all have them.

The Enemy's missiles are as varied as the weaknesses of man. Some of the most seen are 1. The doubting of Scripture and the goodness of God. 2. The accusation of past sins. 3. Discouragement. 4. The evil foreboding regarding the future. 5. A strong incitement to sin. 6. A flash of burning anger. 7. An overwhelming sense of despair. The possibilities are almost limitless. The Shield of Faith must be raised against such assaults! "I give no consent to these thoughts! I choose the Lord Jesus Christ. Satan, take your blasphemies and leave me."[15] I will trust what God has said to be true. All other messages I will filter through what God has said in His Word. All will be judged according to "thus saith the Lord." "But only uplift the Shield of Faith, bearing the blood-red escutcheon of the cross, and there are plenty of the knights of Hell who are ready to unhorse you. On, champion, on! In the name of Him that is with you. No lance can pierce that shield; no sword shall ever be able to cut through it; it shall preserve you in all battle and in all strife; you shall bring it home yourself; through it you shall be more than conqueror."[16]

## Take the HELMET of SALVATION

The Helmet of Salvation is that piece of armor that protects the mind. Don't ever forget, the battle in this invisible war is in the mind *(I Cor. 2:16)*. The whole body receives its direction from the head. The Apostle Paul is no doubt quoting from *Isaiah 59:17*.

*And He (God) put on righteousness like a breastplate And a helmet of salvation on his head.* Remember, *As a man thinketh in his heart so is he (Prov. 23:7 KJV).*

*For the weapons of our warfare are not of the flesh, but divinely powerful for the destruction of fortresses, (the pulling down of strongholds). We are destroying speculations and every lofty thing raised up against the knowledge of God, and WE ARE TAKING EVERY THOUGHT CAPTIVE to the obedience of Christ (2 Cor. 10:4-5).*

We are told in God's Word:

*And do not be conformed to this world, but be transformed by the renewing of your mind, that you may prove what the will of God is, that which is good and acceptable and perfect (Romans 12:2).*

The battle for God's will to be done in your life is in your mind! The Helmet of Salvation keeps the head protected in battle.

Since the command is addressed to those who are already children of God, it cannot have reference to the initial act of receiving salvation. It rather refers to realizing the fullest possible benefits of the salvation, which is already a cherished possession.[17] Our Lord has given through the work of Christ on Calvary every thing and more that is needed for the child of God to live in victory. Salvation is the person of Christ. When the aged Simeon took the baby Jesus into his arms and praised God, one of his expressions of praise was, *"My eyes have seen your salvation" (Luke 2:30).* The psalmist declared, *"The Lord is my light and my salvation" (Psalm 27:1).* Peter proclaimed, *"Salvation is found in no one else" (Acts 4:12).* Salvation is a Person more than a condition or state of being.[18]

The believer is to take and receive the work of Christ for his victory. It is Christ who has won the victory over the Enemy. It is Christ who has disarmed the rulers and authorities. It is through the shed blood of Calvary that Satan and all his attempts to steal, kill and destroy are foiled *(Col. 1:13-15).*

Salvation and all its benefits are a gift from God. God's Word tells us that this wonderful salvation is God's work:

*And we know that God causes all things to work together for good to those who love God, to those who are called according to His purpose. For whom He foreknew, He also predestined to become conformed to the image of His Son, that He might be the firstborn among many brethren; and whom He predestined, these He also called; and whom He called, these He also justified; and whom He justified, these He also glorified. What then shall we say to these things? If God be for us, who is against us? He who did not spare his own Son, but delivered him up for us all, how will He not also with Him freely give us all things (Romans 8:28-32)?*

Dear brother and sister in Christ, understand all that God has done for you in Christ. This is your Helmet of Salvation. **1. He knew you! 2. He chose you! 3. He has a plan for you! 4. He called you! 5. He justified you! 6. He glorified you!** It's all a gift from God. Receive it. Put your Helmet of Salvation on and leave it on!

## Take the SWORD of the SPIRIT,
## The WORD OF GOD

The sword is the last piece of the parts of God's armor for the Christian in spiritual battle. Why is the sword the last piece mentioned? We cannot be ready to use our aggressive weapon against Satan's kingdom until all of the other parts of the armor are in place. We must remember whom we are fighting against. Our Enemy is God's Enemy. Satan is the most powerful of all created beings. He was a formidable foe to even the warring Archangel, Michael *(Jude vs. 9)*. One cannot trifle with Satan's kingdom. A careless, unprepared advance against Satan's kingdom that lacks full awareness of our union with Christ, the ministry of the Holy Spirit, and the provision of our armor may prove disastrous.[19]

The Sword of the Spirit is the Word of God. I have always believed that the written Word of God could not be separated from the living Word of God. The Bible claims for itself to be "God breathed." The very life and breath of God abides in the Word of God. I am deeply grateful to our Lord that the largest non-Catholic denomination in America, in whose churches I serve, has finally come to this fundamental understanding of the nature of the Word of God. Through many years of battle over the institutions and agencies of the Southern Baptist Convention, our people have come to understand that the nature of the Scriptures is that of the nature of God. Some wonder why we fought for so many years over the matter of the authority and inerrancy of the Bible. I can't speak for others, but for me it was always clear. If we give up the Word of God, in the invisible war we lose our primary offensive weapon. Without the Word of God as the Sword of the Spirit, defeat is certain. The writer of Hebrews says:

*"the Word of God is living and active. Sharper than any dou-bled-edged sword, it penetrates even to dividing souls and spir-it, joints and marrow; it judges the thoughts and attitudes of the heart" (Hebrews 4:12).*

Think of it, through the Word of God, the work of God is done. The Sword of the Lord is able to separate that which is holy from that which is unholy. The Sword of the Lord is able to penetrate the heart of man and determine that which is of the flesh and that which is of the spirit. Wow, what power! No psychiatrist however educated is able to do that.

Only God's Word is used by God to determine the truth or its absence in the life of a man. There is no substitute for the use of the Word of God against Satan. The great Scottish preacher, John Knox said it well, "Christ might have repulsed Satan with a word, or by commanding him to silence, as He to whom all power was given in heaven and earth; but it pleased his mercy to teach us how to use the sword of the Holy Ghost, which is the Word of God, in battle against our spiritual enemy."[20] Even Jesus recognized the use of the Word of God as His sword against Satan in his amazing encounter with him in the wilderness *(Luke 4:1-3)*.

To be able to use the Word of God in spiritual warfare, the believer must first know the Word of God. Dear brother and sister in Christ, get into the Word and stay in the Word! Come to know the Scriptures. Not as a matter of legalistic ritual, but as a pattern for life, internalize the Word of God. Build your days on the foundation of the Word of God. You must know your sword well before you attempt to use it in battle.

The word used here for the "Word of God" is "rhema." This word refers to the word from God. It is a personal word from God to you personally. For every lie the Enemy uses against the believer, God has an answer in His Word. This answer is your "rhema." How will I know that the answer is from the Lord? He will speak to you through His written Word. The Enemy can't use the Word of God to bring God's will in your life. Only the Spirit of God will bring to you a personal word from the written Word that will be used of the Holy Spirit to bring you His will. Remember, the Devil is about destruction based on lies. Our Lord has given us His Word that it might bring forth life.

The Devil and his evil angels are eternally fearful of the Word of God. All demons tremble in the presence of the well-dressed spiritual warrior wielding the Sword of the Spirit. All of Satan's lies are exposed and expelled with the Word of God. All the ground that the Devil's imps have gained in our lives, they have stolen through deceit and lies. The Word of God is without a doubt the most powerful weapon in the believer's arsenal in the invisible war. Remember, *And you shall know the truth, and the truth shall make you free (John 8:32)*. In Jesus' prayer for the church, He makes it clear as to the nature of the Word of God. *Sanctify them in the truth; Thy word is truth (John 17:17)*. Whether you and I debate the truth of the Word of God, in Heaven and in Hell the debate is over. The Word of God is the truth of God used by the Spirit of God. It is the Sword of the Spirit. Take it up and let the Spirit of God who is within you use it to destroy the works of the Enemy.

## Prayer as a Weapon

*With all prayer and petition pray at all times in the Spirit, and with this in view, be on the alert with all perseverance and petition for all the saints (Eph. 6:18).*

As we come to the end of the study of our spiritual armor our Lord has provided in Him for the invisible war, the weapon of prayer. This too can be offensive as well as defensive in spiritual battle.

Prayer is not getting God's attention. We have God's attention through Christ *who is at His right hand of God, who also intercedes for us (Romans 8:34).* Prayer is not an avenue by which we can get God to do what we want or desire Him to do. Prayer is not some kind of "gimme gimmick." God cannot be manipulated to accomplish our selfish agendas. Prayer is linking our will with the will of the Father through the union we have in Christ through the Holy Spirit that dwells within us.

## Prayer and Fasting

*Then the disciples came to Jesus privately and said, "Why could we not cast it out?" And He said to them, "Because of the littleness of your faith; for truly I say to you, if you have faith as a mustard seed, you shall say to this mountain, Move from here to there, and it shall move; and nothing shall be impossible to you. But this kind does not go out except by **prayer and fasting"** (Matt. 17:19-21).*

I must admit to you that when it came to fasting I was at best confused. Those who openly talked about fasting made what I believed to be two significant errors.

**1. They talked about it openly.** Jesus taught his disciples that when they fasted to do it in private. No one was to know about it except the Lord *(Matt. 6:16).*

**2. They talked as if it were a way to get into God's presence.** My dear friend, we already have access to the Throne Room of Heaven. The Holy of Holies is now available through our union with Christ. The veil of the Temple of God has been torn in two. If we have to do any kind of work to get into God's presence, then Jesus died in vain. He did it for us. In our union with Christ, we have ready access to the Heavenly Father *(Eph. 2:5-6)*.

Well what's the deal about fasting? Here it is, don't miss it. When Jesus fasted in the wilderness for forty days, He knew He was to do battle with Satan. Growing up I always believed that Jesus was "bushwhacked," surprised by the temptations of the Devil. I probably watched too many "Saturday morning Westerns" on television. The Scriptures tell us a much different story. Jesus *was led about by the Spirit in the wilderness (Luke 4:1)*. Jesus' encounter with the Devil was no surprise. Jesus was God. He knew what was about to happen. But Jesus was very much flesh. And He knew it. He knew that if He was going to win the battle over the temptations of the Enemy, He had to deal with His flesh first. Jesus' forty day fast in the wilderness was His time of spiritual preparation for the truth encounter that was to take place. The desire to feed the flesh is as basic to our lives in the flesh as it gets. To deny the flesh food, is to as Paul puts it:

*Now those who belong to Christ Jesus have crucified the flesh with its passions and desires (Gal. 5:24).*

Fasting is a basic fundamental way of crucifying the flesh. Fasting is the act of putting the flesh aside so that the Enemy cannot use it against us in the invisible war.

In a time of attack on my family, the Enemy had come against one of my sons. There was obvious bondage as a result of the lies of the Enemy he had believed. For months, we were being led and taught by the Holy Spirit about this invisible war in which we were engaged. The Lord told me several times to fast for my son. I told the Lord, No. How could I fast if I didn't understand it? Jesus kept bringing the passage in *Matt. 17* to my heart. He kept telling me to be obedient to Him and to bring my petitions before Him through prayer and fasting. I finally obeyed.

While serving as an interim pastor in a small country town in North Central Texas, I asked one of the men, who I knew loved me and loved the Lord to stay late and pray through the matter with me. I asked him to stay with me as together we would go before the Lord with our tears until He brought us a peace concerning my son. That night, as we were praying, a spiritual breakthrough was finally experienced. In the union that was ours in Christ, as we called on the Lord to have his will in my boy's life, everything the Enemy had done to keep my son from freedom was stirred up, big time. Although final victory did not come until some time later, now we were on our way to victory. God was clearly at work exposing the darkness.

It is here that two verses become clear as to the importance of getting the flesh out of the way in spiritual warfare:

*Therefore it says, "God is opposed to the proud, but gives grace to the humble" (James 4:6).*

Nothing will cause more humility in our lives than to put aside the desires of the flesh. Here is the eternal truth that must be grasped in the invisible war. Exalt the flesh; the Devil will bring you into defeat. Submit the flesh to the purposes of God and the Devil will be defeated. *And they overcame him because of:*

**1. The blood of the Lamb** *and because of* **2. The word of their testimony,** *and* **3. They did not love their life even to death** *(Rev. 12:11).*

Do you see it? Look at number three. There it is. They had put aside all the desires of the flesh. They did not care even if it brought them death. When the flesh is laid aside, the Enemy has nothing to work with.

Not only does the Word of God in the Book of Ephesians tell us to pray in this spiritual battle, but also it tells us how and when to pray. *With all prayer and petition* **pray at all times.** In 1983 I had the wonderful opportunity to attend the International Conference for Itinerant Evangelists. This convocation was held in Amsterdam, Holland sponsored by the Billy Graham Evangelistic Association. My Father and I and our wives were able to attend this historic and holy meeting. During the conference we had a time of questions and answers with Evangelist Billy Graham. One of the questions was, "During the day how often do you pray?" The great evangelist said, "I never stop praying. I'm praying right now as to how to answer your questions." The Bible tells us to *pray without ceasing (I Thess. 5:18). Men ought always to pray (Luke 18:1).* Live your life in sweet communion with the Lord Jesus Christ. In this battle we are in, we must *pray at all times.*

The next admonition given in the text concerning our prayer in spiritual warfare is *pray in the Spirit.* What does praying in the Spirit mean? Is it speaking in tongues? Is it some kind of heavenly language by which we can get more done through prayer? Nowhere does the Bible teach that speaking in an unknown so-called heavenly language makes prayer more effective in the presence of God. The truth of the matter is we must be extremely careful in opening up ourselves to any foreign spirit to control any area of our lives. Just because the experience is supernatural doesn't mean it is of God. We must be obedient to the admonition:

*Beloved, do not believe every spirit, but test the spirits to see whether they are from God (I John 4:1).*

Praying in the Spirit is simply letting the Spirit of God control the time and the agenda of the prayer. Let God tell you what to pray for. Let God tell you what is important to Him. Praying is not just talking. Prayer is as much listening as it is talking. Jesus said, *My sheep hear my voice (John 10:27).* Do you know Him? Do you know His voice when He speaks? My experience in the invisible war has taught me how to listen. I'm finally learning how to listen to that still small voice. The best biblical explanation of praying in the Spirit is found in Romans.

*And in the same way the Spirit also helps our weaknesses; for we do not know how to pray as we should, but the Spirit Himself intercedes for us with groanings too deep for words (Romans 8:26).*

Here is the Spirit of God taking over the prayer of the saints as we join together with Him that God's will be done.

**Pray with all perseverance.** Don't be discouraged in the battle. Keep praying. Keep trusting. God always hears and answers our prayers that are prayed in the Spirit. His ways are not our ways and His thoughts are not our thoughts *(Isaiah 55:9)*. He sees the beginning from the end. He is Alpha and Omega. His timing is always on time. My brother and sister in Christ, keep on praying. Keep on trusting. Trust God for that wayward child, *it is His will that none perish but for all to come to repentance (2 Peter 3:9)*. Believe the words of Jesus when he said:

> *"Ask, and it shall be given to you; seek and you shall find; knock and it shall be opened to you" (Luke 11:9).*

Don't stop praying. Keep on asking. Keep on seeking. Keep on knocking. Our Lord promises to answer our prayers and petitions that are brought in the name and will of our Lord Jesus.

The last word in the text concerning our spiritual armor is to **pray *for all the saints***. Why? There is not a single soul in the body of Christ who is not vulnerable to the Enemy's schemes of deception and destruction. No one is better than anyone else. That's why we all needed to be saved. That's why we all need the Savior. Don't stop praying for every believer. We must have your prayer support.

Take every piece of the armor of God and put it on. Walk in victory as you battle the forces of darkness. Your victory will only be found in your union with the Lord Jesus Christ. Join with Christ in the Throne Room of Heaven through praying in the Spirit:

> *Nevertheless not my will, but Thine be done (Luke 22:42).*

## *Putting on the Armor of God*

My Dear Heavenly Father, I come to You in the name of the Lord Jesus Christ, my master and savior. I thank You that You have provided all I need to ward off the attacks of the Enemy in my life through my union with Christ in the heavens. I choose to cover myself with the armor of God, which You have promised me in Your Word.

I put on the Girdle of the Truth of God. However painful it may be, I choose to hear Your truth, face Your truth, believe Your truth, trust Your truth, and tell the truth. Speak to my heart that I may hear from You what I need to know and believe what You have said in Your Word is true.

I put on the Breastplate of Your Righteousness. All of my right-eousness is filthy rags except what You have done in my life to make me right with You. I receive Your working in my life to make me like Jesus.

I receive the shoes that represent my willingness to readily go where You want me to go that I may represent You and Your peace to a world that does not know the peace of God. If there is any area in my life where I am not at peace with You, show me and I will gladly con-fess it so I may be cleansed. I ask You to bring into my life through the fruit of Your Spirit, the peace of God. And I desire to be at peace with all men. If there is someone that I need to make peace with, please let me know who it is, and how best to humble myself before them, that they might see Christ in me.

I take up the Shield of Faith. Thank You that this Shield is able to quench all the arrows aimed at me dipped in the flames of Hell. I praise Your holy name that my victory over the Enemy has been won by Christ Jesus. I do not fight this battle toward victory; I fight this war from the victory of Calvary's Cross. I choose to believe what You have said in Your Word is true. I choose to obey You when You speak.

I receive from You every provision needed for spiritual battle through the gift of Your salvation. I place on my head the Helmet pro-vided for me through the shed blood of Your Son. Thank You for pro-tecting my head in this battle. I choose to take every thought captive to the obedience of Christ.

Now that I have the armor that covers my body in this battle against your Enemy, I am ready to take up the Sword of Your Spirit, which is the Word of God. Whatever lies the Enemy will hurl at me, give me from Your heart Your Word to ward off his lies. Make the Scriptures alive in my hand and in my heart. May Your Word separate the lies and the working of the Enemy in every area of my life from the truth of God that is able to set me free.

As I go into battle with the Enemy, I go only in the union that is mine with Christ. I will pray without ceasing as You tell me how and what to pray. I will trust You to keep on praying until You answer according to Your will. And I will pray for all my brothers and sisters that You have joined with me in Your body until all are set free in the name of the Lord Jesus Christ.

I praise Your mighty and Holy name that You are able to do exceedingly abundantly above all that I ask or think according to the power that works within me. I thank You that there is only one Lord and You are He. I thank You that each piece of Your spiritual armor represents Christ Jesus and my union with Him. Thank You that I am more than a conqueror through Christ who loved me and gave Himself for me. I praise Your name that the battle is already won in Christ Jesus. Amen!

# Chapter 6

# Deliverance from the Devil

*"He (the believer) must wrestle not with flesh and blood, but against principalities and powers. He must have weapons for his warfare-not carnal-but mighty through God to the pulling down of strongholds. He must go forth to attack the castles of the Enemy, and to put them down, to drive the Canaanite out of the land."*
— *Charles H. Spurgeon*

Deliverance is the sovereign work of grace by our Lord Jesus. He is the one who came to *set the captives free (Luke 4)*. He is the one that was *manifest that He might destroy the works of the Devil (I John 3:8)*. He is our deliverer. He taught us to pray, *Deliver us from the Evil One (Matt. 6:13)*. In simple outline form here are the principle truths that are involved in setting the captives free.

A. **DISCOVER** through Discernment the work (or ground) of the Devil. **RECOGNIZE** the work of the Devil *(I John 3:10, James 3:11-12)*. (See Appendix A, Case 3, pg. 254, Case 2, pg. 251.)

B. **DENOUNCE** the work of the Devil.

- **RENOUNCE** *(2 Cor. 4:2)*.
- **REPENT** Turn from sin and turn to God for forgiveness *(Acts 8:22-23)*.

- **RESIST** *(James 4:7).*
- **REPLACE** the lies of the Enemy with the **TRUTH** of **GOD'S WORD** *(John 8:32).* (See Appendix A, Case 5, pg. 258.)

**C. DECLARE** out loud your commitment to Christ *(Romans 8:35-39).*

- Your **Position** in Christ – Victor not a Victim *(Col. 2:15, Eph. 6).*
- Your **Posture** of Victory – **Humble** yourselves before God *(James 4). Reckon yourself dead to sin (Romans 6:11).*
- **Proclaim** your Victory – *(Rev. 12:11).*

**D. DELIVER** through **DISPOSING** the Enemy *(Luke 8:26-33).* (See Appendix A, Case 6, pg. 261.)

- **RECLAIM for** Christ the area stolen by the Enemy *(Eph. 4:26-27).*
- **REFILL** the empty area with the Holy Spirit *(Luke 11:22-26).*
- **RENEW** the mind through the Word of God *(Romans 12:1-2, Phil. 4:8, 2 Cor. 10:5).*
- **REJOICE** with all of heaven in the work of the Lord Jesus Christ *(Luke 15:7,10,32).*

## *The Prayer God Answers*

*The effectual fervent prayer of a righteous man availeth much (James 5:16 KJV). Now to Him who is able to do exceeding abundantly beyond all that we ask or think, according to the power that works within us (Eph. 3:20).*

Before any attempt to set the captives free is approached, before any confrontation with the rebel prince is launched, the believer **must** understand the eternal truths concerning the prayer that God answers. (See Appendix A, Case 1, pg. 249.)

*1. God Answers the Prayer that is prayed under the Sacrifice of Christ.*

Since the attack on America on September 11, 2001, our nation has been in a state of shock and sorrow like we have not known in our lifetime. In an effort to heal our nation's sorrow, a prayer meeting was scheduled in Yankee Stadium. Expectantly I watched with millions of others as the prayer meeting was broadcast on national television. Maybe you were as shocked and hurt as I was as the name of Jesus was only mentioned once in the two hours of this so called "prayer meeting." What a waste. Prayers can only reach the Throne Room of Heaven through the sacrifice of Christ:

*I am the way, the truth, and the life, no one comes to the Father* ***except by me*** *(John 14:6, KJV).*

*And whatever you ask* ***in my name*** *that will I do, that the Father may be glorified in the Son (John 14:13).*

*Truly, truly, I say to you, if you shall ask the Father for anything, He will give it to you* ***in my Name*** *(John 15:16, 16:23).*

It is only through our union with Christ made possible through His sacrifice on Calvary for our sins that we are able to approach the Holy of Holies with our petitions. *...and raised us up with Him, and seated us with Him in the heavenly places in Christ Jesus (Eph. 2:6).* This passage is a direct reference to verse 20 of Chapter One that tells us that only through our union with Christ made available through His blood sacrifice for our sins are we able to come and be received before a Holy God.

## 2. God Answers the Prayer that is Specific.

*You have not because you ask not (James 4:2). ...but in everything by prayer and supplication with thanksgiving let your requests be made known to God (Phil. 4:6).*

Why are we to be specific when we pray? Isn't God omniscient? Doesn't He already know what is going on? Prayer is not getting God's attention. We have His undivided attention through our union with Christ. Prayer is a time of getting our hearts in tune with the heart of

God. Prayer is not some self-centered exercise of manipulating God to do what we want.

Prayer is not some "name it and claim it, blab it and grab it" means by which we seek to fill our own selfish desires, as some would teach. No, no! Prayer is exercising our union with Christ to join our hearts with the will and heart of our Heavenly Father.

*If you ask Me anything in my Name, I will do it (John 14:14).*

Prayer is working together with God to see His will accomplished on earth as it is in Heaven.

*Truly I say to you, whatever you shall bind on earth will be bound in heaven; and whatever you loose on the earth shall be loosed in Heaven (Matt. 16:19).*

### 3. God Answers the Prayer that is prayed in the Spirit

*And in the same way the Spirit also helps our weaknesses; for we do not know how to pray as we should, but the Spirit Himself intercedes for us with groanings to deep for words (Romans 8:26).*

Once again it is through our union with the Lord Jesus that our prayers become effective prayer. The Spirit of God who dwells within each believer is the one who teaches us how to pray and what to pray. It is through this holy relationship with God that effective prayer resides. There are times in all of our lives when our hurts are so deep, our sorrows so overwhelming that we don't know if we can pray, much less what to pray. These are the times when our prayer time becomes a time of healing and sweet communion with the Lord. It is the Holy Spirit that will take over the prayer "closet." There is no night so dark that our Lord is not present. There is no tear-stained pillow that our Lord does not share our grief (*Isaiah 53:4-5*). It is through the precious ministry of the Paraclete, The One Who Stands along our side, the one who never leaves us or forsakes us, the Holy Spirit, that enables us to be in communion with God in prayer. Even in the passage concerning our Armor of God within the Spiritual Battle we find ourselves, we find this admonition:

*With all prayer and petition pray at all times **in the Spirit** (Eph. 6:18).*

## 4. God Answers the prayer that is Offered in Submission to His will.

*God is opposed to the proud, but gives grace to the humble (James 4:6).*

Herein lies the key to effective prayer:

*You ask and do not receive, because you ask with wrong motives, so that you may spend it on your pleasures (James 4:3).*

If we ever expect God to hear and answer our petitions they must be presented to Him in complete humility and submission to His will. Fasting comes into focus at this point. Fasting is not an attempt to become super spiritual. Fasting is not some kind of "work" to get into God's presence. Fasting is simply putting aside our flesh so it cannot influence our communion with the Lord. God answers the prayer that is presented in total submission to His will.

*And this is the confidence, which we have before Him, that, if we ask anything according to His will, He hears us (I John 5:14).*

## Deliverance from Strongholds

*"For though we walk in the flesh, we do not war according to the flesh, for the weapons of our warfare are not of the flesh, but divinely powerful for the destruction of (strongholds) fortresses. We are destroying speculations and every lofty thing raised up against the knowledge of God, and we are taking every thought captive to the obedience of Christ" (2 Cor. 10:3-5).*

A stronghold is a fortress, a "beach-head" that Satan has been allowed to build within our lives. It is ground that has been given over to the Enemy through continual unconfessed sin and an unrepentant heart. We are warned by Holy Scripture:

> *Be of sober spirit, be on the alert. Your adversary, the Devil prowls about like a roaring lion, seeking someone to devour (I Peter 3:8).*

Our archenemy, Satan is continually looking for a place to take advantage in our lives for the ultimate purpose to *steal, kill, and to destroy (John 10:10).* Sin always separates us from a Holy God and His protection, not His grace and love *(Romans 8:35-39).* God's Word tells us:

> *Be angry, and yet do not sin; do not let the sun go down on your anger, and do not give the Devil an opportunity, a place (Eph. 4:26-27).*

This word translated "opportunity" or "place" is "topos." We get the word "topography" from this word. It literally means a place or ground by which the Devil can get an advantage in our lives to defeat and ultimately destroy us.

Herein lies the truth concerning strongholds. They are places in our lives given to the Devil by sin, disobedience and unbelief. Spiritual warfare is the struggle between believing the lies of the Enemy, (who is the Father of Lies, *John 8:44*), and the truth of the Word of God *(John 17:17, Psalm 119:89, 2 Tim. 3:16, John 8:32).*

Think of a stronghold in the terms of how the Bible refers to it. It is a fortress. I like to think of it as a tower or a wall. It is a place given to the Enemy through believing his lies. The Enemy fortifies these fortresses through time. It is a place behind which the Enemy hides while doing his evil work of stealing, killing and ultimate destruction. Rarely is the demonic exposed and seen, but their evil work is clearly seen. (See Illustration B, The Pulling Down of Strongholds, The Enemy's Fortresses – Hiding Places, to help visualize the nature and function of these strongholds, pg.145) The structure of these strongholds is explained on page 147-148 in the Stronghold Structure Section of the Stronghold Prayer. These strongholds although invisible are real structures, real fortresses where the Enemy has been allowed by our sin and unbelief to do his evil work. Once they are torn down the evil ones will have to find

manifestation of the Holy Spirit. I belong to God and the Evil One cannot touch me. I ask that no other voice be heard but the voice of the Lord Jesus. All others must be silenced in the presence of Holy God. I ask the Lord to reveal to me His truth, as the Holy Spirit will guide me. (See Appendix A, Case 5, pg. 258.)

## STRONGHOLD PRAYER

1.  **I bring the bindings, judgments, anathemas, and coverings of the blood of the Lord Jesus Christ to bear.**

2.  **Whatever structure, level, spirits, materials, motors, batteries, light, shadow, or never.**

3.  **Whatever the demons, demon creatures, ancestral spirits, and spirits of living flesh, animal spirits and nature spirits, or any other spirits we may not know about whatever their foundations, formations, and functions.**

4.  **Whatever the assignments, curses, or judgments, ties, deceptions, destructions, triggers, batteries and programming, without or within us, without or within the family, without or within covens, whatever the location or place, whatever their times, foundations, formations, or functions.**

5.  **Declaring them null and void and without effect. Sending them back to their point of origin, with judgment, pain, and condemnation in the name of the Lord Jesus Christ.**

Pray the "Stronghold Prayer" over each area of the "Stronghold Structure." Think of the stronghold as a tower with its separate parts.

## STRONGHOLD STRUCTURE

A.  **Environment (*2 Cor. 10:3-5*)**                    **70x7x7 to 2nd***
    **System of thought contrary to the teaching of the Word of God. Ideas learned as a child without biblical basis.**

**B. Place (topos) given to the devil**    70x7x7 to 7th
   **(*Eph. 4:26-27*)  (Anger)**
   **Non-biblical ideas we act on to create sin in our lives.**

**C. Walls (*James 1:13-15*)**    70x7x7 to 3rd
   **Sinful thoughts, sinful emotions, sinful behaviors that hurt others and us.**

**D. Foundation (*Isaiah 53:4-5*)**    70x7x7 to 4th

   · **Griefs – Normal emotions to express loss**
   · **Sorrows – Things that happen we wished had never happened**
   · **Wounds – Unhealed damage to spirit or body that is continual pain, abusive action or trauma.**

**E. Cornerstone (*Isaiah 53:4-5*)**    70x7x7 to 5th
   **Iniquity (Hebrew word), way of life built on lies.** [1]

*As you pray, applying by faith the truth of the Word of God in each area of the stronghold, call on the Lord to bring to bear all of the power of God needed to destroy all the works of the Enemy. These mathematical formulas represent the power of God used (as discovered in the counseling room by those in deliverance ministry) to break down each piece in the structure of the Enemy's stronghold. (See Appendix A, Case 6, pg. 261.)

### PRAYERS FOR DELIVERANCE

The following are prayers of deliverance. They have been compiled and expanded from a collection of prayers used by those who have been for many years in deliverance ministry. They are intended to be a guide. Words are not magic. We cannot fool God. He knows our hearts. If these prayers reflect the desires of your heart as you humble yourself before God, you will find these prayers most helpful on your way to full freedom in Christ. A careful study of James Chapter 4 will help you understand the attitude of the heart that is needed to receive an answer from our Lord. Remember, "You have not, because you ask not." Be specific when you pray.

### Prayer of Deliverance from False Religions, False Teachings, and Rituals
#### (I Cor. 10:20)

All that the Enemy does is a carefully designed counterfeit to the work and truth of God. It is critically important to renounce (verbally reject) old past or present involvement with occult practices, cult teachings, and rituals, as well as non-Christian religions. You must renounce any activity or group which denies Jesus Christ or offers guidance through any source other than the absolute authority of the Bible. Any group that requires dark, secret initiations, ceremonies, promises, or pacts should also be renounced. Begin this step by praying aloud:

### Prayer

Dear Heavenly Father, I ask You to bring to my mind anything and everything that I have done knowingly or unknowingly that involves occult, cult, or non-Christian teachings or practices. I pray that all of Satan's deceptions will be seen for what they are in my life. I want to experience Your freedom by renouncing these evil things in which I have been involved. In Jesus' mighty and holy name I pray, Amen.

Lord, I confess that I have participated in_____. I know it was evil and offensive in your sight. Thank You for your forgiveness. I renounce any and all involvement with_____, and I cancel out any and all ground that the Enemy gained in my live through this activity. In the name of my Lord Jesus Christ I pray, Amen.

### Prayer of Deliverance from Idolatry
#### (I John 5:20-21, Matt. 4:10, Exodus 20:3
#### Matthew 22:37, Rev. 2:4-5, Deut. 5:7-8)

### Prayer

Dear Lord God, I have allowed other things and other people to become more important to me than You. I am so sorry I have offended You and Your Word when You have said, I "shall have no other gods" before You. I confess to You that I have not loved You with all my heart and soul and mind. As a result, I have sinned against You, violating the first and greatest commandment. I repent and turn away from this idolatry and now choose to return to You, Lord Jesus, as my first love. Please forgive me for not trusting and loving You. As I come before You, please show me anything or anyone I have allowed to become an idol in my life. I renounce each of them; and, in so doing, cancel out any and all ground Satan may have gained in my life through my idolatry. In the name of Lord Jesus Christ, the one true God, Amen.

In the name of the true and living God, Jesus Christ, I renounce my worship of the false God of (name the idol). Please forgive me. As I have sought my answers except from Your truth, I have sinned against You. Please forgive me for believing Satan's lies. I choose to worship only You, Lord. I ask You, Father, to enable me to keep this area of (name the idol) in its proper place in my life. I choose to seek first the kingdom of God and Your righteousness. You and You alone are Lord. There is one Lord! And You are He! I ask that all assignments and evil spirits sent by Your Enemy would be cast out of my life. I call on You, Lord Jesus, to come and set the captives free. Thank You that You have come to destroy the works of the Devil in my life. All demons must come to attention in the presence of the Lord Jesus. There will be no manifestations except the manifestation of the Holy Spirit. You may not separate. You may not divide. You may not get reinforcements. You must face the judgment of the Lord Jesus Christ. I bind every spirit involved in my idolatry with the three-fold cord that cannot be broken in the Name of the Father, Son, and Holy Spirit. You must go where Jesus tells you to go, when Jesus tells you to go.

### *Special Renunciations for Satanic Ritual Involvement*

1. I renounce ever signing are having my name signed over to Satan. I announce that my name is now written in the Lamb's Book of Life.

2. I renounce any ritual where I was wed to Satan. I announce that I am the bride of Christ.

3. I renounce any and all covenants, agreements, or promises that I made to Satan. I announce that I have made a new covenant with Jesus Christ alone that supersedes any previous agreements.

4. I renounce all satanic assignments including duties, marriage, and

children. I announce and commit myself to know and do only the will of God, and accept only his guidance for my life.

5. I renounce all spirit guides assigned to me. I announce and accept only the leading of the Holy Spirit.

6. I renounce any giving of my blood in the service of Satan. I trust only in the shed blood of my Lord, Jesus Christ.

7. I renounce ever eating flesh or drinking blood in satanic worship. By faith, I take Holy Communion, representing my Savior, the body and blood of the Lord Jesus.

8. I renounce all guardians and satanic parents that were assigned to me. I announce that God is my heavenly Father and the Holy Spirit is my guardian by whom I'm sealed.

9. I renounce any baptism whereby I am identified with Satan. I announce that I had been baptized into Christ Jesus and my identity is now in Him alone.

10. I renounce any sacrifice made on my behalf by which Satan may claim ownership of me. I announce that only the sacrifice of Christ has any claim on me. I belong to Him. I have been purchased by the blood of the Lamb.[2]

Now that the stronghold of the Enemy has been broken, and now that the evil spirits are gone, ask the Lord to cleanse with His blood the areas vacated by the Enemy and to put a seal of His blood on that area. Now ask the Lord to fill you with His Spirit.

### *Prayer of Deliverance from the Work of Covens*
*(Eph. 5:11-14, Romans 13:12)*

Satan's work is done on the earth in many different ways and through many different levels of evil. One of the avenues of perpetrating evil on the earth is through the workers of iniquity who have signed on as disciples of Satan. Through their lust for illicit power and money they do the Enemy's evil bidding. They join groups of other highly demonized individuals called covens. In these covens demonic activities are carried out usually in secret. Their function is to carry out the evil purposes of Satan on the earth as it is in Hell.

Covens are doing their evil work among us. They are at work in our churches. They are at work in politics. They are at work wherever you find money and power. The following is an outline of their evil work.

### The Structure and Purposes of Satanic Covens

1. Coven Leader

2. Coven Members

3. Formations
   Operation
   Rituals

4. Outcomes
   Breaking the will and Word of God, Old and New Testament.

   | A | B |
   |---|---|
   | Afflict | Rob, Steal |
   | Harass, Terrorize | Kill |
   | Torment, Accuse | Destroy |
   | Oppress | |

5. A. Perversion of all human power, authority, wealth, influence, attributes and time.

   B. To give Satan control- To turn all these over to Satan.

The following is an example of how to pray against the works and the workers of iniquity functioning in covens.

### Prayer

Dear Lord Jesus, I thank You that You are able to do exceeding abundantly above all that I could ask or even think. As I pray I ask for Your protection. I put on the Armor of God provided by You that is my protection against the forces of darkness (See Chapter 5). I bring to bear in the name of the Lord Jesus Christ of Nazareth the blood of the Lord Jesus, the Word of God, and the power of Almighty God a billion times a billion times a billion. Put it on the evil ones heads the same torment and destruction You put upon Satan's head at Calvary. Raise it to the billionth power for every moment the evil ones resist. Put them in the circle of Your blood. Pour Your blood over them and down their throats 800 billion times per second. Make them obey Your Word and bow before You as the master and ruler of all creation.

I ask You Lord Jesus to pour Your blood over the workers of iniquity and all their evil outcomes. Pour Your blood over the coven leaders and the coven members. Separate by Your blood and by Your power their ability to work together for evil. Pour Your blood over the formations, operations and rituals made in the unholy covenants with the Enemy. Lord Jesus, I ask that You would stop the ability of those who would attempt through unholy power to break the will and Word of God, the Old and New Testament. I ask You, Lord Jesus to shut down the power of those who would afflict, harass, terrorize, torment, accuse, oppress and the like, and all those who would rob, steal, kill and destroy. Pour Your blood over them and their ability to perpetrate the evil purposes of Your Enemy. Pour Your blood over the evil ones who would attempt to pervert all human power, authority, wealth, influence and attributes and turn all these over to Satan. I ask You, Lord Jesus to shut down the evil ones ability at any level to function in this place, over my family and in my life. I ask all of this in the mighty all powerful name of my Lord Jesus Christ.

### Prayer of Deliverance from Deception
*(John 14:6, 16:13, 17:17, Ephesians 4:15,*
*John 8:32-36, 44, 2 Timothy 2:26, Revelation 12:9)*

### Prayer

Dear Heavenly Father, I know that You want me to face the truth, tell the truth, believe the truth, trust the truth, and live in accordance with the truth. Thank You that it is the truth that will set me free. I now know I have been deceived by Satan, the father of lies. Through believing his lies, I have deceived myself as well. Father, I pray in the name of the Lord Jesus Christ, by virtue of his shed blood and resurrection, asking You to rebuke all of Satan's demons that are deceiving me. I have trusted in Jesus alone to save me, and so I am your forgiven child. Therefore, since You accept me just as I am in Christ, I can be free to face my sin and not try to hide. I ask for the Holy Spirit to guide me into all truth. I ask You to *Search me, O God, and know my heart; try me and know my anxious thoughts; and see if there be any hurtful way in me, and lead me in the everlasting way (Psalm 139:23-24).* In the Name of The Lord Jesus Christ, who is the truth, I pray. Amen.

### Prayer of Deliverance from the Spirit of Fear
*(2 Timothy 1:7)*
(See Appendix A, Case 4, pg. 256.)

Fear is extremely powerful. It reveals the very opposite of the faith the Lord has for us. He has not given us a spirit of fear. Fear weakens us, causes us to be self-centered, and clouds our minds so that all we can think about is the thing that frightens us. But fear can only control us if we let it. God, however, does not want us to be mastered by anything, including fear *(I Corinthians 6:12).* Jesus Christ is to be our only master. He is the only true Lord. All others are imposters *(John 13:13; 2 Timothy 2:21).*

Fear can manifest itself in many different ways. Thoughts of inadequacy, rejection, paranoia, lack of trust, fear of men (because of abuse), fear of women, and the like. When a person is controlled by the spirit of fear, he may so manipulate his life and those around him to create a false sense of success and security. These fears can often be a cover for the chief cause of our fears. For instance, I have found in many cases where fear is in manifestation that the root spirit, the root cause is a spirit of abandonment. In order to begin to experience freedom from the bondage of fear and the ability to walk by faith in God, pray the following prayer from your heart:

### Prayer

Dear Heavenly Father, I confess to You that I have listened to the Devil's lies and have allowed fear to master me. Please forgive me for not living by faith in You. Thank You for forgiving me each time I refused to believe Your Word. Right now I renounce the spirit of fear and all other spirits that have their assignment with fear. I ask You to bind them

with the three-fold cord that cannot be broken, in the Name of the Father, Son and the Holy Spirit. You must come to attention and receive the judgment of God. You will go where Jesus tells you to go when Jesus tells you to go. There will be no manifestations except the manifestation of the Holy Spirit. All voices must be silent in the presence of Holy God. I believe Christ has not given the spirit of fear but of power, love, and the sound mind. Lord, please reveal to my mind now all the fears that have been controlling me so I can renounce them and be free to walk by faith in You. I renounce the (name the fear) because God has not given me a spirit of fear. I choose to live by faith in the God who has promised to protect me and meet all my needs as I walk by faith in Him. I thank You for the freedom You give me to walk by faith and not by fear. You have never left me nor forsaken me. Please forgive me for believing the lie that You left me. Thank You for Your never-ending faithfulness to me according to Your Word *(Heb. 13:5)*. In Jesus powerful name, I pray. Amen.
*(2 Cor. 4:16-18; 5:7; Psalm 27:1; Matthew 6:33,34; 2 Timothy 1:7)*

After you have finished renouncing all the specific fears you have allowed to control you, pray the following prayer:

## *Prayer*

Dear Heavenly Father, I thank You that I can trust Your Word. I choose to believe Your truth, even when my feelings and circumstances tell me to fear. You have not given me a spirit of fear. You have told me not to fear, for You are with me, to not anxiously look about me, for You are my God. You will strengthen me, help me, and surely uphold me with Your righteous hand. You are my strength. I pray that when I am faced with the choice to fear or to trust You, You will strengthen me to trust in You. I pray this with faith in the name of the Lord Jesus Christ, my Master. Amen *(Isaiah 41:10)*.

## *Prayer of Deliverance from Bitterness*
### *(Eph. 4:31-32, Heb. 12:5)*

Bitterness only destroys the one who allows its spiritual cancer to remain in his/her heart. We need to forgive others so Satan cannot take advantage of us. The Bible teaches that we must forgive others with the same love that our Heavenly Father has forgiven us. If you have not allowed the Lord to forgive any sin in your life, do so right now. Once you are right before God then ask God to bring to your mind the people you need to forgive by praying the following prayer out loud *(2 Cor. 2:10-11)*.

### *Prayer*

Dear Heavenly Father, I thank You for the riches of Your kindness, forbearance, and patience toward me, knowing that Your kindness has led me to repentance. Please forgive me for my unwillingness to trust You to take care of my hurts. Thank You that you bore my pain and carried my sorrows. You were wounded for my iniquities, and by Your stripes I am healed. You alone are Lord. You can and will handle all wickedness and unrighteousness. You alone are the judge and will reconcile all things to Yourself. You have said in Your Word that vengeance is Yours, You will repay. Through my disobedience in not trusting You, I have not allowed the Holy Spirit to manifest His love in me and through me to others. I confess I have not shown Your love, kindness, and patience toward those who have hurt me. Instead, I've held on to my anger, bitterness, and resentment toward them. Because You have forgiven me, I now can forgive those who have hurt me. Please bring to my mind all the people I need to forgive in order that I may forgive them now. In Jesus mighty name I pray, Amen *(Romans 2:4)*.

Say, "Lord, I choose to forgive (name the person) for (what they did or failed to do) because it made me feel (share the painful feeling)."

After you have forgiven each person for all the offenses that came to your mind, and after you have honestly expressed how you felt, conclude your forgiveness of that person by praying out loud:

Lord, I choose not to hold on to my resentment. I thank You for setting me free from the bondage of my bitterness. I relinquish my right to seek revenge and ask You to heal my damaged emotions. I now ask You to bless those who have hurt me. Please Lord, do a great work of Your love and mercy in their life. May they come to serve You with all their hearts. For the sake of the glory of Your name, I pray. Amen.

### *Getting Rid of Bitterness*

We are most like Satan when we are bitter and angry. We are most like Christ when we unconditionally love and forgive those who have hurt us. Bitterness is a powerful chief demonic system that allows the Enemy ground to destroy ultimately everyone and everything it touches. I have learned that Bitterness is much more than just a powerful emotion even though emotions are involved. Bitterness is like an octopus. It has many tentacles that hang on for ultimate control and power. Each arm or tentacle must be removed individually before Bitterness will leave. If one of its underlings is allowed to hang on, Bitterness will hang on.

Get alone with our Heavenly Father. Ask Him to silence all other voices but His. Humble yourself and ask Him to tell you where any of the underlings of Bitterness listed below are still at work in your heart. When He tells you, agree with Him. Confess each one out loud. Ask Him to forgive you for cooperating with the Evil One through His demonic system of Bitterness. When all areas of cooperation with the underlings are confessed before God, Ask the Lord by His power, by His blood, and by His Word to remove Bitterness from you. Once it's done, ask the Lord to give you the same love for the one who has hurt you that our Lord has so freely expressed toward you in the sacrifice of His Son, Christ Jesus. It's all a gift. Receive it!

### *Bitterness is a Principality- the Chief Demon*

### *Underlings:*
- Un-forgiveness- to enhance the normal feeling of un-forgiveness.
- Resentment- Plays the record of the wrong.
- Retaliation- Plotting to get even for wrong done.
- Anger/Wrath/Rage- Physical Manifestation of Defilement.
- Hatred- Stage of elimination- Carries Out (domestic violence)
- Violence- Bitterness in Motion- Full blown manifestation.
- Murder- The full completed work of Satan. (We can murder someone with our tongues and in our heart. Mitigated murder is still murder.)[3]

### *Prayer of Deliverance from Rebellion*
### *(I Samuel 15:23)*

Rebellion is the sin of witchcraft. Whether rebellion against civil government *(Romans 13:1-7, I Timothy 2:1-4, I Peter 2:13-17)*, parents or legal guardians *(Eph. 6:1-3)*, teachers or school officials *(Romans 13:1-4)*, employers *(I Peter 2:18-23)*, husbands *(I Peter 3:1-4)*, church leaders *(Hebrews 13:7)*, or God *(Daniel 9:5,9)*, it's still rebellion and God's Word forbids it. Ask the Lord to bring to your mind all the ways you have been rebellious; use the following prayer to specifically confess that sin:

### Prayer

Lord, I confess that I have been rebellious toward (name) by (Say what you did specifically). Thank You for forgiving my rebellion. I choose now to be submissive and obedient to Your Word in the name of my Lord Jesus Christ. Dear Heavenly Father, You have said that rebellion is as the sin of witchcraft and insubordination is as iniquity and idolatry *(I Samuel 15:23)*. I choose to turn from rebellion and turn to You. Cleanse my heart of all rebellion by the New Covenant in Your blood.

In my rebellion I now know I have sinned against You. I ask Your forgiveness for my rebellion and pray that by the shed blood of the Lord Jesus Christ all ground gained by evil spirits because of my rebellion would be canceled. All spirits assigned to rebellion must come to attention. You may not separate, you may not divide, and you may not call on reinforcements. You must face the judgment of God. I ask the Lord to bind all evil spirits under the assignment of rebellion in the name of the Father, Son and the Holy Spirit. You will go where Jesus tells you to go, when Jesus tells you to go. I pray that Christ will shed His light in my life that I may know the full extent of my rebellion. Cleanse me with your blood that was shed on Calvary for my sin. Heal the wounds left by the work of the Enemy. I ask You to fill me with Your Holy Spirit. May Your presence fill all the areas that the Enemy has now left. In the name of Christ Jesus my Lord. Amen. (See Appendix A, Case 7, pg. 264.)

### Prayer of Deliverance from Pride
*(Prov. 16:18-19, James 4:6-10, Phil. 2: 3-8)*

Pride separates us from God. That separation always leads to death for only in God is there life. "God resists the proud, but gives grace to the humble." God will not humble you. Humility is your choice. Without genuine humility true deliverance and victory in the Lord is impossible. Ultimately, all sin comes down to pride. The Devil knows that our pride can be the most effective area to attack to keep us from believing and trusting God. In the believer's life there is a constant battle between the flesh and the spirit *(Romans 6-8)*. Pride allows the flesh to rule. Remember, a man cannot serve two masters. *Proverbs 3:5-7* says:

*Trust in the Lord with all your heart, and do not lean on your own understanding. In all your ways acknowledge him, and he will make your paths straight. Do not be wise in your own eyes; fear the Lord and turn away from evil.*

*I Peter 5:1-10* warns us that serious spiritual problems will result when we are proud. Pray the following prayer to express your commitment to living humbly before God:

**Prayer**

Dear Heavenly Father, You have said that pride goes before destruction and an arrogant spirit before stumbling *(Prov. 16:18)*. I confess that I have been thinking mainly of myself and not of others. I have not denied myself, picked up my cross daily, and followed You. I have not lived my life as a living and holy sacrifice unto You. I have not allowed the Holy Spirit to fill my life with the humility of Christ. As a result I have given ground to the Devil in my life. I have sinned by believing I could be happy and successful on my own. I confess that I have placed my will before Yours. I have centered my life around myself instead of You. I have ruled on the throne of my life instead of allowing Jesus to be the Lord of my life. I have been selfish in my relationship with you and with others. I repent of my pride and selfishness and pray that all ground gained in my members by the enemies of the Lord Jesus Christ would be canceled. I choose to rely on the Holy Spirit's power and guidance so I will do nothing from selfishness or empty conceit. With humility of mind, I will regard others as more important than myself. And I choose to make You, Lord, the most important of all in my life. Please show me now all the specific ways in which I have lived my life in pride. Enable me through love to serve others and in honor to prefer others. I ask all of this in the mighty and able name of Jesus, my Lord. Amen. (See *Matthew 6:33, 16:24, Romans 12:10*)

Now that you have made a commitment to God in prayer, ask Him to show you any specific ways you have allowed pride to rule in your life. As He shows you these pride areas in your life, pray this prayer out loud:

### Prayer

Lord, I agree I have been proud in (name the area). Thank You for answering my prayer. Thank You for showing me every area of pride that needs Your cleansing. Thank You for forgiving me for my pride. I choose to humble myself before You and others. I choose to place all my confidence in You and none in my flesh. I choose to follow and serve only You all the days of my life. You alone are worthy of all praise. Please forgive me for allowing any self praise to find a place in my heart. In the name of the Lord Jesus Christ I pray. Amen.

## Prayer of Deliverance from Bondage

The wages of sin is always DEATH. No one is exempt from this eternal truth. Unconfessed sin always leads to habitual sin. Habitual sin most often leads to spiritual bondage. People who get caught in the "revolving door" of sin-confess-sin-confess may need to follow the instructions of *James 4:1-10.*

*If we confess our sins, He is faithful and righteous to forgive us our sins and to cleanse us from all unrighteousness (I John 1:9).*

Confession is not saying, "I'm sorry" but saying "I did it." Confession is agreeing with God that He is right in what He says and that you have been wrong. Only the sorrow that leads to repentance (a change of thinking, which is believing the truth of God) will bring God's deliverance *(2 Cor. 7:10).*

### Prayer

Dear Heavenly Father, You have told us to put on the Lord Jesus Christ and make no provision for the flesh in regard to its lust *(Romans 13:14).* I acknowledge that I have given in to fleshly lusts, which wage war against my soul *(I Peter 2:11).* I thank You that in Christ my sins are forgiven, but I have transgressed Your holy law and given the Enemy an opportunity to wage war in my members *(Romans 6:12,13; James 4:1; I Peter 5:8).* I come before You to acknowledge all sins of the flesh and to seek Your cleansing *(I John 1:9).* Please forgive me for not agreeing with You when You told me these evil thoughts and actions were wrong. I now believe You. Lord, Jesus, You alone can cleanse me of my sin. I put my faith in Your Word and ask that You will come and do in my life what You alone can do. Please reveal to my mind the ways that I have transgressed Your moral law and grieved the Holy Spirit. In Jesus' precious name I pray. Amen.

The deeds of the flesh are numerous. You may want to open your Bible to *Galatians 5:19-21* and pray through the verses, asking the Lord to reveal the ways you have specifically sinned. It is our responsibility to not allow sin to reign in our mortal bodies by not using our bodies as instruments of unrighteousness *(Romans 6:12-13)*. If habitual sexual sins, such as pornography, masturbation, sexual promiscuity, are controlling your life, come humbly before the Lord Jesus and ask Him to break these areas of bondage in your life.

### Prayer

In the Name of the Lord Jesus Christ, I call upon You, Lord to silence all other voices but the voice of the Lord Jesus. Lord, I ask You to reveal to my mind every sexual use of my body as an instrument of unrighteousness. I pray this knowing that You are able to do exceeding abundantly above all that we ask or think according to the power that works within me. Amen.

As the Lord brings to your mind every sexual use of your body, whether you were willing or unwilling, (rape, incest, or any sexual molestation), renounce every sexual involvement.

### Prayer

Lord, I renounce (name the specific use of your body) with (name the person) and ask You to break that (soul-tie) bond. Lord Jesus, I call on You to break all soul-ties that have remained as the result of any of my sexual involvement that was not of You. Please separate me to serve only You. I give You my body for the glory of Christ. I rededicate my body as the dwelling place (the Temple) of the Holy Spirit. (See Appendix A, Case 4, pg. 256.)

Now commit your body to the Lord by praying:

*Prayer*

Lord, I renounce all these uses of my body as an instrument of unrighteousness and by so doing ask You to break all bondages that Satan has brought into my life through that involvement. I confess my participation. Through the New Covenant in Your blood, I now present my body to You as a living sacrifice, holy and acceptable to You. I reserve that sexual use of my body only for the marriage partner that You have chosen for me. I renounce the lie of Satan that my body is not clean, that it is dirty or in any way unacceptable as a result of my past sexual experiences. Lord, I thank You that I am totally cleansed and forgiven through the shedding of Your blood for my sin. Thank You for loving and accepting me unconditionally. Because You have accepted and forgiven me, I forgive and accept myself. In the name of the Lord Jesus Christ, I Pray. Amen.

## Prayers of Deliverance for Specific Needs

### Homosexuality
*(Lev. 18:22, 20:13, Romans 1, I Tim. 1:9-10, I Cor. 6:9)*

*Prayer*

Dear Heavenly Father, You have created me. I am not a mistake. I am not a piece of junk. Lord, I renounce the lie that You have created me or anyone else to be homosexual, and I affirm that Your Word clearly forbids homosexual behavior. I accept myself as a child of God and declare that You created me a man (or woman). I renounce any bondages of Satan that I have perverted my relationships with others. I ask You to bring to attention all evil spirits that have gained any ground in my life. I ask You to bind them with a three-fold cord that cannot be broken in the Name of the Father, Son, and the Holy Spirit. All spirits working under the assignment of homosexuality must go where Jesus tells you to go when Jesus tells you to go. I announce that I am free to relate to the opposite sex in the way that You intended. Please release my body from all bondage of the Enemy to serve the one and true living God *(Romans 12:1-2)*. In the Name of The Lord Jesus Christ, my Creator and my Lord, Amen.

## Abortion
### (Psalm 139:13-16)

**Prayer**

Dear Heavenly Father, I confess that I have believed Satan's lies. I am so sorry I joined the Devil's rebellion against You by allowing the child that You gave me to be killed. I am so sorry that I was more concerned about what people would think of me than what they would think of You. Lord, I confess that I did not assume stewardship of the life You entrusted to me, and I ask Your forgiveness. You have promised that if we confess our sin You are faithful and just to forgive us our sin and to cleanse us from ALL unrighteousness *(I John 1:9).* I choose to accept Your forgiveness. Because You who are just have forgiven me, I choose by faith to forgive myself. I do love the child You gave to me. Please let my baby know I am so sorry. Please let my baby know that I do love him/her. I now commit that child to You for Your care in eternity. I look forward to seeing my child one day when we shall gather in Heaven around Your Throne. In the name of the Lord Jesus Christ, I pray. Amen.

## Suicidal Thoughts
### (Deut. 5:17, I Cor. 6:19-20)

**Prayer**

Dear Heavenly Father, Please forgive me for not believing Your Word. I renounce the lie that I can find peace and freedom by taking my own life. Please forgive me for being so selfish and thinking only of myself. I give my grief, pain and sorrows, and my wounds to You for You have carried them in Your body *(Isaiah 53:4-5).* Satan is a thief, and he comes to steal, kill, and destroy. Please forgive me for not believing Your truth and believing Satan's lie. I now know that if You wanted me dead, I would be, for You are life. You have the keys to Hell and death *(Rev. 1:18).* I choose life in Christ, who said He came to give me life and to give it abundantly. In the name of my Lord Jesus Christ, I pray. Amen. (See Appendix A, Case 1, pg. 249.)

## Eating Disorders or Self Mutilation
### (Psalm 139:14, I Cor. 10:20-21)

Eating disorders such as anorexia nervosa, bulimia, and or cutting oneself, self-mutilation becomes a blasphemous ritual of spiritual cleansing without the blood of Christ. Even though we may not realize the blasphemies we have been involved in by not believing God's Word, Satan joins us to his rebellion through our unbelief. Humble yourself as you go before God to ask His forgiveness.

### Prayer

Dear Heavenly Father, I renounce the lie that my worthiness is dependent upon my appearance or performance. I renounce cutting myself, purging, or defecating as a means of cleansing myself of evil, and I announce that only the blood of the Lord Jesus Christ can cleanse me from my sin. I ask You to cleanse all the ground that the Enemy has taken in my life because of my sin and disobedience. I ask You to bind all evil spirits involved in this unholy ritual of trying to cleanse my sin without You. It is You, Lord, and You alone are able to cleanse my sin. I ask the Lord to bind all evil spirits with the three-fold cord that cannot be broken in the Name of the Father, Son, and the Holy Spirit. All spirits that have found refuge in my life must go where Jesus tells you to go, when Jesus tells you to go. I renounce the lie that I am evil or that any part of my body is evil. I announce the truth that I am totally accepted by Christ just as I am. Dear Lord, release my body as a living sacrifice unto the glory and praise of the Lord Jesus Christ. Amen *(Romans 12:1-2)*.

### Substance Abuse, Drug Addiction
*(Rev. 21:8)*

The word for sorcery in the Scriptures is "pharmachia." We get our word "pharmacist" and "pharmacy" from this word. It implies the physical, behavioral, and spiritual manipulation by the use of drugs. The use of drugs for manipulating behavior is becoming involved in witchcraft, sorcery. Drugs are not evil in and of themselves. However, the placing of our trust in a drug over faith in Christ is spiritually dangerous and can have devastating effects. Addiction by definition assumes someone is "out of control." When someone is out of control, someone else is in control. Remember Spiritual Warfare is about dominion. Who is in control? Whenever you find addiction, you will find a wound. The addiction is the symptom not the cause. Even though addictions are extremely dangerous spiritually, physically, mentally, and emotionally, the hurt behind the addiction must be healed for deliverance to be possible.

*Prayer*

Dear Heavenly Father, I confess that I have misused substances (alcohol, tobacco, food, prescription or street drugs) for the purpose of pleasure, to escape reality, or to cope with difficult situations resulting in the abuse of my body, the harmful programming of my mind, and the quenching of the Holy Spirit. I have profaned my body, which is the temple of the Holy Spirit. I have been involved in witchcraft through allowing the Enemy to control my body through the use of _____. Please forgive me for believing the lies of Satan. I ask Your forgiveness, and I renounce any satanic connection or influence in my life through the misuse of chemicals or food. Thank You for carrying my grief, pain and sorrow, and all my wounds in Your body on Calvary. I cast my anxiety onto Christ who loves me, and I commit myself to no longer yield to substance abuse but to the Holy Spirit. I ask You, Heavenly Father, to fill me with Your Holy Spirit. In the name of my Lord Jesus Christ, I pray. Amen.

After you have confessed all known sin, pray:

*Prayer*

I now confess these sins to You and claim through the blood of the Lord Jesus Christ my forgiveness and cleansing. I cancel all ground that evil spirits have gained through my willful involvement in sin. I ask You to gather all wicked spirits that have found a place to work their evil in my life. I pray that You will bind them with the three-fold cord that cannot be broken, in the Name of the Father, Son, and Holy Spirit. All wicked spirits must go where Jesus tells you to go, when Jesus tells you to go. I thank You, Lord, that You are able to do exceeding, abundantly above all that I ask or think according to the power that You have invested in me through Your Holy Spirit. I ask this in the wonderful name of my Lord and Savior, Jesus Christ. Amen.

## *Divorce*
### *(Malachi 2:16)*

*Prayer*

Dear Heavenly Father, please forgive me for my disobedience in my marriage that ended in divorce. I believe Your Word when it says that You hate divorce. Please show me the ways I have been deceived by the Enemy to believe his lies instead of Your truth. Please forgive me for not believing that You are able to do exceeding abundantly above all that we ask or think according to the power that works within me.

As the Lord shows you every area of disobedience in your part of the marriage, confess it to Him.

Lord, I agree with You that I have been wrong and selfish. I am so sorry I have not believed You. Please forgive me for trying to fix my life my way. Please forgive me for not keeping my vows I made to You. I am so sorry that I have dealt treacherously with You and the mate You gave me. I ask You to cleanse my life of every vestige of hurt and bitterness. Please forgive me for being so selfish and hurting my children. I ask You to come and heal all the hurts caused by my divorce. I pray that You will take charge of my life. If it pleases You, put my marriage back together for Your glory. Please cleanse me from any working of Satan in my life as the result of my divorce. In the Name of the Lord Jesus Christ I pray, Amen.

### Prayer for Deliverance from Ancestral Curses
*(Exodus 20:5, Numbers 14:18, Jeremiah 32:18)*
(See pages 67-73)

None of us knows what works of Satan may have been passed on to him from his ancestry. Therefore it is well for every child of God to make the following "Renunciation and Affirmation." It is advisable to speak it out loud.

### Renunciation and Affirmation
*(Eph. 1:7, Col. 1:13, Gal. 2:20, Romans 6:4, Gal. 3:13, Eph. 2:5-6)*

As a child of God purchased by the blood of the Lord Jesus Christ, I here and now renounce and repudiate all the sins of my ancestors. As one who has been delivered from the power of darkness and translated into the Kingdom of God's dear Son, I cancel all demonic working that has been passed on to me from my ancestors. As one who has been crucified with Jesus Christ and raised to walk in newness of life, I cancel every curse that may have been put upon me. I announce to Satan and all his forces that Christ became a curse for me when he hung upon the Cross. As one who has been crucified and raised with Christ and now sits with Him in heavenly places, I renounce any and every way Satan may claim ownership of me. I declare myself to be eternally and completely signed over and committed to the Lord Jesus Christ. All this I do in the Name and authority of the Lord Jesus Christ.[4]

### Prayer of Deliverance for your Home or Room
*(Deuteronomy 7:26, Isaiah 1:16, 2 Cor. 7:1,*
*Psalm 51:1-2, Proverbs 3:33)*

This prayer of spiritual cleansing of a home or a room is far more than a superstitious little ritual. This is a powerful claiming of your home, your child, and all aspects of his life for God. It's standing up and proclaiming, *As for me and my house, we will serve the Lord (Joshua 24:15).* It is saying, "My home is sanctified and set apart for God's glory." One does not know what horrible sins may have been committed in the place of your home. The Enemy may have gained ground (dominion) given over to him through sin and great sorrow. Taking this ground back and giving it to its rightful ruler, the Lord Jesus Christ, is being obedient to our Lord and sharing in His authority to accomplish His will *(I John 3:8, Eph. 2:4-6).*

### Prayer

Heavenly Father, I acknowledge that You are the Lord of Heaven and earth. In Your sovereign power and love, You have given me all that I have. Every good and perfect gift comes from You. Thank You for this place to live. Thank You for this place of refuge for me and my family. I ask for Your protection from all the attacks of the Enemy. As a child of God, raised up and seated with Christ in the heavenly places, I command every evil spirit claiming ground in this place, based on the activities of past or present occupants, including me, to leave and never return.

I renounce all curses and spells directed against this place. I ask You, Heavenly Father, to post Your holy, warring angels around this place to guard it from any and all attempts of the Enemy to enter and disturb Your purposes for my family and me. I thank You Lord, for doing this in the name of the Lord Jesus Christ, Amen.

### Prayer for the Cleansing of a Child's Room

After removing and destroying all objects of false worship, pray this prayer aloud in every room if necessary:

### Prayer

Lord Jesus, I invite Your Holy Spirit to dwell in this room, which belongs to (name of child). You are Lord over heaven and earth, and I proclaim that You are Lord over this room as well. Flood it with Your light and life. Crowd out any darkness which seeks to impose itself here, and let no spirit of fear, depression, anger, doubt, anxiety, rebelliousness, or hatred (name anything you've seen manifested in your child's behavior) find any place here. I pray that nothing will come into this room that is not brought by You, Lord. If there is anything here that shouldn't be, show me so it can be taken out.

I ask that You will post Your holy guardian angels in this place. From the North and the South, from the East and the West, from above and below, I call on You to bring your protection in this place through the New Covenant in Your blood. Fill this room with Your love, peace, and joy. I pray that my child will say, as David did,

*"I will walk within my house with a perfect heart. I will set nothing wicked before my eyes" (Psalm 101:2-3).*

I pray that You, Lord, will make this room a holy place, sanctified for Your glory.

For more information concerning the spiritual cleansing of your house and property study the material in the book *Spiritual House Cleansing*, by Eddie and Alice Smith, Regal Books, 2003.

### *PRAYING FOR OUR CHILDREN*

Satan is a legalist. He brings to the battle for the control and ultimate destruction of our lives his legal right or ground to continue his evil. These rights are given to Him by the Word of God. Satan can only do what the Scriptures allow Him. The Scripture says:

*Be angry, and yet do not sin; do not let the sun go down on your anger, and do not give the Devil an opportunity (Eph. 4:26-27).*

To disobey this or any scriptural admonition is to say to Satan, "I'm giving you the legal right, the Scriptural right to destroy me."

Any area of unbelief or disobedience in our lives gives Satan and His minions the legal right to proceed to steal, kill, and destroy. The Word of God speaks of a certificate of decrees that are against us;

*Having canceled out the certificate of debt consisting of decrees against us and which was hostile to us; and He has taken it out of the way, having nailed it to the cross (Col. 2:14).*

Hallelujah, what a wonderful Savior! Oh, what He has done for you and me. As I have stated, the victory is already won for us in Christ, but the battle still rages. You will find as you pray for your children that you will have great authority as long as they are in your home and under the age of maturity. However, once they are gone to college or out of your home the battle in the prayer closet can become more intense.

Below is a contract, a legal document that I have found to be extremely effective especially as we battle for our children. Let me encourage you to get each of your children to sign this document and give it to you. When you are in the heat of the battle, pull it out. Remind Satan that you too have a legal right given to you by God and by your children to war on their behalf. It's extremely powerful.

### My Commitment to Christ
### My Prayer Covenant with my Parents

I _____ do hereby declare my holy commitment to Jesus Christ as my Lord and my Savior. As a child of God purchased by the blood of the Lord Jesus Christ, I here and now announce to Satan and all his forces that Christ became a curse for me when He hung on the cross for my sin. All my sin, past, present and future was placed upon Christ when He died on Calvary. It was on an old Roman cross where Christ paid the penalty for all my sin. When Jesus said, "It is finished", He meant that the price of my sin that God demanded was paid in full.

I do hereby give my full consent to my Guardians, Father, _____ and my Mother, _____ to battle on my behalf against the forces of darkness according to the leading of the Holy Spirit in their lives. I request for them to pray in my behalf and plead my case before the Righteous Judge of all Creation, Yahweh, God. Through the power given to them through their union with Christ Jesus, I do hereby allow them to stand in my behalf as the need would arise under the leadership of the Holy Spirit.

Because the Word of God says, *"That if two of you agree on earth about anything that they may ask, it shall be done for them by My Father who is in heaven. For where two or three have gathered together in My name, there I am in their midst" (Matt. 18:19).* I do hereby declare my faith in the Word of God by requesting them to pray on my behalf expecting our mighty Lord and Savior, Jesus Christ to hear their prayer and answer their prayer according to His sovereign will.

Signed, Sealed, and committed this day all under the authority of the Lord Jesus Christ.

Signed_____

Date_____

## PRAYING THE WORD OF GOD
## IN ENGAGING THE POWERS OF DARKNESS

The Word of God is the revelation of God. In it we have the manifestation of the presence and power of almighty God. The Scriptures claim for themselves to be "theopneustos." The word comes from two words; theo which means God and pneustos which means breath. It literally means all Scripture comes to us from the very breath of God.

*All Scripture is inspired by God and profitable for teaching, for reproof, for correction, for training in righteousness; that the man of God may be adequate, equipped for every good work (2 Timothy 3:16-17).*

The explanation of the relationship between the Word of God and God is given in the Gospel of John.

*In the beginning was the Word, and the Word was with God and the Word was God (John 1:1).*

We find these words in Hebrews as to what the Scriptures claim for themselves.

*For the word of God is living and active and sharper than any two-edged sword, and piercing as far as the division of soul and*

*spirit, of both joints and marrow, and able to judge the thoughts
and intentions of the heart (Hebrews 4:12).*

In the Scriptures and through the Scriptures we have the very presence of God. We must not separate the living Word of God from the written Word of God. Each is the living presentation of the presence and power of God. In a wonderful supernatural way God is able to use our faith by using the Scriptures as a powerful weapon of warfare. The best example we have is the way Christ Jesus used the Scriptures in *Luke 4* to resist and rebuke the Enemy. Along with the previous methods spelled out in this chapter, the Word of God can be used as a prayer to confront the powers of darkness. The following are examples of how to pray the Word of God in the battle of control over strongholds of the Enemy. These Scriptures listed here are just a sampling of how to use the Word of God in the process of spiritual cleansing. These particular scriptural passages have been found to be extremely powerful and effective in the cleansing process.

As you pray the Scriptures over a person and the battle in which they find themselves with the powers of darkness, Ask the Lord Jesus to cause the Word of God to become the sharp two-edged sword in the spirit world He promises them to be in *2 Tim. 3:16-17, John 1:1, Heb. 4:12, Eph. 6:17, Heb. 4:12, Jude, Col. 3, James 4, Psalm 35, Psalm 103.*

### Prayer

Dear Lord Jesus, I come to You as Your child. As a joint-heir with Christ Jesus, I thank You that You are able to do exceeding abundantly above all that I could ask or even think. I thank You, Lord Jesus that I am a victor not a victim. I thank You that everything that I need to be free in Christ has been made available to me through the shed blood of Calvary. I thank You, Christ Jesus that it was for freedom that You came to set me free. You came to destroy the works of the Devil. As I pray Your Word over this matter, I ask You to use Your Word as a sharp two edged sword, separating righteousness from unrighteousness, good from evil and the truth of God from the lies of the Enemy. I ask You Lord Jesus to make the evil ones hear and obey the Word of God. May what is done here today bring glory to Your holy name. May Your cleansing work cause all of the holy angels to rejoice and all the evil ones to be tormented even to the very pit of hell itself. As I pray these

Scriptures back to You, I ask Lord Jesus, that You would use them to confront, rebuke and dismantle the evil ones and their strongholds. As I pray the Word of God use each word to set this captive one free for Your glory alone.

### Jude 1

*1 Jude, a bond-servant of Jesus Christ, and brother of James,*
*To those who are the called, beloved in God the Father, and kept for Jesus Christ:*
*2 May mercy and peace and love be multiplied to you.*
*3 Beloved, while I was making every effort to write you about our common salvation, I felt the necessity to write to you appealing that you contend earnestly for the faith which was once for all delivered to the saints. 4 For certain persons have crept in unnoticed, those who were long beforehand marked out for this condemnation, ungodly persons who turn the grace of our God into licentiousness and deny our only Master and Lord, Jesus Christ.*
*5 Now I desire to remind you, though you know all things once for all, that the Lord, after saving a people out of the land of Egypt, subsequently destroyed those who did not believe. 6 And angels who did not keep their own domain, but abandoned their proper abode, He has kept in eternal bonds under darkness for the judgment of the great day. 7 Just as Sodom and Gomorrah and the cities around them, since they in the same way as these indulged in gross immorality and went after strange flesh, are exhibited as an example, in undergoing the punishment of eternal fire.*
*8 Yet in the same manner these men, also by dreaming, defile the flesh, and reject authority, and revile angelic majesties. 9 But Michael the archangel, when he disputed with the devil and argued about the body of Moses, did not dare pronounce against him a railing judgment, but said, "The Lord rebuke you." 10 But these men revile the things which they do not understand; and the things which they know by instinct, like unreasoning animals, by these things they are destroyed.*
*11 Woe to them! For they have gone the way of Cain, and for pay they have rushed headlong into the error of Balaam, and perished in the rebellion of Korah.*
*12 These men are those who are hidden reefs in your love*

*feasts when they feast with you without fear, caring for them-selves; clouds without water, carried along by winds; autumn trees without fruit, doubly dead, uprooted;* [13] *wild waves of the sea, casting up their own shame like foam; wandering stars, for whom the black darkness has been reserved forever.*

[14] *And about these also Enoch, in the seventh generation from Adam, prophesied, saying, "Behold, the Lord came with many thousands of His holy ones,* [15] *to execute judgment upon all, and to convict all the ungodly of all their ungodly deeds which they have done in an ungodly way, and of all the harsh things which ungodly sinners have spoken against Him."* [16] *These are grum-blers, finding fault, following after their own lusts; they speak arrogantly, flattering people for the sake of gaining an advantage.*

[17] *But you, beloved, ought to remember the words that were spoken beforehand by the apostles of our Lord Jesus Christ,* [18] *that they were saying to you, "In the last time there shall be mock-ers, following after their own ungodly lusts."* [19] *These are the ones who cause divisions, worldly-minded, devoid of the Spirit.*

[20] *But you, beloved, building yourselves up on your most holy faith; praying in the Holy Spirit;* [21] *keep yourselves in the love of God, waiting anxiously for the mercy of our Lord Jesus Christ to eternal life.*

[22] *And have mercy on some, who are doubting;* [23] *save others, snatching them out of the fire; and on some have mercy with fear, hating even the garment polluted by the flesh.*

[24] *Now to Him who is able to keep you from stumbling, and to make you stand in the presence of His glory blameless with great joy,* [25] *to the only God our Savior, through Jesus Christ our Lord, be glory, majesty, dominion and authority, before all time and now and forever. Amen.*

### Colossians 3

[1] *If then you have been raised up with Christ, keep seeking the things above, where Christ is, seated at the right hand of God.* [2] *Set your mind on the things above, not on the things that are on earth.* [3] *For you have died and your life is hidden with Christ in God.* [4] *When Christ, who is our life, is revealed, then you also will be revealed with Him in glory.*

*5 Therefore consider the members of your earthly body as dead to immorality, impurity, passion, evil desire, and greed, which amounts to idolatry. 6 For it is on account of these things that the wrath of God will come, 7 and in them you also once walked, when you were living in them. 8 But now you also, put them all aside: anger, wrath, malice, slander, and abusive speech from your mouth. 9 Do not lie to one another, since you laid aside the old self with its evil practices, 10 and have put on the new self who is being renewed to a true knowledge according to the image of the One who created him 11 a renewal in which there is no distinction between Greek and Jew, circumcised and uncircumcised, barbarian, Scythian, slave and freeman, but Christ is all, and in all.*

*12 And so, as those who have been chosen of God, holy and beloved, put on a heart of compassion, kindness, humility, gentleness and patience; 13 bearing with one another, and forgiving each other, whoever has a complaint against anyone; just as the Lord forgave you, so also should you. 14 And beyond all these things put on love, which is the perfect bond of unity.*

*15 And let the peace of Christ rule in your hearts, to which indeed you were called in one body; and be thankful. 16 Let the word of Christ richly dwell within you, with all wisdom teaching and admonishing one another with psalms and hymns and spiritual songs, singing with thankfulness in your hearts to God. 17 And whatever you do in word or deed, do all in the name of the Lord Jesus, giving thanks through Him to God the Father.*

*18 Wives, be subject to your husbands, as is fitting in the Lord. 19 Husbands, love your wives, and do not be embittered against them.*

*20 Children, be obedient to your parents in all things, for this is well-pleasing to the Lord.*

*21 Fathers, do not exasperate your children, that they may not lose heart.*

*22 Slaves, in all things obey those who are your masters on earth, not with external service, as those who merely please men, but with sincerity of heart, fearing the Lord. 23 Whatever you do, do your work heartily, as for the Lord rather than for men; 24 knowing that from the Lord you will receive the reward of the inheritance. It is the Lord Christ whom you serve.* [25] *For he who does wrong will receive the consequences of the wrong which he has done, and that without partiality.*

### James 4

[1] *What is the source of quarrels and conflicts among you? Is not the source your pleasures that wage war in your members?*

[2] *You lust and do not have; so you commit murder. And you are envious and cannot obtain; so you fight and quarrel. You do not have because you do not ask.* [3] *You ask and do not receive, because you ask with wrong motives, so that you may spend it on your pleasures.*

[4] *You adulteresses, do you not know that friendship with the world is hostility toward God? Therefore whoever wishes to be a friend of the world makes himself an enemy of God.* [5] *Or do you think that the Scripture speaks to no purpose: "He jealously desires the Spirit which He has made to dwell in us"?* [6] *But He gives a greater grace. Therefore it says, "GOD IS OPPOSED TO THE PROUD, BUT GIVES GRACE TO THE HUMBLE."*

[7] *Submit therefore to God. Resist the devil and he will flee from you.* [8] *Draw near to God and He will draw near to you. Cleanse your hands, you sinners; and purify your hearts, you double-minded.* [9] *Be miserable and mourn and weep; let your laughter be turned into mourning, and your joy to gloom.* [10] *Humble yourselves in the presence of the Lord, and He will exalt you.*

[11] *Do not speak against one another, brethren. He who speaks against a brother, or judges his brother, speaks against the law, and judges the law; but if you judge the law, you are not a doer of the law, but a judge of it.* [12] *There is only one Lawgiver and Judge, the One who is able to save and to destroy; but who are you who judge your neighbor?*

[13] *Come now, you who say, "Today or tomorrow, we shall go to such and such a city, and spend a year there and engage in business and make a profit."* [14] *Yet you do not know what your life will be like tomorrow. You are just a vapor that appears for a little while and then vanishes away.* [15] *Instead, you ought to say, "If the Lord wills, we shall live and also do this or that."*

*16 But as it is, you boast in your arrogance; all such boasting is evil. 17 Therefore, to one who knows the right thing to do, and does not do it, to him it is sin.*

## Psalm 35

*1 Contend, O LORD, with those who contend with me; Fight against those who fight against me.*

*2 Take hold of buckler and shield, And rise up for my help.*

*3 Draw also the spear and the battle-axe to meet those who pursue me; Say to my soul, "I am your salvation."*

*4 Let those be ashamed and dishonored who seek my life; Let those be turned back and humiliated who devise evil against me.*

*5 Let them be like chaff before the wind, With the angel of the LORD driving them on.*

*6 Let their way be dark and slippery, With the angel of the LORD pursuing them.*

*7 For without cause they hid their net for me; Without cause they dug a pit for my soul.*

*8 Let destruction come upon him unawares; And let the net which he hid catch himself; Into that very destruction let him fall.*

*9 And my soul shall rejoice in the LORD; It shall exult in His salvation.*

*10 All my bones will say, "LORD, who is like Thee, Who delivers the afflicted from him who is too strong for him, And the afflicted and the needy from him who robs him?"*

*11 Malicious witnesses rise up; They ask me of things that I do not know.*

*12 They repay me evil for good, To the bereavement of my soul.*

*13 But as for me, when they were sick, my clothing was sackcloth; I humbled my soul with fasting; And my prayer kept returning to my bosom.*

*14 I went about as though it were my friend or brother; I bowed down mourning, as one who sorrows for a mother.*

*15 But at my stumbling they rejoiced, and gathered themselves together; The smiters whom I did not know gathered together against me, They slandered me without ceasing.*

*16 Like godless jesters at a feast, They gnashed at me with their teeth.*

*17 Lord, how long wilt Thou look on? Rescue my soul from their ravages, My only life from the lions.*

*18 I will give Thee thanks in the great congregation; I will praise Thee among a mighty throng.*

*19 Do not let those who are wrongfully my enemies rejoice over me; Neither let those who hate me without cause wink maliciously.*

*20 For they do not speak peace, But they devise deceitful words against those who are quiet in the land.*

*21 And they opened their mouth wide against me; They said, "Aha, aha, our eyes have seen it!"*

*22 Thou hast seen it, O LORD, do not keep silent; O Lord, do not be far from me.*

*23 Stir up Thyself, and awake to my right, And to my cause, my God and my Lord.*

*24 Judge me, O LORD my God, according to Thy righteousness; And do not let them rejoice over me.*

*25 Do not let them say in their heart, "Aha, our desire!" Do not let them say, "We have swallowed him up!"*

*26 Let those be ashamed and humiliated altogether who rejoice at my distress; Let those be clothed with shame and dishonor who magnify themselves over me.*

*27 Let them shout for joy and rejoice, who favor my vindication; And let them say continually, "The LORD be magnified, Who delights in the prosperity of His servant."*

*28 And my tongue shall declare Thy righteousness And Thy praise all day long.*

### Psalm 103

*1 Bless the LORD, O my soul; And all that is within me, bless His holy name.*

*2 Bless the LORD, O my soul, And forget none of His benefits;*

*3 Who pardons all your iniquities; Who heals all your diseases;*

*4 Who redeems your life from the pit; Who crowns you with lovingkindness and compassion;*

*5 Who satisfies your years with good things, So that your youth is renewed like the eagle.*

*6 The LORD performs righteous deeds, And judgments for all who are oppressed.*

*7 He made known His ways to Moses, His acts to the sons of Israel.*

*8 The LORD is compassionate and gracious, Slow to anger and abounding in lovingkindness.*

*9 He will not always strive with us; Nor will He keep His anger forever.*

*10 He has not dealt with us according to our sins, Nor rewarded us according to our iniquities.*

*11 For as high as the heavens are above the earth, So great is His lovingkindness toward those who fear Him.*

*12 As far as the east is from the west, So far has He removed our transgressions from us.*

*13 Just as a father has compassion on his children, So the LORD has compassion on those who fear Him.*

*14 For He Himself knows our frame; He is mindful that we are but dust.*

*15 As for man, his days are like grass; As a flower of the field, so he flourishes.*

*16 When the wind has passed over it, it is no more; And its place acknowledges it no longer.*

*17 But the lovingkindness of the LORD is from everlasting to everlasting on those who fear Him, And His righteousness to children's children,*

*18 To those who keep His covenant, And who remember His precepts to do them.*

*19 The LORD has established His throne in the heavens; And His sovereignty rules over all.*

*20 Bless the LORD, you His angels, Mighty in strength, who perform His word, Obeying the voice of His word!*

*21 Bless the LORD, all you His hosts, You who serve Him, doing His will.*

*22 Bless the LORD, all you works of His, In all places of His dominion; Bless the LORD, O my soul!*

## *Prayer of Deliverance from Mammon and its False Religious System of Christian Materialism*

Much of the Christian world in America has been seduced by a strategically crafted deception of the Evil One called Christian Materialism. It is a compromised religious system that leaves the believer powerless in the supernatural war with the powers of darkness. Christian Materialism attempts to give religious justification for our selfish desires to possess and use those possessions for the purpose of illicit personal power and control. In its essence, it is a toxic brew of worldly philosophies and practices mixed with religious traditions and Christian-like verbiage for the purpose of making it acceptable to its vulnerable carnal target. It is a carefully crafted cover for the invasion of a false god called Mammon. This chief demon seeks to bring us into spiritual bondage through the offering of this alluring false religious system as a substitute for our worship of the Lord Jesus Christ.

As in any false religious system, Christian Materialism looks good, it sounds good, and of course it feels good. However, when it's covering of religious traditions and ecclesiastical rituals are removed, we find a deadly demonic scheme whose purpose is to steal, kill and destroy. The only way to clearly recognize the Enemy's deceptions is when we measure them by God's truth revealed to us in His Word.

One of the false tenets of Christian Materialism is ***God wants you to have money. Therefore the possession of money is a sign of God's favor and blessing.*** Of course money may be an indicator of God's blessings, but not always. Why would God, who is wise and good, give riches to someone who was not spiritually mature enough to honor Him with those riches *(Luke 16:10-13)*?

We can observe the influence of this false religious system in many church practices. One such practice is the choosing of leaders on the basis of their worldly possessions. The Bible warns us about this dangerous practice. Jesus said in *Matt. 23, vs. 10-12, "And do not be called leaders; for One is your Leader, that is Christ. But the greatest among you shall be your servant. And who ever exalts himself shall be humbled; and whoever humbles himself shall be exalted."* Instead of looking to those who might help finance our selfish agendas, we should be looking first and foremost to those whose lives manifest the Spirit of Christ with a humble servants' heart for positions of leadership. Jesus said of Himself, *"...the Son of Man did not come to be served, but to serve,..." (Matt. 20:28).* Many a pastor's spiritual integrity has been compromised because they have embraced at some level the crafty deception of Christian Materialism. Instead of shepherds, Jesus calls them hirelings *(John 10:12-13)*.

Does not the stark contrast of the scriptural record speak clearly of the incompatibility between true Christianity and materialism? There is a constant warning throughout the Bible concerning putting our trust in riches for temporal and selfish purposes *(Prov. 30:8, Matt. 6:21, James 5:1-6)*. Jesus called riches deceitful *(Matt. 13:22)*. We must always be reminded that the one we call the "rich young ruler" wanted eternal life but never received it because He could not obey the Lord with regard to his great riches *(Luke 18:18-25)*. The Christ of Calvary we have decided to follow was a man of virtually no worldly possessions. Jesus had no place to lay His head *(Matt. 8:20)*. He was buried in a borrowed tomb. He said of His ministry that the Spirit of God had anointed Him to preach the gospel to the poor *(Luke 4:18)*. Peter had neither silver nor gold *(Acts 3:6)*. Paul, as an itinerant evangelist, lived in places he did not own. Today he might even be considered homeless. By the criterion of Christian Materialism, Christ, Peter and Paul would be disqualified for leadership in many churches today. The Bible also gives a clear warning concerning such prejudice with regard to the favoring of the wealthy over the poor in the church *(James 2:1-5)*. As a counterfeit dollar is rarely recognized except by those familiar with the authentic dollar, this counterfeit religious system of the Enemy can only be exposed through the authentic truth of God's Word.

It is also critically important to ask, "Where does the money come from?" Some chosen for leadership in the church today have and are receiving their riches by disregarding and disobeying God's Word. In Christian Materialism the end justifies the means. It doesn't matter how you get money. Since "God is all about you having money," just get it. Selfish gambling practices, crooked and corrupt business deals, and some have even received their wealth through the sorrow and pain of the neglected and vulnerable *(2 Tim. 3:6-9)*. Even in the face of the teaching of Scripture concerning the prohibition of usury practices among those in the family of God *(Deut. 23:19-20)*, many churches have chosen their leaders among the ranks of the scripturally disobedient. You see if the money (or anything else we possess), has been received from a wicked or ungodly source, or through the disobeying and disregarding of God's Word *(2 Tim. 3:6-9, Deut. 23:19-20)*, it may have unholy and demonic attachments to it for the purpose of stealing God's glory. In such case it must be spiritually cleaned up through prayer and repentance while dedicating it to the glory of the Lord Jesus Christ alone or it may need to be discarded *(2 Cor. 6:14-18, Acts 19:18-19).*

Another false tenet of Christian Materialism is ***prosperity is the result of the abundance of money and worldly possessions***. "But Rob," you ask, "Don't the Scriptures teach prosperity?" Of course they do! In *3 John vs. 2 we read, "Beloved, I pray that in all respects you may prosper and be in good health, just as your soul prospers."* Here is the problem. We have allowed our worldly environment instead of Scripture to falsely define prosperity. There are 11 words in the Bible that are translated prosper or prosperity. Not one, that's right, not one is necessarily related to money. These words given to us by the Holy Spirit translated prosperity mean to go on well without hindrance. Prosperity means to go in peace.

You may be asking, "Are you saying that money is evil?" Absolutely not! It is not money that is evil. ***For the love- the worship of money*** *is a root of all kinds of evil, and some by longing for it have wandered away from the faith, and pierced themselves with many a pang (I Tim. 6:10).* The question is not whether or not we possess money. The question is better asked, "Does money possess us?" What is our attitude, the condition of our heart concerning money? Some of the most selfish people I have ever known were those without money. And some of the most spiritually poor people I have ever known had great worldly wealth. On the other hand, some of the most spiritually rich people I have ever known had great wealth, and because of their commitment to Christ their wealth could not possess them. Is it the desire of your heart to honor the Lord Jesus in the handling of whatever He has given you? If not, there is a spiritual rat in the wood pile. *And whatever you do in word or deed, do all in the name of the Lord Jesus, giving thanks through Him to God the Father (Col. 3:17).*

True Christian stewardship comes down to ownership and gratitude. It is Christ who is Lord of ALL *(John 3:31, Eph. 1:20-22, Phil. 2:9-11).* Everything belongs to Him. *The earth is the Lord's and all it contains, the world, and those who dwell in it (Psalm 24:1).* He is Jehovah Jireh - Our Provider. He is the God of our provision. It is His nature to provide for His own *(Matt. 7:9-11, Phil. 4:19).*

*Blessed be the God and Father of our Lord Jesus Christ, who has blessed us with every spiritual blessing in the heavenly places in Christ (Eph. 1:3).*

And in *James 1:17* we are told, *"Every good thing bestowed and every perfect gift is from above, coming down from the Father of lights, with whom there is no variation, or shifting shadow."*

As the Heavenly Father allows us to share in His provision, it is to be used in gratitude and glory to Him. Do you see it? ALL THINGS exist for God's glory alone *(Col. 1:16)*. When we allow anything or anyone other than our Lord Jesus Christ to receive the glory for what He has done and for which He alone deserves, we become accomplices in Satan's rebellion. Here is what all of us must face hopefully sooner rather than later. We can't have it both ways. No matter what we have been taught through the false religious system of Christian Materialism, no one has ever been or will ever be able to serve God and Mammon - Riches *(Matt. 6:24)*. When the two are bundled together by the strands of false religious practices the result becomes a convoluted contaminated counterfeit used by the Enemy.

We're not off the hook just because Christian Materialism is a crafty deception. Each of us must look carefully at any area where we might have believed the lies of the Enemy rather than the truth of God's Word. Our very freedom in Christ is at stake. No matter how many times we say it or how hard our flesh wants to believe it, God will not contradict His Word. Remember, all the Enemy needs to invade the church and bring his evil corruption upon her is our disobedience to the Word of God. In the practice of Christian Materialism one will discover an absence of the manifestation of God's power which always results in spiritual defeat.

The following prayer is a prayer of confession and repentance concerning any unbiblical relationship to Mammon and the practice of Christian Materialism that has or/is being used of the Enemy in your life.

## RENUNCIATION of MAMMON
## And any Involvement in the
## False Religious System of Christian Materialism

A Declaration of my commitment to Christ as my Provider
*(Phil. 4:19, Rom. 8:17, Matt. 6:19-21, 25-34,*
*7:9-11, 13:22, James 5:1, Prov.30:8)*

## *Prayer*

As a child of God purchased by the blood of the Lord Jesus Christ, **I hereby renounce** any claim Satan and all His forces may claim ownership of me with regard to my finances. I come before my Heavenly Father through the shed blood of Calvary to ask forgiveness and repent of my disobedience and unbelief.

**I repent** that I have exchanged the value of the Kingdom of Heaven for the desires of my heart. I repent for laying up treasures on earth *(Matt. 6:19-21)*.

**I repent** for loving money, for serving riches, for my greed and covetousness *(I Tim. 6:10)*.

**I repent** for making money my defender, security and protection *(Matt. 13:22)*.

**I repent** for believing that chants, spells, fate, superstition and luck will provide the money I need *(Deut. 18:10-12)*.

**I repent** for the dishonest ways I have gained wealth. *(Gal. 5:19-21, Eph. 2:2-3)*.

**I repent** for seeking, accepting, treasuring or profiting from money received from the sorrow and pain of others *(2 Tim. 3:6-9)*.

**I repent** for my robbing God by the withholding of His tithes and my offerings *(Malachi 3:8-11)*.

**I repent** for not feeding the poor nor taking care of the widows and orphans *(James 1:27)*.

**I repent** for my critical spirit concerning the supporting of missionary and evangelistic ministries *(3 John)*.

**I repent** for any and all the ways I have allowed myself to worship at the false altar of Mammon. I ask the Lord Jesus to break all ties to Mammon either as a result of my disobedience or that which has been assigned to me as the result of my ancestors disobedience *(Matt. 6:24)*. (See Chapter 2, pgs 67-73)

**I hereby affirm** that My Creator and Heavenly Father is my provider. I receive all that God has for me through my inheritance as a joint-heir with His Son, Christ Jesus. I asked the Holy Spirit to help me see money from God's eyes. Help me worship our Heavenly Father for every financial need He meets according to His riches in glory by Christ Jesus. Only give me that which brings glory and honor to You, Lord Jesus.

Name_____ Date_____

# CASTING OUT DEMONS
## A Suggested Procedure

The following suggested procedure in the ministry of deliverance is taken from *The Deliverance Ministry* by George A. Birch, Horizon Publications, Camp Hill, PN, 1988. George and Grace Birch became involved in the ministry of deliverance while serving as missionaries in China and Borneo under the China Inland Mission/Overseas Missionary Fellowship. Later in their retirement years in White Rock, British Columbia, Canada, they led hundreds of people out of spiritual bondage to victory in Christ.

"The suggested procedure for casting out demons in the Name of the Lord Jesus Christ is not a ritual and should not be regarded as being the only way. In sharing this method Grace and I trust that not only will you find it helpful and easy to follow, but that you will also look to the Holy Spirit to guide you in adapting it to your particular circumstances."

The Lord will lead in all matters of deliverance. This is His work. You will find you are the assistant nurse in the service of the master surgeon. Deliverance is not about you. Deliverance is not about the Devil. Deliverance is about the Lord Jesus Christ.

### *Prerequisites for Involvement*

The authority our Lord Jesus gave to the seventy disciples in *Luke 10:19* was not confined to a few select persons, but is available to every born-again child of God with the following qualifications:

1. A firm assurance of his own eternal salvation in Christ Jesus *(John 10:27-30)*.

2. Faith in God to move "mountains" *(Mark 11:22-24, 16:17)*.

3. A good knowledge of the Word of God *(Hebrews 4:12)*.

4. A recognition that Satan has already been defeated by Christ *(Col. 2:13-15, Heb. 2:14)*.

5.  A humble dependence on and trust in God. Pride brings defeat *(Prov. 3:5-7).*

If possible, it would be well to be associated with a well-qualified leader in this ministry before taking the lead if one is a novice. However, any believing Christian need not fear to confront the Enemy if the circumstances call for it.

### *Making the Appointment*

Often someone will phone and say, "I have a friend who I think needs deliverance. He has asked me to make an appointment for him." I will explain to such a caller that we always insist that the counselee make his own appointment. In this way he takes responsibility and cannot say afterward that he went along just to please someone. The phone call also offers an important introduction to the future counselee.

1.  He will state why he is calling or I will ask why he thinks he needs deliverance.

2.  I will ask what the main problems are and will write these down along with the caller's name, address and phone number.

3.  I will ask if he is a Christian and when he received Christ.

4.  I will quote some encouraging Scripture and have prayer together over the phone.

5.  I will assign him Scripture to read and a verse to memorize.

6.  I will tell him that there are two conditions for deliverance: a full submission to God *(James 4:7),* a willingness to deal thoroughly with sin *(James 4:8).*

7.  If he is a Christian, I will assure him that the Lord does have deliverance and freedom for him.

8.  We will set up a date and time for an appointment. This call serves as a preliminary session and is often a great comfort to

the afflicted one and will cause him to come to the first appointment with great hope of deliverance.

## THE PREPARATION

My wife and I work together in the counseling ministry. She is the secretary and keeps a record when we deal with demons. I make a list of problems and sins and she records the names of the demons as they are given and records their responses to the commands given, with their words in quotes.

## THE PROCEDURE

We try to limit each session to about three hours. It is important that you as the leader be in control of the time scheduled and that neither the spirits nor the counselee be allowed to unnecessarily prolong the session. A second appointment would be preferable.

1. First, get acquainted briefly.

2. Have prayer, committing the time to God and asking His guidance and protection.

3. Read *John 10:1-18, 27-30* or another appropriate portion, asking each one present to share in the reading and afterward to choose a verse or two from the portion and give a brief meaning of the verses. This reveals the spiritual state of the counselee.

4. If the counselee is not a Christian, lead him to make a personal commitment to Christ.

5. Have a round of prayer, thanking God for His truth contained in the verses shared.

6. Now ask the counselee to share his problems. Make a list of these beginning with childhood to the present, listing traumatic experiences, spiritual, emotional and physical problems.

7. Now read and explain *James 4:7-10*. Point out that there are two conditions to obtaining deliverance: <u>First, we must submit to God</u> (link to *Romans 12:1-2*). I ask the counselee if this is what he wants for his life. If so, I ask him to give his whole life to God in prayer, prepared to follow Christ as Lord, renouncing the world and being renewed in his mind by the work of the Holy Spirit through the Word. The <u>Second condition is that sin must be dealt with</u>, including all sin in thought and deed. Sin spoils our fellowship with God and gives ground in our lives to demons if not dealt with *(Eph. 4:26-27)*. We must take the ground away from Satan.

8. Now read *James 5:13-16* and explain that we do not believe in the Roman Catholic confessional. We have no authority to forgive sin, but that it is essential that all sin must be brought to the light of God's presence and confessed and cleansed away through the blood of Christ. This removes the barrier between God and us and it takes all the ground held by Satan away from him. If the counselee wants us to stand with him in getting free from Satan, we need to know what ground Satan has held in his life.

   We assure the counselee that we keep complete confidence with him and do not sit in judgment on him for we too are sinners saved by grace.

9. If the person is willing to thoroughly deal with all past sin, then read *Galatians 5:19-21* and ask the counselee if he has been involved in any of the sins listed in this passage. Include sexual sins, occult practices and sins to do with interpersonal relationships.

   It is very important for the counselee to see himself objectively and to judge his behavior in the light of God's Word. Some people tend to excuse themselves and to blame their circumstances and others for their sins, adding it to the list of problems already noted. This list is very important because it indicates the areas into which the door has been opened for invasion by the Enemy. In connection with the occult read *Deuteronomy 18:9-15*.

   Now the counselor goes over the list and marks everything which from his knowledge and experience would indicate the possibility of bondage.

10. Read *I John 1:5-9* and have the counselee choose a couple of verses from this portion and explain their meaning. Ask him if he really believes that when he confesses his sin God forgives him. Note verse 9 and ask, "How can God be righteous and just and still forgive our sins?" The answer is that God can forgive us and still be just because Christ Jesus bore all our sins on the cross. The counselee can therefore confess his sins with confidence that the price has been paid and that full forgiveness is for him in Christ.

I suggest that everyone kneel for it indicates humility and a total dependence on God. Instruct the counselee, "I will pray for you first, then you pray to our Heavenly Father, in the Name of our Lord Jesus Christ. You take this list and confess each item as sins and ask for forgiveness. Then you can thank God that you are forgiven and that all your sins have been cleansed through the blood of Christ Jesus." Now ask another person who may be present to pray, giving thanks to God.

11. Then comes the actual confrontation with the demons. Lead the counselee to declare, "I claim the full victory my Lord Jesus Christ won on the cross for me, *having disarmed the powers and authorities, He made a public spectacle of them, triumphing over them by the Cross (Col. 2:15,* NIV*).* His victory for me is my victory. In the Name of the Lord Jesus Christ I cancel all agreement my ancestors or I ever made with Satan. I withdraw all ground Satan ever held in me. I want all demons out of me. I belong; spirit, soul, and body, to the Lord Jesus Christ who purchased me with His precious blood."

The counselor should read *Luke 10:17-21*, explaining that this is a joyful, victorious ministry and there is no place for dread or fear *(vs. 17)*. Also, Satan's defeat is sure and believers have the authority, given by the Lord Jesus Christ, over all the power of the Enemy *(vs. 18-19)*. We are to be looking up, for our names are written in Heaven where Christ is seated at God's right hand far above all principalities and powers and God has put all things under His feet. *(vs. 20)* Since all this is true (we are in Christ, the enemies are under our feet and our Lord has given us the authority to tread on them) then they are defeated. Be Christ-centered, not demon-centered.

Then explain to the counselee: "First, I will make some positive statements about you that you are God's child and you have eternal life, etc. Then I will command the demons to give their names. When I do that, command with me, and at the same time listen for the names. They will come to your mind just like a thought. All you have to do is to speak them out, relaying the answers of the demons to our commands. You will be tempted to think that these are your thoughts but I can assure you that they will not be. You do not need to analyze or screen these responses in any way. I want you just to relay whatever comes to your mind when I say, 'We command in the Name of our Lord Jesus Christ,' the demons to do with the problem indicated will have to respond. Now remember that you are in this battle and you are actively engaged in commanding with us in the Name of our Lord Jesus Christ and the demons must obey."

Explain about the names used by demons. Some give names of people such as "John or Mary." Others will give names of characteristics such as "Hatred," "Anger," or "Depression" etc. Some will use Bible names; perhaps even "Jesus" but that would be a "Jesus" of Satan, not the Lord Jesus Christ. You may think the names sound silly or irrelevant, but they should be relayed without delay and should not be screened. The demons may try to deceive by giving names of demons which have already been cast out, but this is up to the counselor to determine. The names must be relayed without comment or transpositions of any kind. There may also be multiple names in each area and all must be named. The counselee may at a point say, "There aren't any more," but that may be a demon speaking and should be confronted by a command to give its name. We use a signal. If the counselor is getting no responses through the counselee after commanding several times, he may hold up his hand; and if the counselee is conscious that all is quiet and no inner commotion is present, he will return the signal to indicate that.

In prayer, ask the Heavenly Father to lead this battle, through the Lord Jesus Christ, just as Joshua took orders from Christ as He appeared to him as the Captain of the Host of Jehovah before the fall of Jericho *(Josh. 5:13, 6:20)*.

12. Declare aloud: "We are a company of God's children (naming all present). We have been redeemed through the blood of Christ and born of the Holy Spirit into God's family. Our position is seated

with Christ Jesus in heavenly places. God has put all things under Christ's feet, and so they are under ours as we abide in Christ. Our Lord Jesus has given us authority to tread upon serpents and scorpions and over all the power of the Enemy *(Rev. 9)*. We come against you enemies in the Name and the authority of our Lord Jesus Christ and we claim the protection of our Lord that nothing shall injure us."

13.  Then confront the spirits by saying: "In the Name of the Lord Jesus Christ, We bind the strong man, Satan, that he may not interfere in any way. No demons may enter (name of counselee). There is to be one-way traffic only, out and to the pit (Abyss). When commanded, the demons must come forward, speak clearly and tell the truth with no profanity or unclean speech, shouting or screaming. We forbid you demons to control any part of (name of counselee) body or mind or to speak directly through his mouth. You must convey your answers to his mind."

14.  Now deal with the demons directly, maintaining eye contact with the counselee. When the demons are present in a person, they look out of the eyes.

First, make some positive statements about the counselee "(Name of counselee) is God's child. He was chosen in Christ before the foundation of the world. He has heard the voice of the Good Shepherd and has followed Him. He has been given eternal life and will never perish. No one can pluck him out of Christ's hand or out of the Father's hand." Other statements concerning the Christian's position and inheritance may be given. They are a blow to the Enemy and an encouragement to the counselee.

Secondly, command, in the Name of the Lord Jesus Christ, the demons connected with the first problem on the list. You may use such words as: "In the Name of the Lord Jesus Christ we command, if there are demons of fear in (name of counselee), you come forward and give your names."

The counselee usually gets a name or names right away and will repeat the name(s). However, sometimes it takes a while, especially for the first name, and it is necessary to keep on repeating the command.

If there is still no response after a number of commands, then you should read and share from the Word of God and have a round of prayer. Also you may find it helpful to have the counselee repeat the following statements: "I am a child of God. I've been redeemed by the blood of Christ and born of the Holy Spirit. You enemies are under our authority in Christ Jesus and you have to give your names."

As each name is given say, "We bind you (name of demon) in the Name of the Lord Jesus Christ until we send you to the pit (Abyss)."

Command a demon to tell only what can be used against him. We do not consult spirits or carry on frivolous or unnecessary conversations with them as that borders on the occult. After getting a number of names, you may command one to tell, "What is your work that Satan sent you to do in (Name of Counselee)?" or "When did you enter into (Name of Counselee)?" This information is sometimes very enlightening. Command the demons to speak in sentences as this makes it very clear to all that we are dealing with a personality, an evil spirit, not the counselee.

After getting four to six names, you will want to command them out of the person. Have everyone present, including the counselee, repeat the following command, "In the Name of the Lord Jesus Christ, we command you (repeat the names of the demons) to come out of (name of counselee) and go to the pit (Abyss) right now."

It is important that the counselee repeat each word. If he is having difficulty, command the Enemy to release him right now, then have him repeat the whole command word for word. Now praise the Lord that these demons are gone.

It is well at this point to forget the demons for the time and to draw near to God by reading a chapter or so of God's Word, choosing a verse or two and sharing concerning it.

Then continue to command the demons, checking back to the former problem area each time. You may say, "In the Name of the Lord Jesus Christ we command you (names of demons) and all your associated, come out of (name of counselee) and go to the pit (Abyss) right now." This assures that that area is clean before going on to the next.

You may wish to group associated sins together, such as

depression and suicide, anger, bitterness and rebellion, transcendental mediation and (mystical) yoga, etc. Sometimes the Lord will give you discernment and it may not be necessary to take time to get the names. A command such as the following may bring freedom in that area: "In the Name of the Lord Jesus Christ, we command all demons in (name of counselee) to do with (name each sin in a given area), come out of him and go to the pit (Abyss) right now, in the Name of the Lord Jesus Christ."

15. Read *John 2:13-16*. This describes how Christ cleansed the temple in Jerusalem. Explain that there is no longer a temple of God in Jerusalem, but that the Church is the temple of God and every individual believer is a temple of the Holy Spirit and that today through this process he is cleansing the temple of the counselee's body.

When you believe that all the ground has been covered, make the following last command: "All of you demons defiling this temple have to go, not one of you can stay. If there are any demons who didn't go when commanded or any with whom we did not deal, we command you now, in the Name of the Lord Jesus Christ, give your names." Sometimes a few remain. Command them out, including all who may be hiding in any part of the body.

We then instruct the counselee to put on the whole armor of God, to appropriate the almighty power of God and to stand firm against all the fiery darts of the Enemy. We encourage them to memorize Scripture, to read God's Word daily, to affirm the truth of God's Word in their lives, to claim the promises and to trust and obey the Lord. Whenever there is failure, confess it at once to God and keep walking in victory. If any demons still trouble, the counselee should be able to deal with them in the Name and authority of the Lord Jesus Christ.[5]

## The Song of Deliverance
### Psalm 32:7

*The son, the sheep, the coin, all are gone;*
*The father prays through his tears, there is no song.*

*Instead of the song, the silence of sadness rings;*
*My son is lost there is no reason to sing.*

*The darkness of sorrow overwhelms the loving heart;*
*Heaven awaits to sing, joy and gladness depart.*

*The Father waits for the one lost in sin;*
*All is ready, the robe, the fatted calf, the ring.*

*The song will change from sadness to glad;*
*When the son is found, who once was dead.*

*The Song of Deliverance begins,*
*All citizens of Heaven join in its sound;*
*This, my Son was lost but now is found.    RWR II*

For more information concerning prayers for deliverance, study Neil Anderson's "Seven Steps to Freedom." These steps and prayers are found in his work on deliverance entitled, *The Bondage Breaker,* Harvest House, Eugene, OR, 1993. Also Mark I. Bubeck's work on deliverance entitled, *The Adversary,* Moody Press, Chicago, Ill, 1975, is a wonderful resource in praying for deliverance. Jim Logan's book entitled *Reclaiming Surrendered Ground,* Moody Press, Chicago, Ill. 1995, is a must in any study of deliverance. For many years Jim has taught these spiritual truths and helped many hundreds and thousands of God's people find freedom in Christ through the International Center for Biblical Counseling in Sioux City, Iowa. Jim's work was used of God in my life at the moment I needed God's truth the most. I will forever be grateful for these wonderful dedicated men of God who have allowed the Lord to use them to set the captives free.

(For further studies in Deliverance see Appendix A:
*Case Studies from America's Heartland, pg. 249*)

## Chapter 7

# Revival and the Invisible War

*"How, then, should the Lord's praying ones pray at the present time (for revival)? They should pray:*
• *Against evil spirits now blocking and hindering Revival.*
• *For the cleansing and delivering of those who became possessed through deception during the time of later Revivals.*
• *That when Revival is once more given it may be kept pure.*
• *For the preparation of instruments for Revival, trained and taught of God to guard against further inroads of the powers of darkness."*
*— Evan Roberts*

*Restore us, O God of our salvation, and cause Thine indignation toward us to cease. Wilt Thou prolong Thine anger to all generations? Wilt Thou not Thyself revive us again, That thy people may rejoice in Thee (Psalm 85:6)?*

What is revival? What do you think of when you hear the word revival? A pizza party for youth, a hotdog supper for children, a brush arbor, or maybe an old gospel tent with the smell of sawdust in the air is what comes to mind. In 1983, at Billy Graham's International Conference for Itinerant Evangelists in Amsterdam, Holland, I had the blessed privilege of meeting one of God's great servants. Dr. J. Edwin Orr was not only Dr. Graham's mentor and personal counselor, but Dr. Orr was one of the world's great students and professors on revival and spiritual awakening. For many years Dr. Orr not only held crusades and revival meetings around the world, but he also was a faithful professor at Fuller Theological Seminary teaching the history of revival movements and spiritual awakening. When we met, he learned I was a Southern Baptist Evangelist. At that moment he said, "Young Randall, the biggest mistake Southern Baptists have ever made is calling their evangelistic meetings revivals."

For many years I have pondered these words of the great evangelist. I have come to understand that there is much truth to his statement. You see, every time we have a meeting and call it revival and true revival doesn't come, we have helped confuse the next generation of believers. We now have a generation of young people who are beginning to have their children who have never known real God-breathed, heaven-sent, community changing, Christ exalting revival.

As I was praying with a pastor in our town about the revival meeting he had asked me to lead. He said, "Rob, before we pray; what are we praying for? I've grown up in a Baptist church. I've served the church as a deacon and now as pastor. I've been to many meetings through my life. But I don't think I've ever seen a real revival. What are we praying for?" Bro. Jerry was more honest than most of us are willing to be. You who are reading this book have probably never been a part of real revival. What is revival?

*If My People which are called by my name shall humble themselves and pray, and seek My face and turn from their wicked ways, then will I hear from heaven, will forgive their sin, and will heal their land (II Chron. 7:14, KJV).*

We usually interpret this passage as a prayer to fix the problems we see in Washington D.C. and local school boards. Remember, text without context can be pretext. The verse prior to this classic verse used for revival says:

*If I shut up the heavens so that there is no rain, or if I command the locust to devour the land, or if I send pestilence among My people (II Chron. 7:13).*

Revival is the promise of the cleansing of the land through rain.

Revival is the promise of rain. Revival is to the church what rain is to a crop. Revival is to a life what rain is to a flower. Those who have been around farm life at all will confer that it doesn't matter how hard you work in the field. You can plant the seed, till the soil and fertilize the plants. If it doesn't rain, there will be no crops, no harvest. All we do in the church, however noble, however faithful, if we do not have revival there will be no spiritual harvest.

As beautiful as this imagery is, it is not mine. All through the Word of God, the presence of God and his working in our lives is seen as water:

*But whoever drinks of the water that I shall give him shall never thirst; but the water that I shall give him shall become in him a well of water springing up to eternal life (John 4:14).*

In the final words of God inviting men to life in Christ, we read these precious words:

*And the Spirit and the Bride say, "Come." And let the one who hears say, "Come." And let the one who is thirsty come; let the one who wishes take the water of life without cost (Rev. 22:17).*

Just like the ground gets hard and parched and unfruitful without water, our hearts get hard and parched and unfruitful without the revival rain of our Heavenly Father. Without the rain cleansing the ground it cannot bring forth good fruit. In the same way, without the cleansing rain of revival in our lives we too become spiritually unfruitful. In the life of the believer, revival brings forth the fruit of effective prayer. True revival brings forth the fruit of a holy communion with our Lord. True Holy Spirit initiated revival brings forth the fruit of spontaneous praise and worship in all areas of our life. Real revival sent from the Throne Room of Heaven always results in a spiritual harvest of holy and righteous living. When Holy God begins to do a new work in our lives it is always for a new work through our lives. You can have a great evangelistic meeting without revival. But you can't have a real revival that doesn't bring the church of God into the harvest of God.

When God begins to move in the reviving of His church what will He do? What will it look like? What will we experience if we see real revival in our time?

> *But who can endure the day of His coming? And who can stand*
> *when He appears? For He is like a refiner's fire and like fuller's*
> *soap. And He will sit as a smelter and purifier of silver, and He*
> *will purify the sons of Levi and refine them like gold and silver,*
> *so that they may present to the Lord offerings in righteousness*
> *(Malachi 3:2-3).*

Here is the awesome picture of the work of Holy God among His people. Revival is a time of cleansing and purifying. When the Holy Spirit comes to do His work in the church, it is a work of separation. He separates from us everything that is unholy and unrighteous. I have witnessed the refining of gold on an occasion. Just like a refiner's fire, when the heat is turned up, everything that is not the pure metal comes to the surface. Every foreign matter and all impurities are separated from the gold. So when the process is finished all you have left is pure gold. That's the image of real revival. When true revival comes it is a holy time of cleansing. The image in the Scriptures is one who is dirty and God comes to clean him with fuller's soap. A deep cleaning is implied here. A complete cleaning of our sin and disobedience is done by God. Every moment of compromise in our lives, every moment of disobedience to His call, every sin and vestige of darkness is addressed by Holy God during true revival. We don't do the cleaning in revival. God is the one whose cleansing work prepares the church for a new and mighty work.

Look with me at a reporting of the movement of God in the Shantung Revival of the 1930s. This spiritual awakening in China was probably the greatest movement of God in the history of Southern Baptist missions. Meetings lasted five or six hours at a time with nothing but confession of sin, one after another bringing out the hidden as well as the known sins of his life. So deep was the work that hours for eating and sleeping passed unnoticed. And so "Judgment began at the house of God."[1]

Evan Roberts was the best-known evangelist that our Lord used during a spiritual awakening in the great Revival in the Country of Wales in 1904. It is a blessing to read the reports of the moving of God among his people in that great revival. "During its first phase the revival was characterized by penitential weeping and sobbing, the whole congregation in tears, confessing their sin, agonizing in prayer for mercy, pleading for salvation, but three months later a fullness of joy took possession of the people."[2]

As we read the reports of the movement of God, our flesh wants to reproduce the effects of real revival. Just like someone wanting the filling of a wonderful meal without taking the time to labor over the stove to cook. So desperate are we for real revival, we too often settle for anything that promises spiritual filling without paying the price in spiritual preparation. Hear me well. We can no more produce the movement of God among His people anymore than we can produce the rain that cleanses the ground. But we can, and we must produce the conditions by which God will pour out His revival rain among us. Just like the dew on the ground is produced by the atmospheric conditions, if God's conditions are met, the cleansing rain of our Lord will surround us. Evan Roberts said that there were four things necessary to receive revival blessing.

1. If there is past sin or sins hitherto unconfessed, we cannot receive the work of the Holy Spirit. Therefore we must search and ask the Holy Spirit to search.

2. If there is anything doubtful in our lives, it must be removed- anything we were uncertain about its rightness or wrongness. That thing must be removed.

3. An entire giving up of ourselves to the Spirit. We must speak and do all He requires of us.

4. Public confession of Christ.[3]

The lasting social results of revival are even more astounding. For example, judges were presented the white gloves because there was not a case to try. There were no robberies, no burglaries, no rapes, no murders, and no embezzlements. Simply put there was no crime. District councils held emergency meetings to discuss what to do with the police now that they were unemployed. In one place, the sergeant of the police was sent for and asked, "What do you do with your time?" He replied,

"Before the revival, we had two main jobs, to prevent crime and to control crowds, as at football games. Since the revival has started, there is practically no crime. So we just go with the crowds."

As the revival swept Wales, drunkenness was cut in half. There was a wave of bankruptcies but nearly all taverns. There was even a slowdown in the mines. Many Welsh coal miners were converted and stopped using bad language. The horses that dragged the trucks in the mines could not understand what was being said to them hence transportation slowed down for a while until they learned the language of Heaven. The revival also affected sexual moral standards. Through the figures given by British government experts, in Radnorshire and Merionethshire, the actual illegitimate birth rate had dropped 44% within a year of the beginning of revival.[4]

Is it any wonder that the Devil will do anything he can to stop revival? The one thing that can take back the ground previously given to the Devil is revival. It is the revival of our Lord in the people of God that makes the Enemy lose his evil grip on our communities, our churches, and in our lives. Whether it is a personal revival or a corporate revival, Satan hates the very thought of any revival. Real revival among the people of God pushes back the darkness. Real revival exposes the lies and deception of the Enemy. Satan hates the subject of revival more than any other burden of the church. Revivals have jarred and sent into retreat the kingdom of darkness as no other events ever have. Satan will do everything and anything he can to stop a revival. If it should come, he will immediately begin to corrupt and divert the movement from the Spirit of God's great work.[5]

Within the Word of God we see the working of Satan after the moving of the Spirit of God at Pentecost. Through persecution and internal corruption through Ananias and Sapphira, the Enemy was at work to shut down the movement of God *(Acts 5)*.

J.C. Metcalfe has written the foreword to the abridged edition of War on the Saints. He writes, "An aftermath of the Welsh Revival at the dawn of the present century was the rise of a number of extreme cults, often stressing a return to "Pentecostal" practices. Mrs. Penn-Lewis, who had witnessed much of the Revival as the representative of the Life of Faith, saw clearly the peril of these fanatical teachings, and in collaboration with Mr. Evan Roberts, who played so prominent a part in the Revival, wrote a book, *War On the Saints.* In this book these extreme and overbalanced beliefs and practices are categorically branded as the work of an invading host of evil spirits. The word deception might be said to be the key word in the book—a term which is in complete harmony with the findings both of John Wesley and Dr. Henson."[6]

Satan's powers are always focused against revival. He hates the very thought of revival. As soon as revival fires begin to burn, he sends his evil messengers to put out the flame as soon as possible. He will use every possible evil tactic in his arsenal to hinder the work of God in the Church. Remember, all of Satan's work is based upon lies. Deception is his game. He is the arch-deceiver. Let's study some of the ways Satan hinders revival through deception. We must learn to recognize his wicked strategies, lest we remain victims of the invisible war.

## THE ENEMY'S HINDRANCES TO REVIVAL

### The Hindrance of Blindness

*In whose case the god of this world has blinded the minds of the unbelieving, that they might not see the light of the gospel of the glory of Christ, who is the image of God (2 Cor. 4:4).*

Satan has the power through people's unbelief to blind them from the light of the Gospel of Christ. The word used here for blinded is "etuphlosen." The root of this word means smoke or fog. Think of it as Satan bringing his smoke from Hell to surround the unbeliever so that when the light of the Gospel of Christ is shown, he's not able to see it.

### The Hindrance of Stealing the Work of God through Misunderstanding

*When anyone hears the word of the kingdom, and does not understand it, the evil one comes and snatches away what has been sown in his heart (Matt. 13:19).*

Remember, the Devil is an opportunist. As soon as he sees the seed of the Gospel being sown, he looks carefully at those who do not understand it. He swoops down like a hawk stealing away what God has sown in his heart. So the unbeliever will stay in his kingdom of darkness, the good seeds of the Gospel are stolen by God's enemy. How many in our own families have we seen misunderstand the Gospel because of the varied lies of the Enemy?

## *The Hindrance of Inflicting the Body*

Demons can have power over the human body. They can cause DUMBNESS:

> *And as they were going out, behold, a dumb man, demon-possessed, was brought to Him. And after the demon was cast out, the dumb man spoke (Matt. 9:32-33).*

Demons can cause BLINDNESS:

> *Then there was brought to Him a demon-possessed man who was blind and dumb, and He healed him, so that the dumb man spoke and saw (Matt. 12:22).*

Demons can cause INSANITY:

> *And when He had come out only the land, He was met by a certain man from the city who was possessed with demons; and who had not put on any clothing for a long time, and was not living in a house, but in the tombs (Luke 8:26-35).*

Today, we would call him a homeless person that has gone insane, a throwaway of society.

Demons also have the power to lead to SUICIDE:

> *And it has often thrown him both into the fire and into the water to destroy him (Mark 9:22).*

Demons can cause PERSONAL INJURIES:
> *And whenever it seizes him, it dashes him to the ground and he*

*foams at the mouth, and grinds his teeth, and stiffens out (Mark 9:18).*

Evil spirits can impart SUPERNATURAL STRENGTH:

*For it had seized him many times; and he was bound with chains and shackles and kept under guard; and yet he would burst his fetters and be driven by the demon into the desert (Luke 8:29).*

Demons can inflict PHYSICAL DEFECTS AND DEFORMITIES:

*And behold, there was a woman who for eighteen years had had a sickness caused by a spirit; and she was bent double, and could not straighten up at all (Luke 13:11-17).*

Often in revival-time, during a great movement of God among His people, Satan will inflict the body to divert the attention of God's people away from prayer, repentance, and spiritual cleansing. How many prayer meetings have been focused only on the physical healing of people rather than their spiritual healing? According to the Word of God, the Lord won't even hear our prayer for physical healing until our sins are confessed. There must be a spiritual healing before there can be power in praying for the sick:

*Therefore, confess your sins to one another, and pray for one another, so that you may be healed. The effective prayer of a righteous man can accomplish much (James 5:16).*

Even our wrongful praying for the sick can hinder real revival. He will use any and all power at his disposal to hinder the work of God.

## *The Hindrance of Diversion*

As we have already studied in Chapter 1, one of the schemes of the Devil is to divert the attention of the believer away from the work of God. From drawing attention away from the work of God to the work of men, to bringing into view good things so we will miss the best things of God, he has a thousand different ways of diversion. The desire to please ourselves rather than God is often exploited by Satan. How quick is the flesh willing to settle for its immediate pleasure. Often we are so anxious to receive satisfaction that we do not test what is being satisfied. Remember, the flesh has an appetite that is never completely satisfied. The pleasing of people rather than God is a tool of diversion we see often in the Church. It would be impossible for me to recount the hundreds of times in a revival meeting, when a prominent leader of the Church had left town on vacation during the most important event on any Church calendar. The person as well as the church may not be aware, but the Enemy has used his tool of diversion to keep the leadership of the Church from revival. All it takes for the Enemy to divert from the purposes of God is to bring into our lives so called "good things" without it being from God.

## *The Hindrance of Discouragement*

As in Elijah's life, discouragement is never far from the plan and purpose of God in and through the believer's life *(I Kings 19)*. If God has called you to do a task for Him, the Enemy will do all he can to discourage you from the task. Leading others to be obedient to the Lord and His call upon their lives is never an easy task. As in every spiritual pursuit, success is directly related to our being yielded to the Holy Spirit in our lives. Our Lord never asks us to do anything that He does not give the strength to accomplish the task. As you call on others to work in the revival effort, you must earnestly pray for them. Remember, you cannot be the Holy Spirit in their lives. Only with God's help can we be successful. Only through His strength can we accomplish the task of reaching people for Christ. Evangelism is clearly a partnership between the believer and the Holy Spirit of God *(2 Cor. 6:1-2)*.

In every revival I have ever seen or with which I have been a part, there is one person that God gives the vision for the meeting. It is this person from which the Lord will expect the most. You must remember God has given you the burning desire for revival in the church. This revival vision will not necessarily be shared by others. Even those you want to share the vision may never come to understand it fully. Do not be disappointed when others don't seem to share your vision. They may never come to see your vision. God gave it to you. It is not your vision they will come to believe in, it is your walk with the Lord in which they will put their confidence. It is through your heart and exercised faith that others may get a glimpse of Heaven's vision for revival.

The Devil knows that the eternity of thousands of people is at stake. He will do everything possible to discourage you from trusting the Lord. He will do all he can to keep you from exercising your faith in the vision God has given. If he can stop the revival effort, he will. Learn to recognize his working. If someone's idea means fewer people will be reached for Christ, that idea did not come from God. If someone's idea means you don't need faith to accomplish the task, that idea did not come from the Lord.

Leadership can be a time of great loneliness. With God's presence you will never be alone. Always remember that, Heaven's resources are at your disposal. God gave you the vision for the revival. God will help you accomplish every task for His glory. There is never anything He tells us to do that He does not give us the authority and ability to accomplish. There is nothing He will ask of you that He cannot accomplish through you. Trust Him and be unshakable with what God has told you. Don't allow discouragement to set in. My Father used to say that one of the tricks of the Devil is to get us to focus on what is not going on rather than to place our focus on what the Lord is doing. Recognize the flaming missile of discouragement. Don't let it penetrate your life.

## The Hindrance of Division and Isolation

The Devil is Diobolos, the divider, the separator. Through his lies, Satan is able to bring division to the Church. Division is clearly a tool of the Enemy to keep the Church from experiencing real revival. As we look at the Church today, division abounds: division in our denominations, division in our churches, and division in our homes. All of it is a tactic of the Enemy to keep the Church from the cleansing of our Lord. For the church to know genuine revival there must be at the very least a desire for unity. As long as we have our attention on others, we cannot be focused on God. Bitterness toward a fellow believer will be used of the Enemy to gain ground in our lives and keep us from real revival cleansing *(Eph. 4:27)*. Remember, we have one enemy, God's enemy,

Satan. We wrestle with his evil powers *(Eph. 6:12)*. Our struggle is not against flesh and blood.

Once again in Elijah's life we see how the isolation of God's prophet from God's people led to a spirit of suicide:

> *But he himself went a day's journey into the wilderness, and came and sat down under a juniper tree; and he requested for himself that he might die, and said, "It is enough; now, O Lord, take my life, for I am not better than my fathers" (I Kings 19:4).*

Remember this is Elijah, the prophet of God that the Lord uses as his example of a righteous man *(James 5:17-18)*. Yet when isolated he was vulnerable to depression.

## The Hindrance of the Counterfeit

Satan is the great counterfeiter. Whatever God desires to do in the life of a believer, Satan believes he can do it better. When controlled by the flesh, the believer is so capable of being deceived by the Enemy. Jesus warns us of the time prior to His coming that many false Christs will come to deceive:

> *For false Christs and false prophets will arise and will show great signs and wonders, so as to mislead, if possible, even the elect (Matt. 24:24).*

The application is clear; believers can be deceived by these false prophets and their false teachings.

The Church's hunger for the supernatural working of our Lord can often lead into great deception. All supernatural manifestations are NOT OF GOD! Sardonic laughter, spasmodic jerks, signs and wonders, super apostles and prophets, and people being "slain in the spirit:" are pointed to as empirical evidence of the power and presence of the Holy Spirit. The form and function of the church is being so radically rearranged that even the secular world has taken note. *Time magazine,* in an article titled "Laughing for the Lord," pointed out that Anglican parishes across England today bear a greater resemblance to "rock concerts" and "rugby matches" than to Christian worship. The article says that sanctuaries throughout the world are littered with bodies as "supplicants sob, shake, roar like lions and strangest of all, laugh uncontrollably."[7] *Newsweek*, in an article titled "The Giggles Are for God," reported that people in churches worldwide were jerking spasmodically, dancing ecstatically, and acting like animals.[8]

Newspapers from the *Orlando Sentinel* to the *Dallas Morning News* have written stories on what is termed the "fastest-growing trend within Christianity." According to the *New York Times*, this trend promotes an "experiential" Christianity that "promises an emotional encounter with God" manifested by "shaking, screaming, fainting and falling into trances."[9] The most notable spiritual movement is known as "The Toronto Blessing." The Toronto Blessing originated in January 1994, at the Toronto Vineyard Christian Fellowship. Services at this church have been held six nights a week now for many years. The movement has had a worldwide impact. As of May 1995, over 250,000 believers from over fifty nations had come to Toronto. These included hundreds of experienced pastors, missionaries, teachers, evangelists, and ministry leaders. Those receiving the blessing in Toronto carried its effects to some 7,000 churches in North America and some 4,000 churches in England. Locally, *Toronto Life Magazine* called the Toronto Blessing the number-one tourist attraction of 1995.[10]

Two godly friends of Dr. Ed Murphy experienced in spiritual warfare attended meetings at The Toronto Fellowship in 1995 and discerned there the presence of counterfeit religious spirits. Through their warfare praying during the service, they were able to shut down the phenomena occurring almost completely, to the consternation of those leading the service.[11] Even in the midst of a great movement of God, the church must always practice vigilance through discernment. History teaches us that the greatest counterfeits of Satan have always come at the time of great revival. It is Satan's desire to hijack the movement of God for the purpose of shutting it down. There is never a time the church can afford to be asleep in the spiritual battle with the forces of darkness, particularly during a supernatural movement of God.

Since the beginning of my adulthood, and subsequent beginnings of my Gospel ministry, there has been a continuous wave of the manifestation of speaking in tongues within the context of evangelical life. Why is it that people seek this particular gift? First of all, people are searching for a validating experience. Too often, the search is not for a better way to worship God or to serve God, but for an experience. Secondly, the tongues movement tends to attract emotionally unstable people. Statistics of two large mental institutions in the United States show that between eighty and ninety percent of the inmates are from branches of the Christian Church that practice speaking in tongues. There are, of course, many exceptions to this. Thirdly, people are searching for reality. They want new life, outreach, changed lives, and new power. They think that they will find this in the gift of tongues. What most people are looking for is really not the gift of tongues, but the things that result from the filling of the Holy Spirit.[12] Most often the results of this counterfeit manifestation of tongues are:

1. **Division**- Invariably, where this counterfeit appears, the church is split right down the middle. People begin to take sides. Those who are psychologically able to enter into the experience become victims of a feeling of superiority and this becomes evident in the way they talk and act, although they try to disguise it. Those who cannot enter into this experience become resentful, or a least suspicious, and schisms and divisions arise.

2. **Diversionary**- It is a trick of the Enemy to distract our attention from the true work of God the Spirit. Even though the claim is often made that it results in greater burden for the lost, this has rarely been observed in experience. Usually, the focus of interest is always tongues, not the Lord or the Gospel.

3. **Devilish**- The Enemy can exploit any spiritual "open door" that is given to him through ignorance. No matter how willing a person is for the working of the Spirit of God, we must never assume that all the supernatural is automatically of God. I am not saying that all of speaking in tongues will lead to demonization. However, it must be noted that in many religions, speaking in tongues is the manifestation of demons. I do believe that there is a language spoken in heaven that is of heavenly origin. Certainly, the language of Heaven is not English or Spanish. And remember, demons are fallen angels. They obviously must know and speak this heavenly language *(I Cor. 13:1)*. Earnest Rockstad, who for many years pioneered deliverance ministry as we see it today, concluded that of the believers that he had dealt with in the

"counseling room" that had this spirit of tongues tested, most all were found out to be a demonic counterfeit.[13]

Without denying the validity of all such manifestations, it must be concluded that all supernatural manifestations must be tested by the criterion of Scripture. I encourage all those who have allowed at any time in their lives a supernatural manifestation like tongues to invade their lives to have this so-called "gift" tested. Just the mention of such testing is an assault to many a believer's spiritual pride. Remember, *God is opposed to the proud, but gives grace to the humble (James 4:6).* However, the Bible makes it plain that we are to test all spirits:

*Beloved, do not believe every spirit, but test the spirits to see whether they are from God; because many false prophets have gone out into this world (I John 4:1).*

Through spiritual confrontation and revelation, the spirit producing the tongue must be identified and tested by the truths of the Word of God.

We must first mention the minimal threefold basis for examination of spiritual experiences. First, the doctrinal content implied, especially with respect to the person of the Lord Jesus Christ, must stand up under the scrutiny of the Word *(I John 4:1-11, I Cor. 12:3, Romans 10:9).* Second, true experiences with the Holy Spirit produce humility, not pride. The believer is drawn closer to the Lord. Holiness of life is increased. Obedience to his Word results *(Gal. 5:22-23).* Love for and tolerance of all believers also occurs *(I John 2-5).* Third, the body of Christ is edified *(I Cor. 12-14).*[14]

As a Southern Baptist Evangelist, it is my conviction that God *is able to do exceeding abundantly beyond all that we ask or think (Eph. 3:20).* Just because God hasn't done it before, doesn't mean He won't do it now:

*For as the heavens are higher than the earth, so are My ways higher than your ways, And my thoughts than your thoughts (Isaiah 55:9).*

What I want you to know is that God can do whatever He wants to in and through His Church. Whatever it takes for our Lord to be exalted and glorified in His Church, He is able and willing to do. Our God is able to raise the dead. Our God is able to heal the sick. He's the only one who can. Our God is able to perform His will, His way, in His Church. AMEN! But the point must be made that what the Lord is able to do, the Enemy is able to counterfeit. All manifestations of the spirit must be tested!

One of the greatest Bible Preachers and leaders Southern Baptists have ever produced is Dr. Jerry Vines. In his wonderful work entitled *Spirit Works* he sets forth a clear straight forward test for every spiritual manifestation and practice within the church.

**1. The Bible Test**. Where is it in the Bible? Bible teaching, not feelings, must be the test of truth. "It's not in the Bible, but I know it happened to me." That's not enough. Does it add to, take away from, ignore, or violate the Bible? Don't seek some experience not promised in the Bible.

**2. The Jesus Test.** Does it bring glory and honor to the Lord Jesus? Is Jesus exalted? Or a movement? Or the Holy Spirit? Roy Fish, long-time Professor of Evangelism at Southwestern Baptist Theological Seminary, has said it well. "The Holy Spirit is to lift us to the level of Christ, not to lower us to the level of animals."

**3. The Character Test.** Is the fruit of the Spirit evident? Does it change and make the person better? Some unusual outward expression is not the litmus test of God working in a person's life. Jesus says, *"By their fruit you will recognize them" (Matt. 7:20)*. The most important evidence of God in one's life is a change. God wants to work in and through us so he can change the world around us.

**4. The Decency and Order Test.** *But let all things be done properly and in an orderly manner (I Cor. 14:40)*. Is this within the guidelines of decency and order? Joy and spiritual excitement in public worship is one thing. Chaos and frenzy are totally different. God is not honored by confusion and turmoil. Ask questions like these: Is there order to the service? Is the service understandable? What about lost people? Will they be drawn to Christ as a result of what occurs? Is this reasonable? Does it violate common sense? Is this within the guidelines of decency and order?

**5. The Evangelism Test.** Does it place the focus on winning people to Christ? Is the purpose and goal to win people to the Lord Jesus? We are not here just to enjoy ourselves. We are here to win lost people to Christ and glorify God. Will this result in lost people being won? If so, there's not a problem. Does it place the focus on winning people to Christ?[15]

The point at which the believer opens himself up to the supernatural, he must be on guard and wear his armor, less he be deceived. Your good intentions are not enough to protect you from the counterfeits of the Enemy. You see, if it was not a good counterfeit, it wouldn't be the work of the Devil. I have had good close friends in the ministry that through their longing for the movement of God have been deceived by receiving only a counterfeit. These counterfeit experiences have left them with nothing more than confusion and discouragement.

If God's desire is that the Church experience revival, why does He allow Satan to attack as he does? Children of God remain content because they are ignorant of their state. My Father used to put it this way, "The problem with revival is, the people who need it the most are those who don't think they need it at all." The good they have blinds them to the greater good, and the greater need of the Church. To arouse them from their self-satisfied condition, God has permitted Satan to sift His people. Remember, Satan cannot go one step beyond the permission of God. Believers will be taught the truth about themselves only by experience; therefore God permits experience. The Church of God must be matured. Only through the fire of sifting will the people of God be urged forward to the battle and victory.[16]

## *The Hindrance of Accommodation and Compromise*

*For my people have committed two evils: they have forsaken Me, The fountain of living waters, To hew for themselves cisterns, Broken cisterns, that can hold no water (Jeremiah 2:13).*

How often have we seen the Enemy shut down the work of God in the Church through accommodation and compromise. God's will is never known through compromise. God's will is never done through accommodation. God's will is done through obedience to Him. Revival is God's will for His people. We desperately need times of spiritual cleansing for the sake of the harvest. Philosophies of the world are strangely fused with the Word of God. The desires of men are the object of revival rather than the desires of God. Often a synthesis is sought instead of God's will whenever differences of opinion arise. Some pastors have built their ministries on accommodation. Is it any wonder revival tarries in their church?

One of the great hindrances to revival in the church today is the "praise and worship" movement. Please do not confuse true praise and worship with the "praise and worship" movement we see that is so divisive. More attention has been given to pleasing the people in terms of their worship style than pleasing our Lord. All across our land, churches are being divided on the basis of worship style. Some churches have gone to a traditional service to accommodate the worship style and personal desires of the older folks. On the other hand, many churches have gone to a contemporary worship service to accommodate the personal desires of younger worshippers. The people of God on both sides are being abused and bruised for the sake of accommodation of the fleshly desires of others within the body. They may think they are being "more spiritual" by singing choruses, or singing hymns, but the result is the dividing of the body of Christ and the hindering of true revival. True worship is never about the worshiper, any more than the sermon is about the preacher. True worship is all about the one who is worthy to be worshiped, God alone. Whatever the style, if the expression exalts the name of our Lord Jesus Christ, it belongs in His Church.

Too often we settle for the compromise. We allow our personal understanding and our personal desires to be satisfied rather than the holy agenda of our Lord. We see this in the devolution of the length of revival meetings in our churches. What once was a priority in the church's calendar, revival meetings are becoming a short and insignificant event. In 1961, Dr. C.E. Autry, former Director of Evangelism for the North American Mission Board of the Southern Baptist Convention, said, "It is the purpose of this Division to lead in a return of the churches to two-week revivals."[17] Being reared in an evangelist's home, I remember the sharing of the great revivals of yesteryear. Wonderful stories of the protracted meetings, where the beginning was scheduled but not the end of the revival meeting. The church would continue in revival meetings until God brought real revival to the church and to the community. Today, some four decades later, we see that many of our churches have fewer and fewer scheduled times to focus on reaching a community to Christ. Some now only have four-day revival meetings. Some churches only have weekend so called revival meetings. Some have even called a single day evangelism rally, "One Day Revivals."

Don't misunderstand me. I believe that God brings His revival to His Church according to His schedule, not ours. You see, it is not God who needs the time; you and I need the time before God for His work to be done in our lives! My Grandfather used to say it this way, "You can't pop corn on a cold skillet." Revival within the church of God is not a matter of coincidence and convenience. Revival cleansing comes from Heaven as a matter of meeting God's conditions. We must do God's will, God's way, on God's schedule.

Remember, evangelism is the natural result of revival. When the Holy Spirit fills the life of the believer, he/she will become God's witnesses:

*But you shall receive power when the Holy Spirit has come upon you; and you shall be My witnesses both in Jerusalem, and in all Judea and Samaria, and even to the remotest part of the earth (Acts 1:8).*

I have a "son in the ministry" that came to Christ in a revival meeting on Thursday night. Jay said that he ran out of excuses after Wednesday night. He told me that if the revival meeting had ended on Wednesday night, he might have never come to Christ. How many thousands of people are still lost without Christ because the Church is only interested in the accommodation of their personal schedules?

It is the heartbeat of my soul that we as believers might come to the place that we will no longer settle for less than real revival. When that day comes, we will give God the time to do His work among His people. Oh, that the day might come that we care more about God's schedule rather than accommodating His work to fit ours. I believe that a church will experience as much revival as they are willing to allow God to bring. Oh, that revival fires of old would burn in every association, in every church, and in every believer's heart. Oh, that we would listen to the voice of the Lord drawing us back to the Lordship of Christ and holiness before Him.

We must decide. Are we going to please men, or please God?

*For am I now seeking the favor of men, or of God? Or am I striving to please men? If I were still trying to please men, I would not be a bondservant of Christ (Gal. 1:10).*

*But Peter and the apostles answered and said, "We must obey God rather than men" (Acts 5:29).*

As long as we settle for personal convenience we are not only compromising our schedules but the plan and purposes of God for His Church. Until the flesh of personal desires is abandoned, we may never know revival in our time. The Enemy will have accomplished his hindering of the Church from living in the victory of spiritual health.

## The Church on the Offensive in the Invisible War

*...and upon this rock I will build My church; and the gates of Hell shall not prevail against it (Matt. 16:18).*

It is necessary, if the Church is to experience revival, she must go on the offensive. The picture in the New Testament of the Church is an aggressive Church. One only needs to read the book of Acts to see a church on fire for God. Revival doesn't just happen. People don't come to Christ coincidentally. Communities are not changed for Christ accidentally. Lives are changed for Christ because of the commitment the Church makes to the union that is hers in Christ. There are three sources of God's power to fight the Enemy available to the Church in this matter we call revival. Let's call them God's "Power Tools" in His Church. They are:

**THE POWER OF *PRAYER*,**
**THE POWER OF *PRAISE*, and**
**THE POWER OF *PROCLAMATION***

### The Power of Prayer

*Now unto Him who is able to do exceeding abundantly above all that we ask or think, according to the POWER that works within us, to Him be the glory in the church and in Christ Jesus to all generations forever and ever. Amen (Eph. 3:20-21).*

We find Jesus in the Temple; as He threw the moneychangers out, He declared:

*"It is written, My House shall be called a house of prayer" (Matt. 21:12).*

The Church is to be a place where the sweet aroma of the prayers of God's people fills the air. When the Church is not praying, it needs revival. The Church is not to be called a house of music or preaching. First and foremost the Church is to be a house of prayer. Paul writes to his son in the ministry, Timothy:

*I exhort therefore, that first of all, supplications, prayers, inter-cessions, and giving of thanks, be made for all men (I Tim. 2:1).*

The prayers of the saints are so powerful and precious to our Lord; they are kept in bowls around the Throne of God. That's right, not our songs, not our sermons, not our money, it is our prayers that are most precious to our Lord *(Rev. 5:8).* In the record of the early church we find:

*they were continually devoting themselves to the apostle's teaching and to fellowship, to the breaking of bread and to prayer (Acts 2:42).*

The Church cannot pray too much when it comes to revival. Jonathan Edwards said, "Much prayer, much revival, little prayer, little revival." Praying is not getting God's attention. We have His undivided attention through our union with His Son, Jesus Christ our Savior. Praying is getting our hearts and lives in tune with God. Praying in a real sense is getting our attention so when our Lord speaks to us we will be ready to hear Him. Prayer is as much listening to our Lord as it is talking to Him.

Dr. A.T. Pierson once said, "There has never been a spiritual awakening in any country or locally that did not begin in united prayer." Let me share with you two examples out of history where great revival came as a result of great prayer. The first was in the wake of the American Revolution. Not many people realize during that time there was a moral slump. Drunkenness became epidemic. Out of a population of 5 million, 300,000 were confirmed drunkards. Fifteen thousand of them were being buried each year. Profanity was of the most shocking kind. For the first time in the history of the American settlement, women were afraid to go out at night for fear of assault. Bank robberies were a daily occurrence.

The Baptists of that day said that they were going through their most wintry season. Each major denomination was in a period of serious decline. The Chief Justice of the United States Supreme Court, John Marshall, wrote to the Bishop of Virginia, James Madison, "That the church, was too far gone ever to be redeemed." Voltaire agreed and Tom Paine echoed, "Christianity will be forgotten in thirty years."

Likewise the colleges of that time were in a great spiritual vacuum. A poll taken at Harvard had discovered not one believer in the whole of the student body. They took a poll at Princeton, which was a much more evangelical place. It was discovered in all the student body there were only two believers and only five did not belong to the filthy speech movement of that day. Students rioted. They held a mock communion at Williams College; and they put on anti-Christian plays at Dartmouth. They took a Bible out of a local church in New Jersey and burned it in a public bonfire. Christians were so few on campus in the 1790s that they met in secret, like a communist cell, and kept their minutes in code so that no one would know.

Kenneth Scott Latourette, the great church historian, wrote: "It seemed as if Christianity were about to be ushered out of the affairs of men." The churches had their backs to the wall, seeming as if they were about to be wiped out. How did the situation change? It came through a concert of prayer.

In New England there was a great theologian by the name of Jonathan Edwards who received a little memorial book by a minister in Edinburgh, Scotland named John Erskine. Edwards was so moved by the appeal of Erskine for the people of God to pray for revival that the New England preacher wrote a response. It finally became a book he called, "A Humble Attempt to Promote Explicit Agreement and Visible Union of All God's People in Extraordinary Prayer for the Revival of Religion and the Advancement of Christ's Kingdom on Earth, pursuant to Scripture Promises and Prophecies concerning the Last Time." Even though this is a long title, don't miss its message. "A Humble Attempt to promote explicit agreement and visible union of God's people in extraordinary prayer for a revival of religion and extension of Christ's Kingdom." Is not this what is missing so much from all our evangelistic efforts today, explicit agreement, visible union, unusual prayer?

This movement had started in Britain through William Carey, Andrew Fuller, John Sutcliffe and other leaders who began what the British called "The Union of Prayer." Hence, the year after John Wesley died, the Second Great Awakening began and swept Great Britain. Out of the Second Great Awakening came the whole modern missionary movement and its societies. Out of it came the abolition of slavery, popular education, Bible societies and Sunday schools, and many social benefits accompanying the evangelistic drive.

For the sake of this presentation, I mention one more example of a great revival of 1858, as a result of great prayer. In 1904 an evangelist by the name of Seth Joshua had come to the Newcastle Emlyn College where Evan Roberts was studying for the ministry. Evan Roberts, then 26, had been a coal miner. The students were so moved that they asked if they could attend his next campaign nearby, so they canceled classes to go to Blaenanerch, where Seth Joshua prayer publicly, "O God, bend us." And Evan Roberts went forward, where he prayed with great agony, "O God, bend me."

Upon his return, he could not concentrate on his studies. He went to the principal of his college and explained, "I keep hearing a voice that tells me I must go home to speak to our young people in my home church." God moved in such power that it is here where the birth of the Welsh Revival came. In five months there were a hundred thousand conversions throughout the country.[18]

All of church history reveals that revival always begins in prayer. Without a movement of prayer there is no movement of God. It is the testimony of time that all great revivals began with great prayer.

Any revival effort must be baptized in prayer. A crusade cannot have too much prayer. For the people of God to experience revival, they must go to the source of all revival, our Heavenly Father. He is more concerned about us having a time of revival and refreshing than we could ever be. Any form of prayer is appropriate and essential. The Scripture verse *Jeremiah 33:3* should be used and promoted as a prayer preparation motto.

*Call unto me, and I will answer you, and show you great and mighty things, that thou knowest not (Jeremiah 33:3).*

## *What Jesus had to say About PRAYER*
### *(Matt. 6:1-15)*

**1.  The Motivation of Prayer- vs. 1-5**
Why do we pray? We pray that God's will is done.  Make certain your motivation is proper when you pray. Make sure your heart it pure when you pray. Remember, *The effective prayer of a righteous man can accomplish much (James 5:16).*

**2.  The Misuse of Prayer- vs. 1-5**
·    A Warning about praying in **public**. *"To be noticed by them"* Our focus can easily become on the surroundings rather than the Savior.
·    A Warning about praying for **personal** gain. Praying for the sake of and in the spirit of PRIDE: *"may be honored by men." "To be seen, noticed by men."*
A prominent deacon in a church where I served as a seminary student told me in private, "Do not call on me to pray in public, I just can't do it. I get too scared." You see he forgot why we pray. When you and I pray, we must get the old man, the flesh out of the way.
·    A Warning about praying **plentiful words.** vs. 7 *"many words"* If we are not careful our prayers can become "meaningless repetition." It's not how much you say when you pray that matters; it's the spirit of your heart when you pray. I've heard some pray in King James English, as if to use the language of the Bible makes our prayer more spiritual. In a Revival meeting during an offertory prayertime, a prayer was said that spoke of revival and how many needed to be saved around the world, I said, "Amen!" The man lost his place and had to start from the beginning to repeat this poem he had learned. Saying poems is not praying.
·    A Warning about the **stewardship of Prayer**: You and I will be held accountable for how and what we pray. Notice in *vs. 1,* "You will have no reward with your Father who is in Heaven." *vs. 2* *"They have their reward in full." vs. 4 "The Father will repay you."*

*vs. 5 "Truly I say to you, they have their reward in full." vs. 6 "Your Father who sees in secret will repay you."* **God is keeping an account** of (as the Scripture says) every idle word, every word that is spoken in prayer. Here is a caution, be careful when you pray.

## 3. The Message of Prayer: vs. 9-13
### Pray *"IN THIS WAY"*

· **Prayer and its Direction:** Our prayers must be to the Father. Which Father? The one whose name is Hallowed, Holy. Don't you ever run into the Throne Room of Heaven irreverently, half-heartedly? He is HOLY!

> *"Our Father who art in Heaven,*
> *Hallowed be Thy name."*

The Father knows what you need, before you ask of Him. We pray to the Father, Our Creator, Our loving Heavenly Father (*Matt. 7:7-11*). Pray to the Father in Jesus Name *(John 14:14, John 16:24)*. Why in Jesus name? Jesus said, *"No one comes to the Father except by me."* It is only through the shed blood of Calvary that sinners can come into the presence of Holy God.

Why do we pray to the Father? He's the only one who can fully meet our every need *(Phil. 4:19)*. Everything belongs to Him. He is all-powerful. *Now unto him who is able to do exceedingly abundantly above all that we ask or think (Eph. 3:20). And this is the confidence that we have in him, that, if we ask any thing according to His will, he hears us (I John 5:14).*

· **Prayer and its Determination:**

> *"Thy Kingdom come,*
> *Thy will be done on earth as it is in Heaven"*

Why do we pray? We pray to get in on God's will being done for our children, our homes, our community, and our schools. I do not fully understand this, but the truth of the matter is that Heaven moves its purposes on the earth when we pray. The old evangelist had a banner over the platform, "Prayer Changes Things." Do you believe it? Churches are blessed when people pray. Lives are changed when people pray. People are saved when people pray. Why? (*Thy will be done*) God's will is that His church be blessed! God's will is that lives be changed, homes be saved! God's will is that people are to be saved! When you and I pray in the Father's will, God is going to act! Here is the promise of the Kingdom of God when all things will finally be as the Father wills.

· **Prayer and its Dependence:**

### *"Give us this day our daily bread"*

How blasphemous it is to call upon the Lord when your trust is not in Him *(Matt. 7:7-11, Phil. 4:19)*. I have met people in my ministry that wanted me to pray over their business even though they were not willing to dedicate their lives to the Lord. God cannot be fooled. He is Lord!

· **Prayer and its Debts:**

### *"And forgive us our debts, as we also have forgiven our debtors"*

Something owed: herein lies the idea of redemption: the price of something owed. Forgiveness: Yes! *For if you forgive men for their transgressions, your heavenly Father will also forgive you. But if you do not forgive men, then your Father will not forgive your transgressions (vs. 14-15)*. Forgiveness is not an option for the one who has been forgiven of Christ. What Christ has given us through His forgiveness we must give to others.

**Observations:**

1. You are most like Jesus when you forgive *(Col. 2:13)*.

2. You can't forgive unless you've been forgiven *(I John 2:9-11)*.

3. Who is the one who loses? The one who owes or the one who is owed? The one who forgives loses the most.

4. Unforgiveness causes broken fellowship with our Heavenly Father:
   a. Hindrance to Prayer- *vs. 14-15 (Mark 11:25)*.
   b. Forgiveness cannot be received from our Lord (*vs. 14-15*).
   c. Receiving Gifts – It is clear that if there exists any un-reconciled matter between brothers, we are to leave the offering and go and make it right with that brother before the offering is given *(Matt. 5:23-24)*.

· **Prayer and its Deliverance:**

*"Lead us not into temptation,*
*but deliver us from evil (the Evil One)."*

There are two parts to the deliverance prayer:
1) Lead us not into temptation- as we have studied in Chapter 3, the believer is vulnerable to the schemes of the Enemy through his temptations. If we can be victorious when tempted by the Enemy, we can live in the victory Christ has given to us at Calvary.

2) But Deliver us from Evil (the Evil One). Our Lord taught us to pray for deliverance from Satan. He came to set the captives free. Jesus came to destroy the works of the Devil. We are to join our Lord through prayer that we will walk in His deliverance from the Enemy, that we might be surrounded by *Songs of Deliverance (Psalm 32:7)*.

· **Prayer and its Declaration:**

*"For Thine is the Kingdom, power and glory forever, Amen."*

Praise the Lord when you pray. It is in Him that the Kingdom of God resides. He is all-powerful. It is our Heavenly Father that deserves all praise and glory both now and forever. In your prayers, praise the Lord!

**4. The Ministry of Prayer**

## *Hindrances to Effective Prayer*

### 1. Unforgiving Heart

*(Matt. 6:14-15)* As we have studied, an unforgiving spirit will not be able to receive the forgiveness of the Lord *(Mark 11:25)*.

### 2. Unbelief

*But let him ask in faith without any doubting, for the one who doubts is like the surf of the sea driven and tossed by the wind. For let not that man expect that he will receive anything from the Lord (James 1:5-7).*

### 3. Selfishness

*You ask and receive not because you ask amiss that you may spend it on your lusts (pleasures) (James 4:3,* KJV*).* R.A. Torrey said that a selfish prayer robs prayer of it power. Often in our crusades, I will meet women who are married to alcoholic husbands. Through the years, many of them have asked me to pray for their husbands. Although I am more than willing to pray for their souls, it is clear in many of the cases, that the call to prayer of these women is less than genuine. Many of them want God to save their alcoholic husbands simply because they are tired of messing with them. God never answers the selfish prayer!

### 4. Unconfessed Sin

*Behold, the Lord's hand is not shortened, that it cannot save; neither His ear heavy, that it cannot hear. But your iniquities have separated between you and your God, and your sins have hid His face from you, that He will not hear (Isaiah 59:1-2,* KJV*).* Sin hinders prayer. Sin always separates us from Holy God. It is through confession that our fellowship with the Father is restored *(I John 1:9)*. (See Appendix B, Making Your Sin List, page 269.)

### 5. Idols

*Son of man, these men have taken their idols unto their*

*heart, and put the stumbling block of their iniquity before their face; should I be inquired of at all by them (Ezekiel 14:3,* KJV). Idols in your heart can cause God to refuse to listen to your prayers. What is an idol? Anything that takes the place of God can be an idol. Our Children can become idols. A wife, a husband, our possessions, the ability to make money, anything that takes precedence over God can become an idol.

### 6. Husbands dishonoring their wives

*You husbands likewise, live with your wives in an understanding way, as with a weaker vessel, since she is a woman; and grant her honor as a fellow heir of the grace of life, so that your prayers may not be hindered (I Pet. 3:7,* KJV). As husbands, we are to love our wives like Christ loved the church and gave Himself for her *(Eph. 5:25).* To do less is to disobey our Lord and enter into sin.

### 7. A Stingy Heart

*He who shuts his ear to the cry of the poor will also cry himself and not be answered (Prov. 21:13).* There is probably no greater hindrance to prayer than stinginess. All we have comes from the Lord. We are to give in the same spirit as our Lord has given to us.

## *Secrets of Effective Prayer*
*So Peter was kept in the prison, but prayer for him was being made fervently by the church to God (Acts 12:5).*

1.  **Pray to God "unto God."** When you pray always remember to whom you are praying. It is Holy God, The Lord of Hosts who answers our prayer.

2.  **Pray with a clean heart before God.** It is necessary to note that we must confess our sins first before we pray for others *(James 5:16).* (See Appendix B, Making Your Sin List, page 269.)

3.  **Pray without ceasing, earnestly, intensely, fervently.**

Leonard Ravenhill the late great revivalist often used the word "travailing" when he would teach on prayer. My grandfather used to use the phrase, "Pray until you've prayed it through." They understood that prayer was work. It took time and effort to bring petitions before the Lord. Pray however long it takes until the prayer burden is lifted by our Lord.

**4. Pray in the Spirit**. Let the Spirit of God take over the prayer agenda. Pray only what the Holy Spirit tells you to pray. Listen to Him in the prayer closet. Let the Holy Spirit take charge of your time in prayer *(Eph. 6:18)*.

**5. Pray with Fasting**- In warfare praying the flesh becomes vulnerable to the attacks of the Enemy. As we have studied in Chapter 5, fasting is a way to get the flesh out of the way. Fasting helps us lay our flesh aside so the Enemy's attacks are futile and our prayer becomes eternally effective *(Acts 14:23, Acts 13:2,3)*.

**6. Pray together with other believers**: *"by the church"* *Again I say to you, that if two of you agree on earth about anything that they may ask, it shall be done for them by My Father who is in heaven. For where two or three have gathered together in My name, there I am in their midst (Matt. 18:19)*. There is great power in prayer. There is greater power in corporate prayer.

## *Prayer Preparation for Revival*

### 1. COTTAGE PRAYER MEETINGS

The Cottage Prayer Meeting is an attempt to encourage unusual and significant prayer for the revival. This is accomplished by gathering people together in homes for the sole purpose of prayer. The home of a member gives an informal atmosphere as well as a warm personal approach to meeting our need for prayer. Depending upon the size of your church, many different prayer meetings should be scheduled. Possible suggested divisions for cottage prayer meetings are:

A. Deacon Family Ministry Groups
B. Sunday School Departments
C. Geographical Areas of Members
D. Choir Ministry
E. Youth Ministry

## 2. PRAYER CHAIN

The Prayer Chain has long been a successful tool of revival preparation. It has been learned it is best to develop a large chart on which to sign up the people. Select Prayer Captains, (One for each hour of the all-day prayer chain). These captains will aid in enlisting people to pray during their assigned hour. The prayer chain can be a great spiritual experience if properly organized. Please don't leave it to chance or it will be ineffective.

## 3. SIMULTANEOUS PRAYER TIME

All of us are encouraged to pray when we are accountable to one another. A specific time set aside every day by the whole congregation will encourage prayer for the revival. A time such as 10:00 should be designated as the time when all will pray for revival. Each time 10:00 rolls around on the clock, A.M. and P.M., all will be challenged to stop and pray for revival.

## 4. PRAYER PARTNERS

Selecting prayer partners is another effective way to involve many in the prayer preparation for revival. A card is to be produced which says: **My Prayer Partner is (Name).** We will covenant together to pray each day for revival. At the bottom of the REVIVAL PRAYER COMMITMENT CARD should be a place for each prayer partner to sign his/her name and turn it in to you the Prayer Chairman.

## 5. MEN'S AND LADIES' PRAYER BREAKFAST

An exciting event that has been used successfully for many years is the Men's or Ladies' prayer breakfast. A time is set aside at the beginning of a day to come together to pray for revival. The meal is cooked and served by a specific group in the church. Example: The men serve the ladies breakfast. The youth serve the breakfast to either the men or the ladies.

## A Suggested Schedule for Revival Prayer Meetings

- Begin by reading Scripture on prayer.
  Examples: *(Jeremiah 33:3, Matthew 18:19, James 1:6-7)*
- The importance of prayer should be discussed. The relationship between prayer and revival should be discussed. Revival is to be seen as the most important event on the church calendar. Our church is spending time in prayer, preparing us and interceding on behalf of others.
- Read *II Chron. 7:14.* Have a time of silent prayer when each person confesses his sins to God and asks for forgiveness.
- Have a time of prayer for the evangelistic team, the pastor, staff, and the church.
- Ask for prayer requests and pray for these, one at a time. The lost and unchurched should be the priority of this prayer time.
- Have a time of prayer when these requests are made for the power and courage to share their faith with those around them.
- Conclude the prayer time with a time of silent prayer when each one present commits themselves to the revival effort. Lead the closing prayer with the prayer that God will do His work in the lives of our families during the revival.

## The Power of Praise and Worship
### Yet thou art Holy,
### O Thou who art enthroned upon the praises of Israel.
### (Psalm 22:3)

In the invisible war, our Lord has given to His people a most powerful weapon of praise. The power and presence of almighty God resides in the praises of God's people. Satan resents hearing God praised by His children. Martin Luther used to say, "Let us sing psalms and spite the Devil." I have no doubt Martin Luther was pretty nearly right, for that lover of discord hates harmonious, joyous praise.[19] As long as the Church can sing her great hymns she cannot be defeated; for hymns are theology set to music. Hymns do not create truth, nor even reveal it; they celebrate it. They are the response of the trusting heart to a truth revealed or a fact accomplished. God does it and man sings it. God speaks and a hymn is the musical echo of His voice.[20]

Remember, Satan is the father of lies. He hates truth. The praises of God's people reveal the truth of God and His work in their lives. The Devil can't handle it.

Why is praise so powerful? *Whoso offereth praise, glorifieth Me (Psalm 50:23).* As we have studied in Chapter 4, all things have been created by God for God. All exists for His glory! When His creation praises Him, His glory is displayed *(Psalm 69:34, Psalm 148, Isaiah 42:10).* Satan's great desire was to rob God of His glory, by receiving what was meant for God for himself. It is an eternally serious matter when God is robbed of His glory. He is to be praised!

> *From the rising of the sun to its setting the name of the Lord is to be praised (Psalm 113:3).*

> *Let everything that has breath praise the Lord. Praise the Lord (Psalm 150:6)!*

Praising the Lord reminds the Enemy that Jesus Christ is Lord and Master of all. All of the schemes of the Enemy against the Church are aimed at robbing God of His glory. A discouraged and joyless church is hampered in her praise. Spurgeon put it this way, "Beloved friend, the Archenemy wants to make you wretched here if he cannot have you hereafter. In this, no doubt, he is aiming a blow at the honor of God. He is well aware that mournful Christians often dishonor the faithfulness of God by mistrusting it. Thus he thinks if he can worry us until we no longer believe in the constancy and goodness of the Lord, he will have robbed God of His praise."[21]

We also see the powerful significance of praising the Lord. When David numbered 38,000 Levites, 4,000 of them were assigned to praise the Lord *(I Chron. 16:4,6,37).* The Levites were appointed to praise in the gates of the tents of the Lord *(2 Chron. 31:2).* As we come into the presence of God we are to praise Him. *Enter into His gates with thanksgiving, and into His courts with praise (Psalm 100:4).* Throughout the Bible the praise of God's people is essential in their relationship to God. The natural result of knowing God and walking with Him is to praise and worship Him.

God responds to the praises of His people. God's power is manifested in the praises of His people. *Out of the mouths of babes and sucklings has*

*thou ordained strength (Psalm 8:2).* Jesus paraphrasing this same passage, put it this way, *Out of the mouths of babes and sucklings thou has
perfected praise (Matt. 21:16).* It is clear that praise is equated with
strength. In *2 Chronicles 20:20-22, KJV,* Jehoshaphat went out to fight a
massive army, and notice how he achieved the victory.

> *So they rose early in the morning and went out into the
> Wilderness of Tekoa; and as they went out, Jehoshaphat stood
> and said, "Hear me, O Judah and you inhabitants of Jerusalem;
> believe in the Lord your God, and you shall be established;
> believe His prophets, and you shall prosper. And when he had
> consulted with the people, He appointed—* Warriors? No. He
> appointed singers, worshippers. *Those who should sing to the
> Lord, and who should praise the beauty of holiness, as they
> went out before the army and were saying, "Praise the Lord, for
> His mercy endures forever." Now when they began to sing and
> to praise, the Lord set ambushes against the people of Ammon,
> Moab, and Mount Seir, who had come against Judah; and they
> were defeated.*

Victory came when they began to sing and praise the Lord. Some
of the many stories of demon manifestations have come from great
worship services. While on a preaching mission in Africa, it became a
common occurrence in the midst of the services to see the tormenting
of demon spirits in the lives of those who needed deliverance. These
manifestations came about primarily during the worship of God's people. And Oh, how the African believers can worship! Satan can't stand
the worship of God's people.

Last summer during a youth camp in Texas, God began to move in
great power among the young people. Much of the schedule was dis-
missed because of the praying and confessing of many who were so
moved of God. My three children were present that amazing week.
They said, "Daddy, the worship of the Lord was constant and genuine."
Many of the young people night after night committed their lives to
Christ. Before the week was over, there were at least three demonic
manifestations. One of them was so dramatic, that the precious young
girl was going to kill herself. All who were present saw clearly how
Satan can't stand the praises of God's people.

Whenever there is a great work of God among His people, it is always accompanied with great praise. As one studies the great revival movements of God, it is impossible to ignore the great music that accompanies the work of God. Music is a great tool to open the heart for the work of God. Of course Satan knows the powerful impact of music on the soul of man. Once as a chief musician in heaven, Lucifer knows very well the power of praise to the Lord *(Isaiah 14:11)*.

## *Music for Revival-time*

Music is an integral part of every revival crusade. The spiritual place of music in a revival crusade cannot be over emphasized. More often than not the people's willingness to hear the message of God is based upon the music and its ability to prepare the heart for God's Word. Each crusade service is to be truly a time of worship where the people of God lift up their hearts in praise to God. Just like the revival message, the revival music must call for repentance and faith in Christ alone for the forgiveness of sins.

All Christian music is <u>not appropriate</u> during the revival service. Two guiding concepts should bring into focus the kind of music appropriate for revival. They are **REMEMBRANCE MUSIC** and **REPENTANCE MUSIC**. Revival music is to aid the Church in remembering the times of commitment in the past. For many, revival is a time of returning to "Bethel," the place of our first commitments to Christ. Music that tells the story of Calvary and lifts up the work of Christ is what is encouraged. Revival music tells who Jesus is and what He did for us. Revival music calls for a commitment of repentance and faith. Revival-time is not a time of celebration; it is a time of mourning. Joy comes after the cleansing time of revival. The style of music may vary, however it must be appropriate for the spiritual needs that will be present in the service. An open-heart surgeon never uses a sledgehammer. Chances are if the music came from the "marketplace," "the top ten" Christian Music Charts, it will have little use in revival.

At the point that music becomes entertainment it ceases to be worship that is acceptable to God. A revival meeting is not a talent show. Revival music is Christ-centered not self-centered. Music is not about us feeling good; it must be about honoring and blessing the Lord. Revival music is not a "show boat" it must be a "life boat." Music during revival-time must lift Christ up so that men might come to know Him as Savior and Lord of their lives. We want people to leave the services saying, "How great our God is," not "how great our talented ones are." However subtle, we must not allow any praise to find a home in the heart of the musician. All praise and all glory must go to our Lord Jesus. If any praise comes to us, we must redirect all of it to the Lord. He alone is worthy to be praised!

### True Worship in Warfare
#### You shall surround me with Songs of Deliverance.
#### (Psalm 32:7)

Praise has a spiritual relationship to deliverance. Paul and Silas were praising God in prison when the prison doors were opened and their chains fell off *(Acts 16:25-26)*. In spiritual warfare praise brings victory. Jericho fell to the trumpets of Joshua *(Joshua 6)*. Judah defeated Israel with a shout *(2 Chron. 13:14-15)*. Singing defeated Ammon and Moab *(2 Cron. 20:22)*. The Psalmist makes it clear, *there is... triumph in thy praise (Psalm 106:47)*. Whenever you go to war against the demonic forces of evil, go praising![22] In every instance of deliverance, where there is the praising of God's people, demons are tormented by it. The worship of our Lord is a sweet healing balm to the afflicted. But to the unholy and wicked it stings like fire.

Worship that works in warfare is that which exalts the Lord. He is to be worshiped. He alone is to be praised. What are the components of true worship that works in the invisible war?

1. **True Worship is SUPERNATURAL.** *God is spirit, and those who worship Him must worship in spirit and truth (John 4:24)*. True worship is not only what we do. It is moreover that which our Lord does in us through the supernatural communion we have with Him.

2. **True Worship is SPONTANEOUS.** *While the whole assembly worshiped, the singers also sang and the trumpets sounded; all this continued until the burnt offering was finished (2 Chron. 29:28)*. What I mean by spontaneous is not that which is unruly

or chaotic. All things in the worship service must be *done properly and in an orderly manner (I Cor. 14:40)*. Spontaneous worship is worship initiated out of a grateful heart. Not some emotional ecstasy worked up by a "cheer leader" calling himself a worship leader. True worship is an **instantaneous** response to the presence and work of God.

3.  **True Worship is SACRIFICIAL.** *I urge you therefore, brethren, by the mercies of God, to present your bodies a living and holy sacrifice, acceptable to God which is your spiritual service of worship (Romans 12:1)*. If our worship is to be used of God in the work of God, it must come from a heart that is totally committed to God. Worship is not just what we do. Worship is what we do because of whose we are. All that we are, all that we possess, and all that we hope to be must be brought to our Lord in true worship.

4.  **True Worship is SANCTIFIED.** *And He will purify the sons of Levi and refine them like gold and silver, so that they may present to the Lord offerings in righteousness (Malachi 2:3)*. As in the previous verse in Romans, worship is to be holy unto the Lord. Worship is to be different, set apart, and holy. True worship is to come from a pure heart living in the righteousness of God.

5.  **True Worship is SUBMISSIVE.** *God is opposed to the proud, but gives grace to the humble. Submit therefore to God. Resist the Devil and he will flee from you (James 4:6-7)*. Submission is not to be confused with passivity. Passivity is one of the great spiritual dangers in the life of the believer. Submission to God is to seek only the will of the Father. Worship is to exalt Christ alone. True worship comes from the heart that has chosen to humble itself before God. Remember, beloved, this one striking point: Jesus Christ will have all of us or nothing. He will have us sincere, earnest, and intense, or He will not have us at all. If you wish to give Christ a little and Baal a little, you will be cast away and utterly rejected- the Lord of Heaven will have nothing to do with you. *Bless the Lord,* then, *all that is within me*

*(Psalm 103:1),* for only such sincere and undivided honor can be accepted by the Lord.[23] When worship comes from a heart totally submitted to the purposes of God, the Devil is in trouble and he knows it.

## The Power of Proclamation
## The Preaching of the Gospel-Evangelism

*For I am not ashamed of the gospel, for it is the POWER of God for salvation to everyone who believes, to the Jew first and also to the Greek. (Romans 1:16)*

*But you shall receive POWER when the Holy Spirit has come upon you; and you shall be my witnesses both in Jerusalem, and in all Judea and Samaria, and even to the remotest part of the earth (Acts 1:8).*

As our Lord has called us to win our world to Christ, He has given the Church the spiritual tools to get the job done. He said:

*All authority has been given to Me in heaven and on earth. Go therefore and make disciples of all the nations, baptizing them in the name of the Father and the Son and the Holy Spirit, teaching them to observe all that I commanded you; and lo, I am with you always, even to the end of the age (Matt. 28:18-20).*

He has not only told us what to do, but our Lord has given us the power to get the job done. The commissioning of Jesus' disciples is preceded with the statement of authority in the heavens. Now that Jesus has been raised from the dead and is now seated at the right hand of God the Father in the seat of absolute authority, He has sent forth His followers not only with a task of winning the world to Christ, but He has given the Church the "authority" and all the power of that authority both in heaven and in earth to be successful in the battle for souls.

Evangelism cannot be clearly understood outside of the invisible war. You see, all of Satan's schemes are designed to rob God of His glory. No greater glory can be given to God than through the changed life of the redeemed. It is man, and man alone, that has been created in the image of God. Because of the sin of our first parents, Adam and Eve, mankind is under the curse of sin *(I Cor. 15)*. Satan wins the war as long as people remain lost in their sin and separation from God and His glory. Because of man's sin, the glory of God intended in and through his life is hindered. Once man's sin is covered by the blood of Jesus, the glory of God can shine. Even at the Cross of Christ, where the payment for all sin was made, Satan in his confused state thought he had God defeated:

*The wisdom which none of the rulers of this age has understood; for if they had understood it, they would not have crucified the Lord of glory (I Cor. 2:8).*

It is at the Cross that sin was ultimately and forever defeated:

*And when you were dead in your transgressions and the uncircumcision of your flesh, He made you alive together with Him, having forgiven us all our transgressions, having canceled out the certificate of debt consisting of decrees against us and which was hostile to us; and He has taken it out of the way, having nailed it to the cross. When He had disarmed the rulers and authorities, He made a public display of them, having triumphed over them through Him (Col. 2:13-15).*

It is at the cross all of Satan's efforts to kill, steal, and destroy became powerless. Because of Jesus' willingness to go the cross and become the sacrifice for all sin, God gave His Son all authority and power. All authority and power over Satan and his underlings, whatever their names, whatever their assignments from Hell, or whatever their evil schemes:

*And being found in appearance as a man, He humbled Himself by becoming obedient to the point of death, even death on a cross. Therefore also God highly exalted Him, and bestowed on Him the name which is above every name, that at the name of Jesus every knee should bow, of those who are in heaven, and on earth, and under the earth, and that every tongue should*

*confess that Jesus Christ is Lord, to the glory of God the Father
(Phil. 2:8-11).*

This power and authority over sin and its resulting death, was given
to Christ by the Heavenly Father. It now has been delegated as a shared
authority to the Church through our union with Him. *And raised us up
with Him, and seated us with Him in the heavenly places, in Christ
Jesus (Eph. 2:6).* Think of it, the Church has been given the authority
of heaven and all the power that goes with that authority to win our
world to Christ.

Through the proclamation of the Word of God the eternal work of
God is done. When the Word of God is shared, the Holy Spirit of God
goes to work:

*For the Word of God is living and active and sharper than any
two-edged sword, and piercing as far as the division of soul and
spirit, of both joints and marrow, and able to judge the thoughts
and intentions of the heart (Heb. 4:12).*

The Word of God is eternal and forever settled in Heaven *(Psalm
119:89).* It is so powerful that it always accomplishes the purpose for
which God intends. Nothing can stop it:

*So shall my Word be which goes forth from My mouth; It shall
not return to Me empty, Without accomplishing what I desire,
And without succeeding in the matter for which I sent it (Isaiah
55:11).*

Satan can't stop the Word of God when it goes forth. All he can do
is try to blind the hearers and stop the Church from telling the truth.
Remember in the war with Satan in the book of the Revelation, he was
defeated by three things. *And they overcame him because of the blood
of the Lamb and because of the word of their testimony, and they did
not love their life even to death (Rev. 12:11).* He is still defeated today
by the same three things. 1. The blood of the Lamb, Calvary. 2. The
word of their testimony. The telling of the truth, which is the proclamation of the Gospel. 3. And they did not love their life even to death.
They had emptied themselves of all their pride and flesh.

There is no greater loss to Satan's kingdom than the salvation of a precious soul. All of his lies and schemes are aimed at keeping people from knowing Christ and His salvation. It is Satan who blinds the unbelieving from the light of the gospel of Christ.

*And even if our gospel is veiled, it is veiled to those who are perishing, in whose case the god of this world has blinded the minds of the unbelieving, that they might not see the light of the gospel of the glory of Christ, who is the image of God (2 Cor. 4:3-4).*

The Enemy of God works on every aspect of the message. The messenger is attacked. The Church is attacked. And the world is blinded from seeing the light of the Gospel.

Is there any hope in this eternal battle for men's souls? YES! A thousand times ten thousand times, YES! The Gospel of Christ is the POWER of God. The proclaiming of the Gospel Truth dispels all of Satan's lies and deceit. The Church has been given the greatest weapon of all to defeat Satan and his demons, the preaching of the Gospel of Christ. It is through the preaching of the Gospel that all of Satan's plans are thwarted. When anyone comes to Christ and trusts Him to save him/her from his/her sin, he is delivered from the domain or kingdom of darkness into the kingdom of Christ. *For He delivered us from the domain of darkness, and transferred us to the kingdom of His beloved Son (Col. 1:13).*

There is no greater battle in the invisible war than the battle for the lost. There is no greater power hurled by Satan and His hosts of demons than in the midst of evangelism. Satan will do anything and everything he can to keep the Church from evangelizing the lost. If the church settles for a false gospel without repentance, Satan wins. If the church sets its mission on anything but winning the lost, Satan wins. If the church is focused inward instead of aiming its ministry to a lost and dying world, Satan wins. If the Church buys into the strategies of the market driven world to establish its place in the community, Satan wins. There is no greater victory in the invisible war than when a person comes to put his/her faith and trust in Christ alone for the forgiveness of his/her sin. When a soul is saved, Satan is defeated.

As I close this chapter on "Revival and the Invisible War," I want to say one final word about taking an area or city for Christ. There have been many methods discussed and debated concerning taking a city for Christ. Methods that are now being used that carry terms of "Spiritual Mapping" and "Prayer Walking." These are methods under the umbrella of what is called "Strategic Level of Spiritual Warfare." This label has been coined by Peter Wagner, Professor of Church Growth at Fuller Theological Seminary. Wagner has written several books on the subject of spiritual warfare. In his book *Warfare Prayer*, he lays out a prayer strategy on how to confront "territorial spirits," "principalities and powers" for the sake of taking a city for Christ.

The best discussion on whether or not we should confront these territorial spirits is in an extremely helpful work entitled, *Three Crucial Questions about Spiritual Warfare* by Clinton Arnold published by Baker Books. The last section of this book is entitled, "Are we called to engage territorial spirits?" The professor handles the issue historically, practically, and biblically for the serious student of these matters. It is a "must read" in this most crucial area of spiritual warfare.

How then should we take our towns and cities for Christ in the invisible war? Should we take them through the confrontation of evil spirits? Should we take them through establishing a rule of righteousness in the schools and courts of our land through political power? Should we take them by building more buildings we call churches and establishing more Christian organizations? Please hear me and hear me well, if we are going to take our cities and towns for Christ we must do it, one soul at a time. It is through one boy and one girl at a time, one merchant, one shopper at a time, one wife, one husband at a time. It is through the power of the proclamation of the Gospel of Christ that the POWER of God resides. Our cities and towns will come to submit to the lordship of Christ when everyone in that city comes to put their complete trust and faith in the Lord Jesus.

It is my conviction based on my study of God's Word, our Lord alone is in charge of the invisible war in which we find ourselves. It is His war and it is His victory. This is His creation and we are His Church. Any program of prayer and confronting the dark powers that is practiced by the sole initiative and determination of the Church, for whatever reason, can be a catalyst for great confusion and ultimate defeat in the invisible war. However, as our Lord leads us, we can ask Him to bind territorial spirits and all works of the Enemy so that the hindrances to revival will cease.

Let us join together in our union with Christ in accepting the responsibility of the authority and power of God given to His Church. However long our Heavenly Father assigns our time on this earth, may we accept nothing less than the victory and freedom that is our birthright in Christ. Today and into the tomorrows, let us live as a praying people. Let us be the people of God committed to the eternal purposes of God. May we not rest until every man, woman, boy, girl, and young person comes to hear the good news of the Gospel of Christ through which all can be rescued from Satan's dark kingdom of death and joyfully presented to our loving Heavenly Father who created all for His Glory.

# Chapter 8

# Questions and Answers
## About The Invisible War

*"There are two equal and opposite errors into which our race can fall about devils. One is to disbelieve in their existence. The other is to believe, and to feel an excessive and unhealthy interest in them. They themselves are equally pleased by both errors."*

*– C.S. Lewis*

*Question: Is there not a danger of becoming too preoccupied with demons?*

*Answer:* Of course there is. This is not a practice for the curious. Curiosity can get a person hurt in the invisible war. Dealing with demons in the flesh can get someone killed. However, it is just as unbalanced to ignore the reality of demons and their work, as it is to go looking for them. Looking for demons "under every pew," and "behind every bush" is ridiculous. But when you are faced with them and their subsequent work, it is spiritually irresponsible to ignore them.

*Question: Why do we have to get involved in deliverance? Can't the Lord take care of these matters without us?*

*Answer:* Of course the Lord can take care of these matters. He is the only one who can. It must be understood that the Church is the Body of Christ. God does what He does in the world through His Body, the Church. The deliverance ministry is not any different than leading someone to faith in Christ. The process of being used by the Holy Spirit is exactly the same. Even though we say, "We win people to Christ," we don't win anyone. It is the Holy Spirit working through us that wins them. There's not just one verse in the Bible from which we get our understanding and methods of evangelism. It's the same in deliverance. One must study the spiritual principles in the Word of God to understand how the Lord uses us in this eternal process of setting the captives free.

We don't deliver anyone from the powers of darkness. The Lord Jesus Christ delivers those who are bound. He chooses to use a willing vessel, a willing Church through whom to do His work. *2 Cor. 6:1* says, *"We are workers together with Him..."* In deliverance we are workers together with Christ.

**Question:** *What about the use of anointing oil in deliverance? Is it necessary?*

**Answer:** I see no biblical foundation for the use of anointing oil in deliverance. In *James Chapter 5* we see the use of oil accompanying the prayers for the sick. The oil I believe had no special healing qualities. The oil was a "helping symbol" in the praying for the sick. Much like baptism is a helping symbol for us today. The water doesn't cleanse our sin. The baptismal waters help us see the picture of the death, burial, and resurrection of our Lord. It is a pictorial of the identification of the new believer in Christ. Much the same way the oil represents the Holy Spirit. I see no danger in using anointing oil in deliverance as long it is seen as a "helping symbol." However, if it is seen as holding some supernatural power it becomes occultish and should be avoided.

**Question:** *What is the gift of discernment? Does a Christian have to have this special gift to be able to do deliverance?*

**Answer:** Discernment is simply the ability to listen to the Lord. He said, *"My Sheep hear my voice."* Deliverance is a work of Almighty

God. No one is able to understand the heart of man. Remember, *"The heart is deceitful and desperately wicked who can know it" (Jeremiah 17:9)?* It is the living Word of God who is the *"discerner of the thoughts and intents of the heart" (Heb. 4:12).* The Lord alone is able to know what is going on in a man's heart. In deliverance He allows us to join Him in the cleaning and healing process. In deliverance, I feel like I am an assistant to a master surgeon. The Lord is in charge. Discernment is listening to the Lord when He speaks.

In *1 Corinthians 12* the Apostle Paul is writing to a church in trouble. The Corinthian Church had begun to fight over which spiritual gift was more important. The flesh had begun to rule in the Church. Each one thought since the Lord had given him or her a certain gift that he/she was more important than his/her fellow believers. I believe that Paul is listing all the different gifts of the Church to show the Corinthian Church that any one particular gift was no more important than any other. The theme of the passage is "The Lord is in Charge of His Church." All the spiritual gifts and their manifestations are for His glory.

We have a tendency to follow the logic of the Church instead of the wisdom of the Scripture. What I mean is, we think, since they thought the gifts were given separately to specific believers, God must only give certain spiritual manifestations to certain believers. I do not think this is so. It is my conviction that our Lord will give any believer at any time whatever is needed for the Lord Jesus to be exalted in and through his or her life. We have been created for the glory of God and His will. All the Lord is looking for is a willing vessel through which His will can be done. As in all the manifestations of the Spirit, you'll have it when you need it.

**Question:** *How can we know for sure if someone has a demon?*

**Answer:** God is the one who reveals the truth concerning the invisible war. He is the one who will tell you if someone has a demon. One of the obstacles we face in our understanding comes from the two images we have of people who are demonized. We have the image of the Gadarene Demoniac. Here he is, living in the tombs, naked, cutting himself, and foaming at the mouth (A homeless insane person). The other image is Linda Blair in the Hollywood movie, *The Exorcist*. The

picture is one whose head is spinning around vomiting green pea soup
all over the walls while spewing vile curses and blasphemies. We
assume that when one has a demon, one of these two manifestations is
what we will see. The truth of the matter is demons do not want to
"manifest." They do their evil work in darkness. The fruit or result of
their work is not invisible, but they will do all they can to keep from
being found out. That is, to stay in darkness. Remember, they are
doomed and damned. And they know it.

**Question:** *Do we actually take authority over evil spirits in deliverance?*

**Answer:** The concept of "taking authority" must be carefully understood. You and I don't have any authority over evil spirits. Only Christ
has the authority over such matters *(Matt. 28:18)*. It is only through our
union with Him that we share in His work of deliverance *(Eph. 2:5-6)*.
It is Christ who takes authority over evil spirits. In deliverance we only
join Him as He takes the authority over evil spirits.

**Question:** *Do you believe in territorial spirits? Are there super
demons that are assigned to geographic locations such as churches,
cities, and the like?*

**Answer:** I do believe that these demons do exist. I believe that Satan
has a kingdom that is carefully designed to do the most damage to the
cause of Christ. Long before I studied spiritual warfare, I became aware
of the concept of the spiritual battle in a given territory. As an evangelist it became obvious that some towns were easier to evangelize in than
others. There was a spiritual resistance in many places that was
stronger than other places. The Bible does indicate in Daniel that these
spirits do exist. Why, the very use of the word "principality" indicates
such spirits.

Because of their greater authority and power, territorial spirits, principalities, must be approached with extreme caution. I do not believe it
is appropriate for the believer to go up against these powerful spirits
unless specifically directed by God. We do not read where Daniel

approached these spirits. We do not read where Paul ever went up against these principalities. To do so could result in tragedy. I do believe however that we can pray for the Lord to confront these spirits so that His will is done in a given place.

## Question: *Do you believe in prayer walking?*

**Answer:** Any approach to prayer that encourages us to come boldly before the Throne is a good thing. As an aid to help encourage our faith, the prayer walk can be very helpful. However, if by prayer walking you mean a strategy by which we challenge the authority of territorial spirits, it can be dangerous and misleading. There is not a biblical basis for such matters. In the Book of Acts we don't see such a strategy in winning people to Christ. They prayed, praised, and proclaimed the Good News of Christ.

Let me refer you to a book written by Dr. Clinton Arnold on the subject. The book is entitled, *Three Crucial Questions about Spiritual Warfare*, Baker Books Publication. The last section of this important work is "Are we called to engage territorial spirits?" The professor does a wonderful work in helping dispel the confusion around such matters.

## Question: *What about Spiritual Mapping?*

**Answer:** Spiritual mapping is a process of isolating areas of darkness within a given area. Once the darkness is recognized, prayer is offered up to dispense "principalities and powers," territorial spirits. The assumption is that if these territorial spirits can be dispersed, our evangelism will become more fruitful. Let me again refer you to Dr. Arnold's work on this matter. It is most helpful.

May I say that any procedure that helps us to become aware of the spiritual battle we find ourselves in and encourages us to believe and trust our Lord is a good thing. However, the idea of going up against these powerful principalities may not be the best idea. Until the "ground is taken back," the sin contract broken, to do such battle with these spirits would be ultimately futile. We can however ask the Lord to bind these spirits that God's will is done in and through His Church.

*Question:* **Is it possible to corporately "remit" the sins of others?**

*Answer:* No. This practice is not biblical. It smacks of Mormonism or some of the pagan practices of the Roman Church. Believers cannot remove the curse of unbelievers. If a Christian leader today publicly confesses his or her city's sins of drug abuse or prostitution, what good does this do if those involved with these evils have not made a confession of faith in Christ. Without faith in Christ, the door is wide open for evil spirits to remain.

Some few years ago, the Southern Baptist Convention publicly prayed for forgiveness for its forefather's participation in slavery. I was extremely uncomfortable with it then and just the mention of this practice makes me very nervous. It is impossible to remit the sins of others. However, if a corporate sin has been committed by a family, church, city, country, etc., it is important to confess that sin corporately. If we have done it together, we can repent of it together *(Neh. 1:6-7)*.

*Question:* **Spiritual warfare seems to me to bring us too close to the occult. Should not a believer avoid such matters?**

*Answer:* We are in a spiritual battle. Whether we like it or not, the Lord has placed us in a hostile environment. This environment is controlled by very powerful personalities with which we must wrestle *(Eph. 6)*. The schemes of the Enemy are darker and more complex than man in his most wicked moment can conceive.

While battling these schemes and assigned evil spirits, the believer will constantly find himself bumping up against the works of darkness, the occult. It is impossible to avoid it. However, just because these matters are revealed for the sake of someone's deliverance, doesn't preclude we have been involved ourselves in the occult.

*Question:* **If it works, then it must be of God, right?**

*Answer:* Our experiences can be deceptive in terms of looking to them for truth. Our flesh can easily be deceived. Every experience, every procedure and approach in the invisible war must be carefully and prayerfully filtered through the truth of God's Word.

Demons are so full of tricks and deception that many are named, "False deliverance" and the like. We cannot believe everything we see, hear, or feel. It is the Word of God that is living and able to discern what is going on in the heart of man *(Heb. 4:12)*. The so-called end does not justify the means when it comes to deliverance.

### Question: *Should deliverance be done in public or in private?*

***Answer:*** In this regard the old adage may be appropriate, "Never say never." Biblically we read where many of the deliverances were public, whereas, many of them were private. Let me say two things here.

1. A stern warning should be given concerning so-called public "deliverance services." The Apostle Paul writing to the Corinthian Church makes the argument that the manifestations of certain gifts of the spirit in public worship could be opened to abuse and misunderstood by those we are trying to reach for Christ *(I Cor. 14:23-26)*. Our flesh is of such nature that we tend to exalt the one who practices the spiritual gift instead of the One who gives the gift. All manifestations of the Spirit of God are for the glory of God and the edification of the whole body of Christ.

2. I believe it is best to handle a deliverance session in private. Deliverance is a "dirty business." The ground that the Devil has been allowed to occupy in the life of the inflicted is most often a sorted and filthy affair. I never cease to be shocked at the horrible evil the Enemy inflicts upon the life of the demonized. There is no personal gratification for the deliverance minister outside the love of our Heavenly Father. The deliverance minister is the "trash collector" in the Church. To protect the individual from the further abuse of the "gossip mill" these matters must be held in strictest confidence and remain private.

### Question: *Is it O.K. to call on angels to help in deliverance?*

***Answer:*** In the Book of Hebrews we find an amazing verse concerning the angels that says, *"Are they not all ministering spirits sent out to render service for the sake of those who will inherit salvation" (Hebrews 1:14)?*

All angels, good and evil, are under the ultimate authority of God. They are on assignment to, "render service," help believers in the receiving of God's will.

It is important to note that we do not control the angels. Only in our union with Christ is the participation with the angels possible. It is never appropriate to call on the angels to help. It is however appropriate to ask the Lord to allow His angels to help in matters of deliverance according to His will. Angels don't have any power to deliver. Only Christ has come to set the captives free. Any practice that brings attention to the work of angels and not to the work of Christ can be spiritually dangerous. We are warned in Scripture that we must worship only God not the Angels *(Col. 2:18)*.

**Question:** *Should not these matters be relegated to the professional counselors?*

**Answer:** There are those Christian counselors for whom I have the highest respect in these spiritual matters. We have much to learn from these men and women who have been called of God to do this work. However, I do not believe that man has answers to man's problems. Only God understands fully what is going on in the hearts of men and women. I know of well-trained, well-educated, so called Christian counselors who are of little or no help in these matters of deliverance from the darkness. One who has received a liberal education in psychology is no more prepared to handle these matters than any otherworldly counselor.

Nowhere in the Scripture do we find where these matters are relegated to the "professionals." Man does not deliver anyone. He doesn't have the power. Only Christ has come *"to destroy the works of the Devil"* *(I John 3:8)*. We are only *"workers together with Him"* *(2 Cor. 6:1)!*

**Question:** *Is it important to stay within your relegated ministry or "authority" when facing the forces of darkness?*

**Answer:** Absolutely! God has called each of us to a specific ministry within His Church. God has set up in His Kingdom certain authority. For instance, the husband is the head of the wife and the home *(Eph. 5:23)*. The pastor is responsible for the flock to which the Lord has made him overseer *(Acts 20:28)*.

In God's economy and for His glory, He has established certain authority under His Lordship. It is necessary for the one who comes up against the powers of darkness to stay within his or her place of spiritual responsibility and authority. Let me explain. I never counsel with anyone outside of my ministry.

Unless the pastor has invited me to come under the umbrella of his church and ministry, I do not go. No matter what I may believe concerning the demonization of a person, unless the inflicted person comes to me there is no encounter. It is extremely important for the one involved in deliverance to stay within his or her relegated authority and assignment given to him from God.

## *Question: Why have Baptists not faced the issue of deliverance?*

*Answer:*  The Randall Family has been serving Southern Baptist Churches in the ministry of Evangelism for over 100 years. My Father and both of my Grandfathers were Southern Baptist preachers. First of all let me say that since Baptists are a congregational people in terms of their polity, no one can speak for all Baptists. To attempt to do so would be foolish at best. You've heard the old sayin', "When you've got two Baptists you have three opinions."

Baptists do and have faced the issue of deliverance. Talk to our thousands of missionaries around the world concerning these matters. Most of our pastors have their "demon stories" from their ministry encounters. I have heard many of them throughout the years as they have come up in our conversations. I do believe that because our educational institutions have been preoccupied with the matter of politics, (raising money), as well as the pressure to comply with the accrediting boards, these matters of dealing with spiritual warfare have been on the "back burner" instead of the forefront of the curriculum. However, let me state that in most of our seminaries such a course has existed. At my seminary, Southwestern Baptist Theological Seminary in Ft. Worth, Texas, these matters were taught for many years in a course called

"Spiritual Foundations for Missions."

Just because we have not gone "public" with these matters, one cannot preclude that Baptists don't believe and practice deliverance. As I have stated in this book, I do believe that since so many of our children are now in spiritual bondage and spiritual jeopardy, we as Baptists can no longer ignore getting them help. Because of the great spiritual needs of this generation, our institutions must begin to teach our leaders how to be used of God to set the captives free.

# Appendix A

# CASE STUDIES From America's Heartland
# IN THE INVISIBLE WAR

These case studies are printed to give this study of the invisible war a place to develop in the hearts of those who will be used by our Lord in the ministry of deliverance. These illustrations are not intended to be a catalyst by shocking those who are intrigued by the invisible war. These are not spooky "campfire" stories. This book is not for the curious. This book is for the one who is seeking biblical truth concerning spiritual warfare. This book is intended for those who seek the victory and freedom that is in Christ Jesus.

These illustrations are not intended to teach "the only way of doing deliverance." Remember, Christ is in charge of deliverance. He will determine what is needed to bring deliverance to the captives. The following stories are just a sampling of the great and mighty things we have witnessed of our Lord. The names of these precious people have been changed to honor their privacy. As you read these case studies, do so with the goal of seeing how the biblical principles laid out in this book are followed in the ministry of deliverance. We serve a great and mighty God!

## Case 1: Texas

As I was traveling to a meeting in a church where I had conducted a revival meeting some eight years before, I was listening to a message on revival preached by the late great revivalist, Leonard Ravenhill. In the message he referred to an evangelist during the late 1930s through the 1940s that would say to the folks each night in his crusades, "Those of you that need prayer for deliverance come to the alter everyone else go home." Each night many would come for repentance and deliverance. They would stay each night for hours dealing and praying with those that would come.

As I preached that night on "The Invisible War," the Lord told me to practice what I had heard on the tape by Ravenhill. So I asked for those to come forward that needed prayer and for everyone else to go home. Two ladies came forward that night. The accompanist and a lady named Linda. The pianist spoke first. I asked, "What do you need prayer for?" She said, "Because I get so angry." "With whom are you angry?" She said, "I'm mad at you for bringing all this stuff out in the open in our church." I asked, "What is the source of your anger?" She began to sob as she said, "My husband. He hurt my children and me because he is so impatient and verbally abusive. I just want him to love me and understand what I have to go through everyday." I asked her "Do you love him?" She said, "Yes." "Do you believe God loves him?" She said, "Yes, I do." "Do you believe God can handle this in your husband?" Through her tears she said, "Yes."

I explained to her that no matter what she did or what she said she was not able to do what needed to be done in her husband. That only God could give him a love for her and their children. Only God could bring about in his life what was needed for God's will to be done in him. When she let the sun go down on her anger, she had given a place for the Devil to work. And that working of the Devil in her life had joined her to the Devil's rebellion against God as she had decided God couldn't handle it without her. Through her unbelief Satan had gained a stronghold. Once the stronghold was discovered and denounced, she received the healing and cleansing the Lord had for her.

The other lady waited patiently while we worked and prayed with her friend. I asked, "Why have you come? For what do you need prayer?" She said, "Look at my wrists." I tried not to show my shock. Scar upon scar as a painful reminder of her hopelessness. She continued to tell me how she felt worthless and had tried suicide many times to end her sorrow. I told her she had believed a lie of the Enemy. That she was special and that God loved her. Jesus had proven God's love for her when He died for all her sin on Calvary. I inquired as to the source of her sorrow. She told me that her daughter had been sexually molested by her second husband. And she believed that if she had been the mother she was supposed to be, it wouldn't have happened. I told her that it wasn't her fault, it was his fault. She had believed a lie all these years. And the Devil had built a stronghold in her life based on lies and deception.

I asked her if she was ready to be set free. She said she was. I took her to *James 4* and showed her the prayers that God answers are only those **1. Specific Prayers** *"You have not because you ask not."*

**2. Unselfish Prayers** *"You ask and do not receive, because you ask with wrong motives, so that you may spend it on your pleasures."* **3. Submissive Prayers** *"God is opposed to the proud, but gives grace to the humble."*

I explained to her that if she wanted to be free just so the pain in her life would end, she would not be set free. The only prayer God answers is the one prayed in God's will for God's will. I told her that it was the Lord's desire to heal and deliver her from all the lies and sorrow of the Enemy. *"He came to set the captives free"* (Luke 4). *"The Son of God was manifest that He might destroy the works of the Devil"* (I John 3:8).

I asked her if she was ready to pray. She said she was. I began to pray and ask the Lord to silence all other voices but His. I took authority over all wicked spirits that were involved in her life. I told them that they could not manifest in any way. There would only be a one-way direction that they could move and that was through the barren desert to the place that the Lord Jesus would send them. I sought the Lord for His will while quoting *Luke 4, I John 3:8, 2 Cor. 2:14, Col. 2:13-15.*

I told her to begin to pray and tell the Lord what is in her heart. She began to cry out to the Lord. She asked forgiveness for believing the lies that she was worthless and no good. She asked forgiveness for carrying the grief and sorrow of her daughter's pain without giving it to the Lord at the Cross of Christ. It was so wonderful to hear her call out to the Lord for His healing and cleansing in her life.

We left thanking the Lord for His work of cleansing in her life. The next night of the revival meeting the pastor said that Linda had given him a sack and told him to give this to Brother Rob she wouldn't need these any more. As I opened the sack, I found a plastic box. When I opened the box there I found her razor blades and homemade noose. Her items of death and sorrow had been given to the Lord. She wouldn't need these any more. Praise the Lord!

## Case 2:  Alabama

As I began my study into spiritual warfare, I learned that the Enemy likes to do his work in darkness. That is he likes to hide. The last thing a demon wants to do is to be found out. This is especially true in the presence of a Christian who has the power in union with Christ to send the demon to the pit. The Bible says that the eyes are the window to the soul. This is never more obvious than in dealing with the demonic. Once they know that you know about them, they can't look you in the eyes. Because in the eyes of the believer is the Spirit of Christ. As a result of this spiritual encounter the demonized person simply can't look at you.

When I discovered this truth, I was preaching a meeting in Alabama. Attending the meeting each night was a well-dressed lady who was attractive (physically) but was repulsive spiritually. She had no color and no joy in her countenance. She was a very troubled woman. As I began to observe her during the week, she never would look at me. I began to wonder, "Maybe she's demonized."

She came to me to tell me that her daughter would be attending the meeting with her. I inquired about her daughter. She told me her daughter had a child and was not married. She also informed me that she had been fighting times of horrible depression and had tried suicide many times. I told her mother I would be praying for them. The Enemy's attacks are about families. When you find the Enemy's work in a life, much of the time you will find the root of that work in the history of the family.

Before the meeting was over she had asked to speak with the pastor and me after the service. As we met with her, we began our time together with a prayer. I prayed that nothing would be heard but what the Lord would want us to hear. No other voices would be heard but the voice of the Lord. All others must be silenced.

She began to share how she had been diagnosed with a compulsive behavior. When she went into a store she went into a trance like state and bought anything and everything. She had sent four husbands into bankruptcy and was on a fifth marriage. I could not imagine her pain and sorrow. Here was an attractive woman with every reason to live but without hope. She shared with me how she felt worthless and didn't deserve to live. She had considered suicide many times.

I began to replace the lies of the Enemy with the truth that God did love her and how she was precious and wonderful in his eyes. I asked her if she had a born again experience. She said she did. She told me of a time when she was a young girl when she trusted Jesus as her Savior. I asked her if she believed that Jesus had saved her as a young girl. She said she did. I proceeded to explain to her that nothing would ever separate her from the love of God in Christ Jesus *(Romans 8)*.

As soon as I heard the words I am no good, I deserve to die. I heard the Lord say "She has been sexually molested." I told her that I needed to ask her a question and that I didn't want her to misunderstand the reason for my asking. She said she understood. I asked, "Have you ever been sexually molested?" She began to openly weep. Through her tears she said she had been by her brother. She sobbed, "It was my fault, and I didn't stop him."

I told her that she had believed a lie all these years. It was not her fault. It was her brother's sin that had caused her this great pain through her life. All of her compulsive behavior was her way of coping with the pain. Behind her pain were the lies (The Father of lies, the work of the Enemy) that kept her from the forgiveness and cleansing of the Lord Jesus. I told her that Jesus came to set the captives free *(Luke 4)*. He came to destroy the works of the Devil *(I John 2:13)*.

I asked her if she wanted to be free. She said she did. I asked her if she wanted to be forgiven from the sin in her life. She said she did. I had her turn to *James Chapter 4*. And I showed her the kind of prayer that God would answer. (See Chapter Six *The Prayer that God Answers* page 140-143.) I explained that the Lord would never free her for her benefit alone. I showed her that God would answer the prayer that was prayed for his glory and for his will to be done.

A light came on and she understood. She said, "Why haven't I heard this before? I've been to many charismatic services for prayer, but no one every explained it to me like this." I asked her if she was ready to pray. She said she was. I began to pray and then asked her to cry out to the Lord. She did. Oh, how she did! I wish you could have heard her call out to our great God through her tears. Each breath of her prayer her new stumbling faith began to grow.

She was set free that night. Hallelujah! Our God is faithful. You shall know the truth and the truth shall set you free! Here is a letter I received from her a couple of months later.

*"Brother Randall, I can never thank you enough. I am not the same person sitting here tonight as I was the first time I heard you speak. I feel normal for the first time in my life. This time it was real. This time my prayers worked, because I did it for the right reasons. I didn't realize my motives in prayer were wrong until we talked. Thank you so much."*

## Case 3: Oklahoma

The Meeting in Southwest Oklahoma was an amazing week. From the beginning song of the first service, God began to move in great power. People were saved in every service of the meeting. The night I preached on the "Invisible War" I invited everyone who needed prayer to come to the altar. I told everyone else to go home.

A young high school girl came to the altar and began to cry out to the Lord as she fell on her face before God. I leaned over to her and said, "I'll be with you shortly. Just stay before the Lord." After the sanctuary cleared, I met with her on the front pew. I asked, "Why have you come? What is going on?" She replied, "I can't control my anger. I get so mad I want to hurt people." "Who do you want to hurt?" I asked. She said, "My friends at school make me so mad. They are so mean to me. I get so mad I can't control my anger." I asked her if she had been saved. Had she had a born again experience? She said she had and told me when it was.

We began to pray, "Lord we only want to hear your voice. No other voice will be heard but the Lord Jesus Christ. All others must be silenced. We only want to know what Christ wants us to know. Lord, please tell us what you want us to know so your child will be free."

As I turned back to her I asked her, "What is the source of your anger?" She told me her mean friends at school. I asked, "What is the real source of your anger?" She looked at me a bit confused. Then the Lord spoke to me and told me that she had been sexually molested by her father as a child. I looked at her and said, "Your father has hurt you, hasn't he?" She said, "How did you know? No one knows that." I told her that there were no secrets in Heaven. That every sin committed was against God. There was only one remedy for sin, the blood of Jesus. Sin could not be cleansed by ignoring or trying to forget it. Only the blood of Jesus can cleanse sin. As the Psalmist prayed, *"My sin is ever before me."* It never goes away until it is dealt with at the cross of Calvary.

She began to weep uncontrollably. I told her that if she wanted to be free, she had to call upon the Lord to do a mighty work in her life to free her from the grief, sorrows, hurts, and consequent bitterness caused by her father's sin against God and against her. I turned to *Isaiah 53* and asked her to read how the Lord carried our grief, sorrows and wounds. By what He did on Calvary we can be healed.

Then I turned to *Eph. 4.* I told her to begin reading in verses 25-27. According to the Word of God every time she went to bed angry, she had given a place for the Devil to work in her life. The place she had given to the Devil was given to him on the basis of believing his lies. I asked her what lies had she accepted of the Enemy. She began to think "God couldn't handle this. I had to carry it." That's right. The Bible says that vengeance is mine says the Lord, I will repay. It is Jesus alone who has the right to judge and execute judgment on all sin. When we decide to carry out our own judgment on a person's sin, we have joined the rebellion in the heavenlies against God. It is as though we are saying, "Jesus blood isn't enough for sin. More blood must be shed." Through the deception of the Enemy, we join his blasphemous rebellion against the work of God in Christ Jesus on Calvary.

We then turned to *James Chapter 4.* I went through the steps of the prayers that God answers. (See Chapter 6, pg 140-143.) I asked her if she was ready to pray for forgiveness. I asked her if she was ready to let go of this hurt and give it to the Lord. Was she willing to let the Lord handle it His way? She said she was.

I began to pray and call on the Lord to come in great power to do only what He could do. I told Satan that he was going to have to let go of any ground he had taken in this child of God's life. And then I asked her to begin to pray. And oh, how she prayed. I wish everyone could have heard this precious young girl cry out to the Lord. We were in the presence of the Lord for some time. It was a wonderful holy moment.

As she was praying, I prayed that she would be able to forgive her Father as Christ had forgiven her. That the sign of her forgiveness would be to call upon the Lord to do a great work in her father's life to save Him. As she cried out to the Lord, here it came. "Oh Lord, Please save my Daddy. Please bring him to yourself. Please do in him what You are doing in my life." I could hardly contain myself. I began to weep and rejoice in the work of the Lord Jesus.

As we finished our time together before the Lord, I told her to stay before Christ in the next hours/days to allow the Lord to do all He wanted to do in her life. She said she would. The next night she came to me before the revival service. She was so excited. She told me that she had asked all her friends to forgive her of her anger against them.

She said that she had called her father. Now she had not seen her father for many years. He was an alcoholic and had become an extremely bitter man. She remembered every time God was mentioned, he would curse Him. She told him what the Lord had done in her life and that she wanted him to know that she loved him and had forgiven him of what had happened between them. She said he was stunned. For the first time in her life he was broken and humbled. He told her that it was obvious that God had done a wonderful work in her life. And he asked her to please pray for him. Praise the Lord! God is so good! Our Jesus Christ is so faithful *(I John 1:9)! If we confess our sins, He is faithful and righteous to forgive us our sins and to cleanse us from all unrighteousness."* The rest of the week she brought her friends to the meeting. Many of them were saved. Hallelujah!

## Case 4: Missouri

The night I preached on the Invisible War in St. Louis was the week of the suicide bombings of the World Trade Center Buildings in New York. The people were extremely sensitive to the Lord. They also had a state of shock about them. The worship service was as good as any I had led in many years. Everyone was in a wonderful state of worship before the Lord.

When I gave the invitation some came for salvation. And then I opened the altar for prayer and repentance. Not many came. In my amazement, I offered the opportunity for more teaching for those who would like to inquire further into this invisible supernatural war.

We went into a conference room next door to the pastor's study. About eight people showed up to learn more from the Word of God. Many questions were asked. After about another hour of teaching, I closed the time with prayer. As we were leaving the room to go home, a young single girl came up to me and asked if she could talk to me.

That began an amazing time of cleansing and deliverance that night. Brenda was a young girl from the country that had come to St. Louis to find work. She told me that she came from an extremely supportive Christian family. She said that she felt like she had a spirit of fear. I ask her why she thought so. She said that when she went to her apartment every night, before she could go to bed she had to check out each closet and under her bed to make sure no one was in her apartment.

We prayed that no other voice be heard but the voice of the Lord. I asked the Lord to stop all other voices but the voice of the Lord. I asked the Lord to reveal only that which He would choose to reveal that this one could be set free by the Truth of God. No longer than I had finished my initial prayer time, The Lord told me that she had been "bar hoping" and sleeping around because of the spirit of fear in her life. He told me that the source of this fear was loneliness.

When I turned back to her I asked her had she been sleeping around and looking for love in all the wrong places. Brenda began to cry uncontrollably. I asked her if she was afraid of being alone. Through her sobbing she shook her head yes. I ask her if she had been born again. She said she was. I asked her to tell me how she came to Christ. She gave a clear born-again conversion experience. I began to quote the Scriptures of the love and faithfulness of the Lord as the Lord brought them to my remembrance. *"I will never leave you nor forsake you"* *(Heb. 13:5). "He that watches over Israel neither slumbers nor sleeps"* *(Psalm 121:4).* I had her read these passages of God's never failing love and abiding presence with His children. I also went to the book of *I Corinthians the 6th Chapter*, and asked her to read *verses 15-20*. She was not argumentative at all concerning her sin. I asked her if she was willing to confess her sin of fornication and adultery, since she had slept with other women's husbands. She said she was.

After a time of "truth encounter" in the Word of God, I went to *James Chapter 4* and began to show Brenda the prayer that God would answer. I had her read this passage as we discussed its eternal truth. I explained to her that God would not hear her prayer of cleansing and forgiveness unless she was willing to humble herself before God. After a time of explaining that she had to be specific when she prayed, I also told her that she had to accept God's will for her life if she expected Him to hear her prayer of deliverance and cleansing.

The crucial moment came when I asked her was she willing to be single for the rest of her life if that is what God's will was for her. She said, "I don't want to be, but if that's God's will I will obey Him." I knew in that moment that God was going to do a mighty work in her life. I began to pray calling upon the God of grace and forgiveness revealed on the Cross of Calvary to come and do only that which He could do in her life. I prayed for a complete healing and deliverance:

*"If therefore the Son shall make you free, you shall be free indeed" (John 8:36).*

Brenda began to cry out to the Lord, while asking His forgiveness for her unfaithfulness to Him. In her brokenness before the Lord, she told Him that she was so sorry for what she had done. She was so sorry for not believing that the Lord would take care of her every need. Since she had become "one flesh" with everyone she had slept with, each "soul-tie," the relationships that had been established in the spirit world, had to be broken. Only God has the power to break these soul-ties *(I Cor. 6:15-20)*.

God did a wonderful work in Brenda's life that night. As she came clean before Him while confessing her sin, the Lord faithfully heard and answered her prayer for deliverance from the bondage of the spirit of fear.

As we left that night, she told me, *"Brother Rob, you have no idea how the Lord has used you in my life. Thank you for allowing the Lord to use you this night in my life."*

## Case 5: Texas

After preaching on the invisible war, I invited, as is my custom, for folks who needed prayer to come forward. I told them that I would stay with them however long it would take to help them pray through their bondages. That night I was overwhelmed with the response. Close to 40 people stayed after needing prayer.

As I inquired as to why the people came for prayer. About a dozen of them were broken hearted for their children who were in darkness. I gathered them together and went through the steps of "The prayer that God Answers." I explained that their children had their own wills. And that God would not violate anyone's will. However, we could cry out to Him and ask Him to mercifully intervene in their lives and bring them to a point of repentance. The altar filled with tears and sobs as these precious parents and loved ones got right with God before they prayed for their prodigals.

The next group was a group of folks that had been involved in witchcraft sometime in their lives. Their ages ranged from early teens to seventy years old. There was not time to deal with each of them individually. I told them that they must repudiate any involvement in witchcraft. They needed to go back to the moment of blasphemy and disobedience and call upon God to forgive them and to clean out any ground that had been given to the Enemy through this unholy involvement in the darkness. I told them that they had any hindrances when they prayed to call me and I would meet them at the church for prayer. None called.

It was beginning to get late so I began to talk to those who were left. Many of them had questions concerning the invisible war. I fielded their questions with the Scripture for a while, until they seemed satisfied.

There were two who stayed after all this time. One was a middle aged women and a teenage boy. I looked at her first and said, "Do you have any questions?" She said "no." She needed prayer. So I asked her what is going on in your life. She said,. "I am a thief, a shoplifter. I am a glutton. I have had drug and alcohol addictions. I've been sexually active outside of God's will." She began to cry, "I'm sick of it. I want to be free." I asked her if she believed that Jesus could set her free. She said she did. I asked her if she was saved, She said she was, and gave a clear conversion experience. I asked her if Jesus set her free tonight would she be willing to serve Him the rest of her life no matter what. She said she was. I referred her to *James 4*, and the prayer that God answers. She was familiar with the passage for she had just heard me teach the others. I asked her if this desire she had to be clean was for her sake or for the Glory of God. She replied, "I want Him to have my life."

So there in the front pew of the auditorium I began to pray. I asked the Lord to come in great power. I prayed *Eph. 3:20-21*. I told the Lord that our hope was only in Him. That if He did not speak, we would not know the truth. That if He did not clean, there would be no cleaning. That if He did not deliver, there would be no deliverance. I prayed that every voice must be silenced in the presence of Holy God. I prayed that no other voice would be heard but the voice of the Lord Jesus. I prayed for the Lord to show us what was going on in her life, and where the Enemy had built a stronghold.

The Stronghold Prayer (See Chapter 6, pg. 147-148) was used. At the end of this powerful prayer, I asked her what the Lord was showing her. She said that she had been sexually molested as a child. I asked her what she saw. She replied, "It's so dark, it's so dark." Through her sobs she cried, "Why did he let this happen to me? He left me all alone. I'm so alone."

There it was, the lie of the Enemy. Every stronghold is based upon a lie or a system of lies. I began to confront the lie of abandonment with the truth of God's Word. But God says, "I will never leave you, no forsake you." I said that if God had abandoned her, even in that horrible moment, that she would be dead. God was life and the giver of all life. That He had never left her because she was still alive. God did not do this awful thing to her. The Enemy did so he could destroy her.

I asked her if she believed the Word of God, or if she was going to continue to believe the lies of the Enemy. She said she believed God's Word. Then I told her to tell the Lord she was sorry for believing the Devil's lies that God had done this awful thing to her and that He really didn't love her. She did. Oh, how she did! I told her to praise the Lord and thank Him for His never-ending love toward her. She did. Oh, how she did!

I asked the Lord upon the authority of His Word to come in great power and to drive out every evil spirit that was involved in this stronghold. I prayed, "Lord, You came to set the captives free. You, Sir, have come to destroy the works of the Devil. We call on You to come and do Your mighty work. Dear Lord, take charge of Thine own. Release this precious child of Yours to Yourself." I asked the Lord to bind each one together with the three-fold cord that could not be broken, in the name of the Father, Son and the Holy Spirit. I declared that they could not split, divide, multiply, or get reinforcements that they would have to face the presence and judgment of Almighty God who was Lord of Heaven and earth.

I declared that they would have to go where Jesus told them to go when Jesus told them to go. That He was in charge. I told the spirits that there would be no manifestations but the manifestation of the Holy Spirit. I called on the Lord to put on all of them the judgment of the sorrow they had put upon this child of God 70x7 times greater.

After a while, I asked her, "What do you see now?" She said, "I see a warm light." I asked that the Lord would come and put His arms of love around her. I asked that the love of the Lord would surround her. I told her to just stay for a while until she was ready to go home. She stayed for another 15 or 20 minutes before the Lord weeping with great joy. Before I left town, I received this note from this precious sister in Christ.

*Dear Brother Rob,*

*Thank you for taking the time to pray with me last night. I know in my head and heart that I gained a great deliverance last night. I felt physically, mentally, emotionally and spiritually that a huge twisted chain had been broken off me. Thank you for being willing to allow God to use you to teach the truth that set me free.*

*May God richly bless you and protect your marriage, family and ministry. Till His Great Appearing!*

*Therefore: John 8:36 If the Son makes you free, you shall be free indeed!*

## Case 6: Texas
## (That same night)

After we finished with what the Lord wanted to do in this lady's life. I looked up and a teenage boy was still waiting for prayer. I looked at my watch and it was midnight. I asked the young man if he needed to pray. He was trembling with emotion. He said he needed to pray with me, and he asked if we could go into a back room to talk. As we went into the back room, his trembling became more and more pronounced. I asked him if he had heard what we had done with the lady. He said he did. I asked him if he was saved. He said he was and also gave a clear conversion experience.

Although this young man was a leader in his youth group and faithful to his church, he told me he was being tormented by the habitual sin of masturbation. I asked him if he was willing to serve the Lord with all his heart. He said that he was. I began to pray that the Lord would come and complete what He had begun in this young man's life that night. I prayed *Eph. 3:20-21*, and declared our total dependence upon the Lord Jesus. I asked the Lord to put us in a circle of His blood as a protection from any evil scheme. I asked the young man to pray and declare his allegiance to the Lord Jesus. With much trembling, He declared his love and commitment to the Lord Jesus.

I asked the Lord to come and show us the basis of the Enemy's stronghold in his life. I declared that no other voice would be heard but the voice of the Lord Jesus. All others must be silenced in the presence of the only true Lord, Jesus Christ. I prayed the stronghold prayer in Chapter 6 and applied the prayer to each area of the stronghold, as I had been instructed by Norm Coad. I declared that no manifestation would be allowed, except the manifestation of the Holy Spirit of God. The only thing we wanted to know is what the Lord would tell us.

I asked the young man what the Lord was showing him. His trembling became more dramatic. He said that he had been sexually abused by his brother as a child. And he began to shout, "Why did God allow this to happen to me?" There it was, the lie of the Enemy. I told him that God did not do this to him, his brother did. God had nothing to do with it. The 18 year-old cried, "How could He love me and allow this horrible thing to take place in my life?" The lies of the Enemy kept coming. I quoted the same Scripture that God had brought to my heart with the previous woman. *"I will never leave you or forsake you."*

I called for the spirit of abandonment to be bound and all other spirits under its authority must be bound with this wicked spirit. I prayed, "I bind abandonment and every spirit under its authority with the three fold cord that cannot be broken, in the name of the Father, Son, and Holy Spirit. You will go where Jesus tells you to go, when Jesus tells you to go.

This young man was tall and skinny. The more we prayed the more his head dipped between his legs until he was almost on the ground. I asked the young man if he had ever tried to commit suicide. He said he had, more than once. How did I know that? The Lord was telling me what was going on in the realm of the spirit. The Bible calls it discernment. It is simply listening to the Lord when He speaks. I must admit, through my study and experience in spiritual warfare, the Lord is teaching me how to listen. Remember, Jesus said, "My sheep hear my voice."

I asked the Lord to bind Murder, Suicide, and Rage and all other spirits on this unholy assignment under them in the Name of the Father, Son, and Holy Spirit with the "Three-Fold Cord" that could not be broken. I reminded the spirits that there would be no manifestations except the manifestation of the Holy Spirit. He was in charge and they had to do what He said. I declared, "You will go where Jesus tells you to go, when Jesus tells you to go."

In a few minutes the attitude of resentment and grief turned into mourning. I told him to tell the Lord how he felt. He began to cry, "I'm so sorry for hating my brother and my father. Please forgive me. Oh, God, please forgive me for blaming you for what has happened to me.

I know you love me and you always have." The trembling ceased.

I asked the Lord to come and wash clean with the blood of Jesus every area in the young man's life where the Enemy had found ground. I asked the Lord to place a seal of His blood over every area that had been cleansed.

I asked the Lord to surround this young man with His loving arms, and to let him know how much Jesus loves him. I looked at my watch. It was 1:30 in the morning. When I walked out of the room, the wonderful pastor of the church was still praying for us. I thought we would go home. I turned around and the young man was not to be seen. The pastor and I went back into the room where we had prayed. There he was face down on the floor, in a pool of joyful tears. He didn't get up for another 20 minutes as he was basking in the work and love of the Lord Jesus.

Hallelujah! Three nights later his brother gave his life to Christ in the revival crusade. You see once the stronghold was torn apart, the Holy Spirit of God was able to move freely not only in His life, but in the life of his family. Praise the Lord!

I received this email from the young man just a few days after the revival meeting in south Texas.

*I met you early in March 2002 at the FBC revival. Allow me to refresh your memory and then fill you in on what God has done in my life. You told everyone to stay after if they needed prayer, so I did. I came up to you and reluctantly told you I had a habitual sin in my life, that of masturbation. It pained me to admit that to anyone, but I was fed up with it and had to do something to rid myself of the sin. So I told you and stayed after. Before you had a chance to get to my problem and me, you encountered a woman confessing her struggle with gluttony. It turned out to be a result of many things, such as sexual abuse during childhood and long-term feelings of anger and inadequacy. It was around 12 A.M. on a school night when God was finally done dealing with her. My turn.*

*During the woman's conversation and confession, I realized where my problem with masturbation had originated. We went to a back room and you prayed over me and talked me through my problems. I was molested as a young child, around the age of 4, by my older brother. For 13 years I have carried that around with me. Because of that shameful incident, I grew to hate my older brother intensely, which I've also carried around for 13 years.*

*My Dad abused my Mom when I was younger, threatening my family who I was never able to protect. And I carried that around all my life. I hated him and didn't really ever want him to be saved because of all he'd done.*

*You allowed Christ to work through you in my life. Now I am free. And when the Son has set you free, you are free indeed.*

This fine Christian young man will be attending Bible college in the Fall as he prepares for the Gospel ministry.

## Case 7: Arkansas

On Wednesday night I preached on the "Invisible War" while conducting a tent crusade in Northeast Arkansas. We probably had the best crowd for the crusade on that wonderful night in late spring. After proclaiming the truth of God and exposing so many of the basic lies of the Enemy, I asked for those who needed Christ to give their lives to Him. Many did. After they left for counseling, I invited anyone who needed prayer to remain after. My appeal was to anyone who had an addiction, bitterness, or any habitual sin that was tormenting them. I told the crowd that I would stay with them to pray however long it would take. I instructed everyone else to go home.

Two people came forward as others were leaving. One was a lady who was in great pain because of bitterness toward a family member. I spent some time with her. We asked the Lord to do a work of cleansing and healing in her life. And He did! God answers the prayer that is prayed in His will. It was wonderful to see how she was willing to call out to the Lord for His work in her life.

After we were done, I looked up and I saw an older teenage boy. He was very nervous. He was physically trembling. He was hard to understand when he spoke. I asked him why he stayed for prayer. He replied, "I am rebellious. After what you said tonight about rebellion, I don't want to live like this any more."

"Son, are you a Christian? Have you ever given your life to Christ?" He told me he had. I told him, "Tell me when you were saved." He gave a clear confession of a conversion experience when a young boy. I asked him if he was willing to live for Christ the rest of his days. I asked him if he was willing to serve the Lord and follow him as his master. I told him that if he wasn't willing to serve the Lord and give Him his life, it would do no good to pray for him and he needed to go home. He assured me that his desire was to follow the Lord and give Him his life.

The young man began to share with me about how he was rebellious in all areas of his life. He and his parents had a continuous struggle. He stayed in trouble at school. All of his relationships in terms of authority were in disarray. I asked him if he knew the source of his rebellion. He said he didn't.

We began to pray and asked the Lord to come and show us what was going on. We asked God to reveal what needed to be known for the sake of his cleansing and healing. I asked the Lord to silence and remove every hindering spirit. I declared, "No other voices will be heard but the voice of the Lord Jesus. All others must be silent in the presence of Holy God." I then asked the young man to confess his sin of rebellion to God. With great struggle, he did. It was extremely hard to understand his trembling voice.

Then I prayed the "Stronghold Prayer" (See Chapter 6, pg.147-148) and asked the Lord to apply His blood over each area of this stronghold in this His child's life. I asked the young man, "What do you see, what is going on?" He said, "I see me in my second grade class. My teacher is walking over to me and making me feel stupid. I asked the Lord bind every spirit that was involved in this matter. I asked him if he believed that he was stupid. He said that he did for many years. I quoted *(Phil. 4:19) But my God shall supply all your needs according to His riches in glory by Christ Jesus.* I quoted *(James 1:5) But if any of you lacks wisdom, let him ask of God, who gives to all men generously and without reproach and it will be given to him. (Phil. 4:13) I can do all things through Him who strengthens me.*

I asked him if he believed the truth of the Bible. He said He did. I told him to tell the Lord. He did. I asked him if the Lord had created him stupid. He said no. I declared that every spirit involved must come to attention. "You cannot divide. You cannot separate. You cannot get reinforcements. You must face the judgment of God. Every evil spirit involved in this stronghold, I bind you together with the three-fold cord that cannot be broken, in the Name of the Father, Son, and Holy Spirit. You will go where Jesus tells you to go, when Jesus tells you to go. You must receive all the pain and sorrow and torment you have placed upon the child of God 70x7 times greater." I asked the Lord to pour the blood of Jesus over every area that the Enemy had found refuge through this painful experience as a second grader. I asked the Lord to put a seal of His blood over the areas He was cleaning.

I asked the young man if there was anything else the Lord was showing him. He began to tell me what he saw. "There is a women taking off her wedding ring and putting it on a night stand beside her bed." I asked him if he recognized the women. He said, "No." I asked him what she was doing now. Was she going to bed with someone? He said, "Yes, a teenage boy." I asked if it was him. He said, "No." I asked, "Do you recognize who they are?" He seemed confused and bewildered. He said, "No."

We called on the Lord Jesus to come and pour his cleansing blood on the hurt and sin He had revealed to this young man. We asked the Lord to bind every evil spirit that had found refuge in the life of this child of God. I prayed, "In the name of the Lord Jesus Christ, and in the authority that is mine in my union with Christ, having been seated with Him in the heavenlies, I bind every spirit involved with the three-fold cord that cannot be broken in the Name of the Father, Son and the Holy Spirit. You cannot multiply. You cannot separate. You cannot go and get reinforcements. You must face the judgment of Almighty God. All of the pain and sorrow that you have put upon my Brother in Christ you must receive 7O x 7 times greater. I pour the blood of Jesus 200 million times per second down your throat. You will go where Jesus tells you to go, when Jesus tells you to go. There will be no manifestations and no resistance. The Lord Jesus has all authority both in heaven and on earth. He is in charge of this matter."

I asked the Lord to pour His blood over all the areas where the Enemy had found a place to work in my Brother's life. I asked the Lord to put a seal of His blood over each area as He was cleansing the places of the Devil's work. I asked the Lord to send an angel to gather together all parts of this one who had been so fractured.

In a little while the struggle was over. I called on the Lord to come and wrap my Brother in his arms and surround him with His love. He left the tent that night tired but cleansed before the Lord.

Let me tell you what I believe the Lord showed to this precious tormented young man. As we asked the Lord to show us what was going on, He did.  As wild as this may sound, I am convinced that the Lord showed this young man his conception. (See Chapter 2, pg. 67-73, The Sins of the Fathers) This boy was born out of an evil rebellion against God. The woman in that bedroom was his mother. The teenage boy she went to bed with was his father. He never knew either one of them. He was given up as a baby for adoption. For the sake of his cleansing, the Lord revealed to him the ground that the Enemy had taken and where he had taken it. Remember, *"You shall know the truth and the truth shall make you free" (John 8:32).*

The next night at the tent I asked if anyone needed to confess his or her sin before the Body of Christ. I asked if there was anyone who needed to share what the Lord was doing in their lives. These two precious people stood and gave testimony of the mighty work of cleansing the Lord had done in their lives. I wish you could have seen this young man. His whole countenance was changed. His earrings were gone. He had a fresh haircut. There was a peace and a profound joy that came from his life, as he was able to stand boldly and praise God for the work God had done in his life to set him free. He declared, "I have given my life anew to the Lord, I have decided to serve and follow only Him."

# Appendix B

# MAKING YOUR SIN LIST

**Before we can effectively pray for our loved ones or those around us, we must first make certain our heart is right with God.**

*Search me, O God, and know my heart;*
*Try me, and know my thoughts;*
*And see if there be any wicked way in me,*
*And lead me in the everlasting way*
*(Psalm 139:23-24).*

The following list is not intended to be exhaustive. It is a guide. As the Lord reveals to you the sin that is in your heart, agree with Him that He's right and you have been wrong. Do not for any reason hang on to your sin or argue with God. It will kill you! Unconfessed sin will allow the Enemy places in your life to steal, kill, and destroy you. Ask the Lord to speak to you concerning these areas in your heart. Ask Him to silence all other voices but His, as He speaks and as you listen. Believe what God's Word says.

*If we confess our sins He is faithful and just to forgive us our sins*
*And to cleanse us from all unrighteousness (I John 1:9).*

If you have already confessed any of these specific sins, forget about it. It's been taken care of by the blood of our Lord Jesus Christ. Don't go digging it back up. It's done.

*There is therefore now no condemnation*
*For those who are in Christ Jesus (Romans 8:1).*

## SINS OF THE TONGUE
Have you made a vow and not kept it? *(Eccl. 5:1-5)*
Have you spoken against anyone (including yourself)? *(Matt. 5:44, Matt. 7:1-2)*
Have you spoken an oath in a secret lodge ceremony or anywhere else? *(Matt. 5:34, Exodus 23:32)*

269

## SINS OF UNFORGIVENESS
Do you hold a grudge against anyone? *(Matt. 6:14-15, Matt. 7:1-2)*
Is there anyone you just can't forgive? *(Matt. 6:14-15)*
Do you resent yourself for any reason? *(Luke 10:27)*

## SINS OF DISSOBEDIENCE
Have you ever said no to the call of God? *(Jonah)*
Are you willing to go anywhere anytime the Lord speaks to you? *(Matt. 4:19-20)*
Have you been involved in the harming of a ministry or minister of the Gospel? *(Psalm 105:15)*
Have you dishonored your wife? *(I Peter 3:7)*
Have you said no to the Lord when He told you to give? *(Prov. 3:27-28)*

## SINS OF REBELLION
Have you ever been involved in any form of witchcraft? *(Deut. 18:10-12, Rev. 21:8)*
Is there any area of rebellion in your life? *(I Samuel 15:23)*
Do you have trouble giving up control? *(Eph. 4:5)*
Are you unwilling to submit to your husband? *(Eph. 5:22-24)*

## SINS OF ANGER
Have you let the sun go down on your anger? *(Eph. 4:26)*
Do you have trouble controlling your temper? *(Psalm 37:8)*
Do you feel you are better than others? *(Romans 3:10)*
Do you try to get your way by arguing? *(Gal. 5:20)*
Do you have a critical spirit? *(Matt. 7:1-2, Romans 14:4)*

## SINS OF UNBELIEF
Does worry often control your thoughts? *(Phil. 4:6)*
Does fear control any area of your life? *(I Tim. 1:7)*
Do you believe God will provide for you? *(Phil. 4:19)*
Do you fear your future? *(Rev. 1:17)*
Do you fear dying or death? *(Rev. 1:18)*
Is there any part of the Scriptures you just don't believe? *(2 Tim. 3:16, Matt. 4:4)*
Do you refuse to live by faith? *(Romans 14:23)*

## SINS OF INGRATITUDE

Is worship a time of great joy or frustration? *(Psalm 111:1-4)*
Do you love the Lord will all your heart, all your soul, all your strength and all your mind? *(Luke 10:27)*
Do you resent God for anything He has or has not done? *(Psalm 143:6-12)*

## SINS OF IMPURITY

Have you committed adultery or fornication? *(Matt. 5:27-28)*
Are you hiding any secret sin in your life? *(Psalm 90:8)*
Could you have stopped an abortion? *(Psalm 139:13-16)*
Does pornography have any part of your life? *(Gal. 5:19)*
Are your thoughts concerning women pure? *(Gal. 5:19)*
Are your thoughts concerning men pure? *(Gal. 5:19)*

## SINS OF GREED

Do you possess anything that is not rightfully yours? *(Eph. 4:28, I Peter 4:15)*
Do you have unpaid debts? *(II Kings 4:7, Romans 12:8)*
Have you robbed god of his tithe? *(Malachi 3:8-10)*
Have you profited through misrepresentation of the value of goods? *(Prov. 21:6)*
Do you love money? *(I Tim. 6:10)*
Do you want what others have? *(Gal. 5:20-21)*
Have you made money or taken advantage through the sorrows of others? *(2 Tim. 3:6-9)*

## SINS OF PRIDE

Are you willing to allow the Lord to manifest His power through you? *(2 Tim. 3:5)*
Are you concerned about your reputation? *(Phil. 2:7)*
Do you have trouble humbling yourself? *(James 4:6)*
Do you have trouble receiving ministry from others? *(James 4:6)*

## SINS OF IDOLATRY

Is there anyone of anything in your life more important to you than Christ? *(Gal. 5:20)*
Do you crave evil things? *(I Cor. 10:5-6)*

Do you have a love for money? *(I Tim. 6:10)*
Do you love the things of the world? *(James 4:4)*

## SINS OF THE SPIRIT
Do you act like everything is alright when it isn't? *(Matt. 23:28)*
Are you too busy to pray? *(I Tim. 2:1)*
Are you neglecting the study of God's Word? *(Matt. 4:4)*
Have you neglected the witnessing of your faith in Christ to others? *(Matt. 28:19-20)*
Have you been unwilling to love others? *(Mark 12:30, Matt. 22:36, I John 3:14)*

> *He who has my commandments and keeps them, he it is who loves Me; and he who loves Me shall be loved by my Father, and I will love him, and will disclose Myself to him.*
> *John 14:21*

# GLOSSARY

In any study of the supernatural, it is necessary that the terms used be clearly defined. There are words such as demon, blasphemy, cult, etc. that carry different meanings to different people. When you encounter such terms in this book, the following list will give you how it is being used by the author.

**Abyss**
Pit, Tartarus, The place of confinement for demons. The place of demons. Demons do not want to be sent to the abyss for they will then be rendered inactive except for some that will evidently be let out at a future date (*Rev. 9:1*).

**Alters**
Alter personality, Dissociation, Fractures, Fragments, Personality Splitting, Segmented Personalities, MPD- Multiple Personality Disorder. God created each human being with one unique personality. However, that personality can be shattered, segmented, broken and smashed into pieces or separate parts, through trauma.

**Anathemas**
To declare that its demise is to the glory of God.

**Ancestral spirits**
The spirits of dead people in Hell.

**Assignments**
A duty or spiteful piece of work allotted to a spirit being who is obligated to complete the allotted task or experience of pain.

**Authority**
The level of power given for the purpose of ruling.

**Batteries**
The most wounded and sensitive part of our personalities that can easily move us into self-defeating thoughts and behaviors that will destroy us.

**Bindings**

To refuse permission to continue.

**Blasphemy**

To willfully lie about God in opposition to Him.

**Cleansing**

To dispel evil spirits or forces of darkness. To be freed from sin and evil.

**Covin, covine, coven**

Demonized individuals who come together to carry out demonic activities, usually in secret.

**Cult**

A system of false religious beliefs or rituals. A false religion.

**Curses**

The natural results of breaking God's laws, a prayer or calling down harm or injury upon someone or something.

**Deceptions**

To mislead, delude, cheat; to lead astray or frustrate by confusing the distinction between true and false, fantasy and reality, leading to confusion.

**Denounce**

To openly declare one's disbelief.

**Demon creature**

A fabricated being, not a true spirit; acts for the demon when he is not present. These just disappear when covered with the blood of the Lord Jesus.

**Demonization, Demonize, Demonized**

Being under the control of one or more demons. One who has or had a demon.

## Demons

Fallen angels who work under Satan's authority to bring Satan's will on earth as it is in Hell.

## Destructions

To bring to nothing by putting out of existence, to kill, to demolish.

## Discernment

The practice of listening to the Holy Spirit as He reveals the thought and intentions of the heart and the workings of Satan.

## Disposing

To cast out. To remove an evil spirit and the evil work of Satan.

## Dominion

Authority, Rule.

## Fasting

The spiritual act of denying the flesh. Preparation for spiritual battle.

## Formation

How and what a particular stronghold of demonic activity is constructed and used to produce a particular outcome, i.e. alcohol plus addiction produces irresponsible behavior, abuse, and death.

## Function

What a particular demonic activity is designed to do; and how the stronghold/structure works.

## Ground

A place given to the Devil to control through sin, blasphemy, and disobedience to God's Word.

## Inerrancy

The belief that God's Word is truth.

**Infidel**
One who opposes the teaching of the Word of God.

**Judgments**
A calamity regarded as sent by Satan by way of punishment; a calamity permitted by God to bring about discipline for godly purposes.

**Legalism**
The false belief that keeping man's rules brings righteousness.

**Levels**
These structures all have essential levels. See stronghold—environment, place to the devil, walls, foundations, cornerstone. For example: A subhead plus alters that are given certain responsibilities within a dissociative personality.

**Light**
That which is in the light. That which is known.

**Loosing**
To allow permission to continue.

**Manifestation**
A public demonstration of the supernatural presence and power of demons or the Holy Spirit.

**Materials**
The behavioral, psychological and spiritual realities from which abnormal personality traits are constructed.

**Motors**
The psychological/spiritual power source that drives personality defects and sinful, self-defeating, self-destructive behaviors.

**Mourning**
The expression of Godly sorrow and repentance.

**New Covenant**

The work of Christ on Calvary. The shedding of the blood of Jesus Christ for all sin.

**Never**

Things that Satan never wants revealed..

**No Gods**

Demons, Devils, Spirits who manipulate the pagan god systems and actually receive homage and worship.

**Occult**

A belief in or study of supernatural powers and the possibility of subjecting them to human control.

**Pharmachia**

The New Testament word for sorcery, witchcraft.

**Pit**

The place of confinement for demons. Abyss.

**Prayer Walking**

The practice of territorial praying to discover and confront territorial spirits.

**Principalities**

Demons of greater power and authority assigned to spiritually significant areas. Territorial spirits.

**Programming**

Developing in a person certain specific responses based on particular stimuli, i.e. as in a computer program; produces activity that is involuntary and /or compulsive.

**Progressivism**

The philosophy that holds all things are progressively getting better. The foundation of Social Darwinism, Pragmatism, and Relativism.

**Reclaim**
To restore the creation to its Creator.

**Reconciliation**
To bring together two opposing positions or beings.

**Relativism**
The teaching system or belief that rejects absolute truth.

**Renounce**
To declare one's opposition.

**Repentance**
To turn. To change one's thinking which changes the direction of his life. To turn from sin and disobedience and to turn to Christ.

**Rhema**
A personal word from God's heart to your heart from His Word.

**Sanctification**
The process of being made holy like Jesus.

**Shadow**
Things which remain hidden by Satan.

**Soul-ties**
Supernatural bondings as a result of sexual intercourse.

**Spirits**
Human spirits, alive or dead, god demons, angels, supernatural beings that are real but not material in nature.

**Spirit of living flesh**
A portion of human spirit projected out of a person: 1) to carry out an assignment; 2) to be projected into another human being as a human tie from one to another.

## Spiritual Mapping
To spiritually define an area for the purpose of confronting territorial spirits.

## Stronghold
The inability to believe the truth because of the ground given to the Devil.

## Structures
All demonic activities within individuals and societies; spiritual/psychological structures to rob, destroy, and kill, i.e. rage, alcoholism, sexual addictions, lying, etc..

## Supernatural
The existence beyond the visible observable realities.

## Sword of the Spirit
The Bible, The Word of God.

## Territorial Spirits
Demons of greater power and authority assigned to spiritually significant areas. Principalities.

## Testing of Spirits
The confrontation of a spirit to determine the source of a spiritual manifestation.

## Theological Liberal
Anyone who holds anything other than the Bible as his final and ultimate authority.

## Ties
To join one being to another by means of transfer of demonic spirits thus gaining a certain amount of control over that person.

## Times
At whatever point in time that a generational curse, assignment, judgment, etc. was loosed—permitted to take effect..

**Topos**

A place given to the Devil to control through sin, blasphemy, and disobedience to God's Word.

**Triggers**

A psychological mechanism that releases a preprogrammed response, i.e. acting out, lying, stealing, inappropriate or antisocial behaviors.

# Endnotes

## Introduction
1 Shearer, Lloyd, The Woman behind the Woman behind Ronald Reagan, Parade Mag., April 1, 1990, pg. 16.

2 Graham, Billy, Angles, Angels, Angels, Doubleday & Co. Garden City, NY, 1975, pg. 7, 25.

## Chapter 1
1 Arnold, Clinton E., Three Crucial Questions about Spiritual Warfare, Baker Books, Grand Rapids, MI, 1997, pg. 110.

2 Ibid. pg. 111.

3 Lewis, Jessie Penn, Roberts, Evan, War on the Saints, Lowe, New York, NY, 1998, pg. 314.

4 Ibid. pg. 314.

5 Ibid. pg. 314.

6 For an English translation, see Knut Schaferdiek, "The Acts of John," in New Testament Apocrypha, vol. 2 Writings Related to the Apostles; Apocalypses and Related Subjects, ed. Wilhelm Schneemelcher, rev. ed., Louisville; Westminster/John Knox, 1989, Pg. 152-209.

7 Arnold, Clinton E., Three Crucial Questions about Spiritual Warfare, Baker Book House Co. Grand Rapids, MI, 1997, pg. 112.

8 Crawford, Mary, Shantung Revival, The China Baptist Publication Society, 1934, pg. 26-27.

9 Lewis, Jessie Penn, Roberts, Evan, War on the Saints, Lowe, New York, NY, 1998, pg. 286.

10 Dickason, C.Fred, Demon Possession and the Christian, Crossway Books, Wheaton, IL, 1987, pg. 22.

11 Warner, Timothy M., Spiritual Warfare, Crossway Books, Wheaton, IL., 1991, pg, 79.

12 Lewis, C.S. The Screwtape Letters, Macmillan, New York, NY, 1961, pg. 9.

13 Dickason, C.Fred, Angels Elect and Evil, Moody Press, Chicago, IL, 1975 pg. 129.

14 Prince, Derek, Spiritual Warfare, Whitaker House, New Kensington, PA, 1987, pg. 11,12.

15 Montgomery, Ruth, A Gift of Prophecy, William Morrow & Company, New York, NY, 1965, pg. 164-5.

## Chapter 2

1 Anderson, Neil, The Bondage Breaker, Harvest House, Eugene, OR, 1993, pg. 22.

2 Ibid. pg. 23.

3 Ibid. pg. 155-158.

4 Manson, Marilyn, The Long Hard Road out of Hell, Regan Books/Harper Collins Publishers, New York, NY. 1998, pg. 22-23.

5Logan, Jim, Reclaiming Surrendered Ground, Moody Press, Chicago, IL, 1995, pg. 61.

6 Ibid. pg. 65.

7 Spurgeon, C.H., Power Over Satan, Whitaker House, New Kensington, PA, 1997, Pg. 27, 30.

8 Prince, Derek, Spiritual Warfare, Whitaker House, Springdale, PA, 1987 pg.25.

9 Spurgeon, C.H., Power over Satan, pg. 89.

10 Logan, Jim, Reclaiming Surrendered Ground, pg. 102.

11 Hochastetler, Dean, Ancestral Sin and Resultant Bondage, Studies and Lectures in Spiritual Warfare, Sioux City, Iowa, International Center for Biblical Counseling, December 1989.

12 Warner, Timothy, Spiritual Warfare, Good News Publishers, Wheaton, IL, 1991, pg. 107.

13 Murphy, Ed. The Handbook for Spiritual Warfare, Thomas Nelson Publishers, Nashville, TN, 1996, pg. 437.

## Chapter 3

1 Basham, Don, Can a Christian Have a Demon, Whitaker Books, Monroeville, PA. 1971, pg. 29.

2 Moreau, Scott, The world of Spirits, Evangel Publishers, Nairobi, Kenya 1990, pg. 90.

3 Arnold, Clinton, The Powers of Darkness, Inter Varsity, Downers Grove, IL, 1992, pg. 128.

4 Anderson, Neil, The Bondage Breaker, Harvest House, Eugene, OR, 1993, pg. 187-8.

5 Dickason, C. Fred, Demon Possession and the Christian, Crossway Books, Wheaton, IL, 1987, pg. 81-127.

6 Rockstad, E. B., Demon Activity and the Christian, Faith and Life Publications, Andover, KS, pg. 7.

7 Anderson, Neil, The Bondage Breaker, Harvest House, Eugene, OR, 1993, pg. 186.

8 Warner, Timothy, Spiritual Warfare, Crossway Books, Wheaton, IL. 1991, pg. 79-80.

9 Ibid. pg. 80.

10 Anderson, Neil, Released from Bondage, Here's Life Publications, San Bernardino, CA, 1991, pg. 16.

11 Murphy, Ed. The Handbook for Spiritual Warfare, Thomas Nelson Publishers, Nashville, TN, 1996, pg. 432-3.

12 Ibid. pg. 433.

13 Swindoll, Charles R., Victory Over Darkness: Winning the Spiritual Battle, Insight for Living, Anaheim, CA. 1981, pg. 23.

14 Bubeck, Mark, The Adversary, Moody Press, Chicago, IL, 1975, pg. 87.

15 Larson, Bob, Larson's Book of Spiritual Warfare, Nelson Publications, Nashville, TN, 1999, pg. 384.

16 Bubeck, The Adversary, Moody, Chicago IL, 1975, pg. 88.

17 Cathey, Sam, Spiritual Warfare, Golden Rule Publications, Orlando, FL., 1987, pg. 18-21.

18 Barnhouse, Donald Grey, The Invisible war, Zondervan Publications, Grand Rapids, MI, 1965, pg. 166-167.

19 Barnhouse, Margaret N., That Man Barnhouse, Tyndale Publications, Wheaton, Ill. 1983, pg. 396-398.

20 Spurgeon, C.H., Power Over Satan, Whitaker House, New Kensington, PA, 1997, pg. 16-17.

## Chapter 4

1 Vine's Expository Dictionary of Old and New Testament Words, Fleming Revell, Grand Rapids, MI: 1981, pg. 332-333.

2 Tozer, A.W., The Warfare of the Spirit, Christian Publications, Camp Hill, PA, 1993, Ch. 3, pg. 1.

3 Murphy, Ed. The Handbook for Spiritual Warfare, Thomas Nelson Publishers, Nashville, TN, 1996, pg. 57.

4 Birch, George, The Deliverance Ministry, Horizon Publications, Camp Hill, PA, 1988, pg. 17.

## Chapter 5

1 Spurgeon, Charles, World Digital Library Edition of The Treasury of David and The collected Works of Charles H. Spurgeon, The Electric Bible Society, 1999, Dallas, TX, pg. 987.

2 Rockstad, Ernest B., The Armor of God, Faith and Life Publications, Andover, KS, 1974, pg. 2.

3 Spurgeon, Charles, World Digital Library Edition of The Treasury of David and

The collected Works of Charles H. Spurgeon, The Electric Bible Society, 1999, Dallas, TX, pg. 294.

4 Lewis, Jesse Penn, The Warfare with Satan, Christian Literature Crusade, Fort Washington, Penn. 1985, pg. 80.

5 Bubeck, Mark, Overcoming the Adversary, Moody Press, Chicago, IL., 1984, pg. 69.

6 Ibid. pg. 71.

7 Jones, D.M. Lloyd, The Christian Soldier, Grand Rapids, Baker Book House, n.d., pg. 184.

8 Lewis, Jesse Penn, The Warfare with Satan, Christian Literature Crusade, Fort Washington, PA, 1985, pg. 82.

9 Rockstad, Ernest, The Armor of God, Faith and Life Publications, Andover, Kansas, 1984, pg. 13.

10 Prince, Derek, Spiritual Warfare, Whitaker House, Springdale, PA, 1987, pg. 67.

11 Lewis, Jesse Penn, The Warfare with Satan, Christian Literature Crusade, Fort Washington, PA, 1985, pg. 82.

12 Bounds, E.M., Winning the Invisible War, Whitaker House, Springdale, PA, 1984, pg. 147.

13 E.M. Bounds, Guide to Spiritual Warfare, Whitaker House, New Kensington, PA, 1984, pg. 149-150.

14 Charles, Spurgeon, World Digital Library Edition of The Treasury of David and The Collected Works of Charles H. Spurgeon, The Electric Bible Society, Dallas, Texas, 1999, pg. 993.

15 Rockstad, Earnest B., The Armor of God, Faith and Life Publications, Andover, Kansas. 1984, pg. 17.

16 Spurgeon, Charles, World Digital Library Edition of The Treasury of David and The collected Works of Charles H. Spurgeon, The Electric Bible Society, 1999, Dallas, Texas, pg. 992.

17 Rockstad, Earnest B., The Armor of God, Faith and Life Publications, Andover, Kansas. 1984, pg. 18.

18 Bubeck, Mark, Overcoming the Adversary, Moody Press, Chicago, IL., 1984, pg. 106-107.

19 Ibid. pg. 115.

20 Knox, John, The Worlds Great Sermons, Funk and Wagnalls Co. New York, NY., 1908, pg. 197.

## Chapter 6

1 Coad, Norman, Coad Word Christian Counseling Services, 1161 S.W. WilshireBlvd. Suite 118, Burleson, TX. 2002.

2 Anderson, Neil, The Bondage Breaker, Harvest House, Eugene, OR, 2000, pg. 208.

3 Wright, Henry W, A More Excellent Way, Be in Health, Pleasant Valley Publications, Thomaston, GA, 2003, pg.92-95.

4 Rockstad, Ernest B, Setting the Captives Free, Tape Lectures and Materials, Faith and Life Publications, Andover, Kansas, 1970.

5 Birch, George, The Deliverance Ministry, Horizon Publications, Camp Hill, Penn., 1988, pg. 203-214.

## Chapter 7

1 Crawford, Mary K., The Shantung Revival, The China Baptist Publication Society, Shanghai, China. 1934, pg. 70.

2 Evans, Eifion, The Welsh Revival of 1904, Evangelical Press of Wales, Bridgend, Wales, 1969, pg. 156.

3 Ibid. pg. 165-6.

4 Orr, J. Edwin, Revival is Like Judgment Day, Message, Oxford Association for research in Revival, 1976.

5 Bubeck, Mark I., The Adversary, Moody Press, Chicago, IL., 1975, pg. 128.

6 Lewis, Jesse Penn, War on the Saints, rev. ed., Christian Literature Crusade, Ft. Washington, PA. 1964, pg. 7.

7 Ostling, Richard "Laughing for the Lord,"Time, 15 August 1994, pg. 38.

8 Brown, Barry; Gordon, Jeanne; Hall, Carol; Woodward, Kenneth L. "The Giggles Are for God," Newsweek, 20 February 1995, pg. 54.

9 Goodman, Walter, "About Churches, Souls, and Show-Biz Methods," New York Times, 16 March 1995, B4.

10 Murphy, Ed., The Handbook for Spiritual Warfare, Thomas Nelson Publishers, Nashville, TN, 1996, pg. 532.

11 Ibid. pg. 533.

12 Dillow, Jody, A Biblical Evaluation of the Twentieth Century Tongues Movement, JD Press, Garland, Texas, 1972, pg. 53-54.

13 Rockstad, Ernest B, Setting the Captives Free, Tape Lectures, Faith and Life Publications, Andover, Kansas, 1970, "Dealing with Demons."

14 Murphy, Ed, The Handbook for Spiritual Warfare, Thomas Nelson Publishers, Nashville, TN, 1996, pg. 446.

15 Vines, Jerry, Spirit Works, Broadman and Holman Publishers, Nashville, TN, 1999, pg.70.

16 Penn-Lewis, Jesse, War On The Saints, Thomas E. Lowe, Ltd. New York, NY, 1998, pg. 299.

17 Annual of the Southern Baptist Convention, 1961, pg. 5.

18 Orr, J. Edwin, Revival is Like Judgment Day, Message, Oxford Association for research in Revival, 1976.

19 Spurgeon, Charles H., Power Over Satan, Whitaker House, New Kensington, PA, 1997, pg, 21.

20 Tozer, A.W. The Warfare of the Spirit, Christian Publications, Camp Hill, PA., 1993, pg.59.

21 Spurgeon, Charles H., Power Over Satan, Whitaker House, New Kensington, PA, 1997, pg. 21.

22 Foster, Neill K., Warfare Weapons, Horizon Books, Camp Hill, PA, 1995, pg. 41-42.

23 Spurgeon, C.H. The Power in Praising God, Whitaker House, New Kensington, PA, 1998, pg. 46-47.

# SCRIPTURE INDEX

# TOPICAL INDEX

# Bibliography

Alsobrook, David. *Understanding the Accuser.*
Ventura: Renew, 1999.

Anderson, Neil. *The Bondage Breaker.*
Eugene: Harvest House, 2000.

_____. *Winning Spiritual Warfare.*
Eugene: Harvest House, 1990.

Arnold, Clinton E. *Powers of Darkness: Principalities and
Powers in Paul's Letters.* Downers Grove: InterVarsity, 1992.

_____. *3 Crucial Questions About Spiritual Warfare.*
Grand Rapids: Baker, 1997.

Barnhouse, Donald Grey. *The Invisible War: The Panorama of the Continuing
Conflict Between Good and Evil.* Grand Rapids: Zondervan, 1965.

Beeson, Ray and Patricia Hulsey. *Strategic Spiritual
Warfare.* Nashville: Thomas Nelson, 1995.

Birch, George A. *The Deliverance Ministry.*
Camp Hill: Horizon, 1988.

Bounds, E.M. *Guide to Spiritual Warfare.*
New Kensington: Whitaker House, 1984

Bounds, E.M. *Satan.*
Grand Rapids: Baker, 1972.

_____. *Winning the Invisible War.*
Springdale: Whitaker House, 1864.

Boyd, Gregory A. *God at War: The Bible and Spiritual
Warfare.* Downers Grove: InterVarsity, 1997.

Bubeck, Mark I. *Overcoming the Adversary.*
Chicago: Moody, 1984.

_____. *The Adversary.*
Chicago: Moody, 1975.

Buntain, Mark. *Waging Spiritual Warfare.*
Springfield: Gospel, 1993.

Cathey, Sam. *Spiritual Warfare.*
Orlando, Golden rule Book Press, 1987.

Chafer, Lewis S. *Satan: His Motives and Methods.* Rev. ed.
Grand Rapids: Kregal, 1990.

Cornwall, Judson. *It's God's War: A Biblical View of Spiritual Warfare.*
Hagerstown: McDougal, 1998.

Day, Peggy L. *An Adversary in Heaven: Satan in the Hebrew Bible.*

Atlanta: Scholars Press, 1988.

Dickason, C. Fred. *Demon Possession & the Christian.*
　　Wheaton: Crossway books, 1987.

_____. *Angels, Elect and Evil.*
　　Chicago: Moody Press, 1975

Downame, John. *The Christian Warfare.* 2nd Ed.
　　London: Printed by Felix Kyngston for Elizabeth Burby, 1608.

Eastman, Dick. *The School of Victorious Warfare.*
　　Colorado Springs: Every Home for Christ, 1995.

Eckhardt, John. *Deliverance and Spiritual Warfare Manual.*
　　Chicago: Crusaders Ministries, 1993.

Ernest, Victor H. *I Talked with Spirits.*
　　Wheaton: Tyndale, 1970.

Evans, Eifion. *The Welsh Revival of 1904.*
　　Bryntirion: Evangelical Press of Wales, 1969.

Evans, Tony. *The Battle is the Lord's: Waging Victorious Warfare.*
　　Chicago: Moody, 1998.

Foster, K. Neill. *Warfare Weapons.*
　　Camp Hill: Christian Publications, 1995.

Frangipane, Francis. *The Three Battlegrounds.*
　　Cedar Rapids: Arrow, 1989.

Garrett, Susan R. *The Demise of the Devil.*
　　Minneapolis: Fortress, 1989.

Gay, Robert. *Silencing the Enemy.*
　　Orlando: Creation House, 1993.

Graham, Billy. *Angels: God's Secret Agents.*
　　Garden City: Doubleday and Co., 1975.

Graves, Kersey. *The Biography of Satan: Or a Historical Exposition of the Devil and His Fiery Dominions.* Kila: Kessinger Publishing, 1993.

Gross, Edward N. *Miracles, Demons, and Spiritual Warfare: An Urgent Call for Discernment.* Grand Rapids: Baker, 1990.

Gurnall, William. *The Christian in Complete Armour [sic]:A Treatise of the Saint's War Against lthe Devil.* Reprint.
　　Carlisle: Banner of Truth, 1995.

Hall, Charles A. *With The Spirit's Sword: The Drama of Spiritual Warfare in the Theology of John Calvin.* Richmond: John Knox Press, 1970.

Hanegraaff, Hank. *Counterfeit Revival.*
　　Dallas: Word Publishing, 1997.

Henton, Richard D. *Christian Warfare.*
　　Tulsa: Vincom, 1992.

Hix, Randy. *Blood War: The Blood Covenant and Spiritual Warfare.*

Costa Mesa: Embassy, 1994.

Horn, Thomas H. *Spiritual Warfare: The Invisible Invasion.*
Lafayette: Huntington House, 1998.

Horsford, Elizabeth-Ann. *Created to Conquer.*
London, Hodr and Stoughton, 1996.

Ing, Richard. *Spiritual Warfare.*
Springdale: Whitaker House, 1990.

Kallas, James. *The Real Satan From Biblical Times to the Present.*
Minneapolis: Augsburg, 1975.

Kirkwood, David. *Modern Myths About Satan and Spiritual Warfare.*
Pittsburgh: Ethnos, 1994.

Koch, Kurt. *Demonology Past and Present.*
Grand Rapids: Kregel, 1973.

————. *The Devil's Alphabet.*
Grand Rapids: Kregel, 1969.

Kuhatschek, Jack. *Spiritual Warfare.*
Downers Grove: InterVarsity, 1999.

Lane, Anthony N.S., ed. *The Unseen World: Christian Reflections on Angels, Demons, and the Heavenly Realm.* Grand Rapids: Baker, 1996.

Larson, Bob. *Larson's Book of Spiritual Warfare.*
Nashville: Thomas Nelson, 1999.

Lewis, C.S. *The Screwtape Letters.*
San Francisco: Harper, 1942.

Lindsell, Harold. *The New Paganism.*
San Francisco: Harper and Row, 1987.

Logan, Jim *Reclaiming Surrendered Ground.*
Chicago: Moody, 1995.

Lovett, C.S. *Dealing with the Devil.*
Baldwin Park: Personal Christianity Chapel, 1981.

Lowe, Chuck. *Territorial Spirits and World Evangelism.*
London: Mentor, 1998.

Lutzer, Erwin W. *Satan's "Evangelistic" Strategy for this New Age.*
Wheaton: Victor, 1989.

MacMillan, John A. *The Authority of the Believer.*
Camp Hill: Christian Publications, 1980.

Malone, Henry *Shadow Boxing.*
Irving: Trophy, 1999.

McCall, Thomas S., Levitt, Zola. *Satan in the Sancturary.*
Chicago: Moody, 1973.

Meyers, Jeff. *God vs. god: Spiritual Warfare in Heavenly Places.*
Springfield: 21st Century Press, 2000.

Miller, Calvin. *Disarming the Darkness*.
        Grand Rapids: Zondervan, 1998.

Moore, Steve. *Insights on Spiritual Warfare*.
        Self Published: Kingdom Building Ministries, 1989.

Moreau, A. Scott. *Spiritual Warfare*.
        Wheaton: Harold Shaw, 1995.

Murphy, Ed. *The Handbook for Spiritual Warfare*. Rev. and Updated.
        Nashville: Thomas Nelson, 1996.

Newport, John P. *Demons, Demons, Demons*.
        Nashville: Broadman 1972.

Nugent, Christopher. *Masks of Satan: The Demonic in History*.
        London: Sheed and Ward, 1983.

O'Grady, Joan. *The Prince of Darkness: The Devil in History, Religion, and the
        Human Psyche*. Shaftsbury: Element, 1989.

Penn-Lewis, Jesse. *Spiritual Warfare*.
        Fort Washington: Christian Literature Crusade, 1998.

Penn-Lewis, Jesse. with Roberts, Evan *War on the Saints*. Unabridged Addition.
        New York: Thomas E. Lowe, 1998

Pentecost, Dwight J. *Your Adversary the Devil*.
        Grand Rapids: Kregel, 1997.

Petzoldt, Ruth, and Paul Neubauer, eds. *Demons: Mediators Between this World
        and the Other: Essays on Demonic Beings from the Middle Ages to the
        Present*. New York: Peter Lang, 1998.

Prince, Derek. *Spiritual Warfare*.
        Springdale: Whitaker House, 1987.

Randles, Bill. *Making War in the Heavenlies: A Different Look on Spiritual
        Warfare*. Published by the author: N.D.

Reapsome, James, and Martha Raepsome. *Spiritual Warfare*.
        Grand Rapids: Zondervan, 1992.

Royster, Roger. *The Word on Spiritual Warfare*.
        Ventura: Gospel Light, 1996.

Rumph, Jane L. *Stories from the Front Lines: Power Evangelism in Today's World*.
        Grand Rapids: Chosen Books, 1996.

Scanlon, Michael and Randall J. Cirner. *Deliverance from Evil Spirits: A Weapon
        for Spiritual Warfare*. Ann Arbor: Vine, 1980.

Schlier, Heinrich. *Principalities and Powers in the New Testament*.
        Freiburg, West Germany: Herder, 1966.

Showers, Ronald E. *What on Earth is God Doing?: Satan's
        Conflict with God*. Neptune: Loizeaux Brothers, 1973.

Shuster, Marguerite. *Power, Pathology, Paradox: The Dynamics of Good and Evil*.
        Grand Rapids: Academie, 1987.

Spurgeon, Charles. *The Power in Praising God.*
New Kensington: Whitaker House, 1998.
_____. *Power Over Satan.*
New Kensington: Whitaker House, 1997.
Stedman, Ray C. *Spiritual Warfare.* Waco: Word, 1975.
Taylor, Jack, *Victory Over the Devil.*
Nashville: Broadman Press, 1973.
Tozar, A. W. *The Warfare of the Spirit.*
Camp Hill: Christian Publications, 1993.
Unger, Merrill F. *Biblical Demonology: A Study of the Forces Behind the Present Unrest.* Wheaton: Van Kampen, 1952.
_____. *Biblical Demonology: A Study of Spiritual Forces at Work Today.*
Grand Rapids: Kregel, 1994.
Unger, Merrill F. *Demons in the World Today.*
Wheaton: Tyndale House Publishers, 1971.
Upchurch, T. Howell. *Strategy for Spiritual Warfare.*
Columbus, GA: Brentwood Christian Press, 1987.
Wagner, C. Peter, Ed. *Engaging the Enemy: How to Fight and Defeat Territorial Spirits.*
Ventura, CA: Regal, 1991.
Warner, Timothy M. *Spiritual Warfare.*
Wheaton: Crossway Books, 1991
White, Thomas B. *The Believer's Guide to Spiritual Warfare.*
Ann Arbor: Servant, 1990.
Wiersby, Warren. *The Strategy of Satan: How to Detect and Defeat Him.*
Wheaton, IL: Tyndale, 1985.
Wimber, John, and Kevin Springer. *Power Evangelism.*
London: Hodder and Stoughton, 1992.
Wink, Walter. *Engaging the Powers: Discernment and Resistance in a World of Dominion.* Minneapolis: Fortress, 1992.
Wise, Terry S. *Fundamentals of Spiritual Warfare.*
Needham Heights: Simon and Schuster, 1996.
Youssef, Michael. *Know Your Real Enemy.*
Nashville: Thomas Nelson, 1997.

**Rob Randall** is a third generation Southern Baptist Evangelist. He has an effective ministry serving churches in evangelistic revival crusades across America as well as an active international crusade ministry. He holds a Bachelor of Arts Degree from Baylor University, a Master of Divinity Degree from Southwestern Baptist Theological Seminary, and a Doctor of Philosophy Degree from Louisiana Baptist University. Rob and his wife Pattie have been married for thirty three years and have their home in the Dallas Fort Woth Metro Area.

**For more information concerning
The Revival and Conference Ministry
Of Evangelist Rob Randall
Contact:**

Rob Randall Evangelistic Ministries, Inc.
P.O. Box 5
McKinney, Texas 75070
robrandall@juno.com
www.robrandall.org